The Birth
of Stalinism

The Birth
of Stalinism

*The USSR on the Eve
of the "Second Revolution"*

By

MICHAL REIMAN

Translated by George Saunders

Indiana University Press
Bloomington • Indianapolis

This book was brought to publication with the assistance of a grant from the
Andrew W. Mellon Foundation to the Russian and East European Institute,
Indiana University, and the Center for Russian and East European Studies,
University of Michigan. A grant in support of the translation was provided by
the Free University of Berlin.

Originally published in German as *Die Geburt des Stalinismus: Die UdSSR am
Vorabend der "Zweiten Revolution,"* © 1979 by Europäische Verlagsanstalt GmbH,
Frankfurt am Main.

Manufactured in the United States of America

Library of Congress Cataloging-in-Publication Data

Reiman, Michal.
　The birth of Stalinism.

　(Indiana-Michigan series in Russian and East European studies)
　Translation of: Die Geburt des Stalinismus.
　Bibliography: p.
　Includes index.
　1. Soviet Union—Politics and government—1917–1936.
2. Soviet Union—Economic conditions—1918–1945.
I. Title.　II. Series.
DK267.R3813　1987　　947.084'2　　85-45885
ISBN 0-253-31196-9

　1 2 3 4 5 91 90 89 88 87

Contents

FOREWORD by Alexander Rabinowitch   vii

TRANSLATOR'S NOTE   ix

PREFACE   xi

1. On the Threshold of Crisis   1

2. The Break with Britain: Conflicts in the Soviet Leadership   11

3. The Opposition Revived   19

4. Economic Crisis and Power Politics   37

5. Social Crisis and Social Repression   51

6. Intermezzo at the Top: The Crisis Continues   67

7. Defeat of the Moderates   85

8. The Stalinist Regime Takes Shape   102

9. The Phenomenon of Stalinism   115

APPENDIXES   123

NOTES   155

INDEX   183

FOREWORD

Inaugurated in 1985, the Indiana-Michigan Series in Russian and East European Studies aims to publish original scholarly research, interpretive studies, and translations in the humanities and social sciences that are genuinely significant contributions to existing knowledge and of broad interest to the field. Previous books in the series include *Mutiny amid Repression: Russian Soldiers in the Revolution of 1905–1906* by John Bushnell (1985); *The City in Late Imperial Russia*, edited by Michael F. Hamm (1986); and *Boris Godunov: Transpositions of a Russian Theme* by Caryl Emerson (1986).

Michal Reiman's *The Birth of Stalinism*, originally published in German in 1979, is an important addition to the series. Born in Moscow in 1930, the son of the prominent Czech historian and Communist Party and Comintern official Pavel Reiman, Michal Reiman received his doctorate from Charles University in Prague. His first major work, a study of Czech social democracy in the nineteenth century, appeared in 1958. In the 1960s Reiman shifted his research to Russian history. In 1967 his book *Ruská revoluce: 23 února–25 října 1917* [The Russian Revolution: February 23–October 25, 1917], was published in Prague; a Russian translation appeared the following year. Based in part on unique documents from Soviet archives, that book, a detailed and comprehensive reinterpretation of the 1917 revolutions from a socialist perspective, constituted a courageous attempt to break with orthodox Stalinist history-writing. The focus of lively debate and controversy among Soviet historians, the book was also of great value to Western specialists.

As a member of the faculty at the Institute for Political Science in Prague during the "Prague Spring," Reiman was closely associated with the Dubček regime; this, and the independence of his historical writings, sealed his fate following the Soviet invasion of Czechoslovakia in 1968, Dubček's ouster, and the reimposition of rigid political and cultural controls. Removed from his academic positions and prevented from continuing his historical research in Prague, Reiman left Czechoslovakia in 1976; he settled in West Germany, where he is now Professor of Political Science at the Free University of Berlin.

Reiman's present work, focused on the dynamics of Stalin's consolidation of power and the earliest stages of the imposition of the Stalinist system, concerns one of the most important and controversial subjects in Soviet history. Fixing his attention on the years 1927 to 1929, Reiman provides a detailed reconstruction and analysis of Soviet high politics during this critical, transitional period. His account makes optimal use of previously little-studied and unpublished documents that he discovered in the political archives of the German Foreign Ministry in Bonn. These include dispatches to the German Foreign Ministry from its representatives in Russia as well as top-secret directives, Central Committee and government protocols and reports, and letters from officials in Moscow to Soviet representatives in Berlin. A fascinating selection of these documents, carefully annotated, is included as an appendix to the present work.

The Birth of Stalinism provides fresh insights into such key historical issues as the fierce struggle for power of the late 1920s; the strengths and weaknesses of the successive oppositions—in particular, the precise chronology and dynamics of Stalin's defeat first of the united opposition and subsequently of the moderates; the impact of ever-deepening economic and social crises on political decision making and vice-versa; the controversy surrounding the growing political role of the security police; and, finally, the origins of Stalin's "cult of personality," the rigid controls, and the extreme forms of coercion and mass repressions of the high Stalin period. Reiman's study is especially useful in clarifying the often highly significant yet previously little-understood connections between foreign policy concerns, including those relating to the Comintern, and internal Soviet politics and decision making.

In Reiman's account, Stalin's political success is founded primarily on cunning, deception, and brilliant political manipulation; he views Stalin less as an original thinker and adapter of Marxist theory to Russian problems in the manner of Lenin than as a clever borrower of the ideas of others and a ruthless, unprincipled opportunist and practitioner of "revolution from above." In Reiman's view, Stalinism, as an all-embracing system, evolved as a gradual response to deepening crises, at one and the same time a product of Stalin's *mentalité* and the natural outcome of Soviet Russia's early development dating back to the October revolution.

The notion introduced by Stephen F. Cohen in his *Bukharin and the Bolshevik Revolution* (New York, 1973), and more recently forcefully argued in his *Rethinking the Soviet Experience: Politics and History since 1917* (New York, 1985), of the continuation of NEP as a viable, ideologically defensible alternative to Stalinism, and of Bukharin as the personal representative of such a course, is implicitly rejected by Reiman. Indeed, in Reiman's account Bukharin emerges as a secondary figure, an ally of Stalin for much of the period under consideration. Also largely dismissed by Reiman is the view, expressed, for example, by Moshe Lewin in his insightful *The Making of the Soviet System: Essays in the Social History of Interwar Russia* (New York, 1985), that policy errors in the mid-1920s, rather than fundamental structural defects connected with NEP, led to the grave economic and social crises of 1927–1929, and that even by the latter date a more moderate "Bukharinist" approach would have achieved more advantageous long-term results at less cost than that adopted by Stalin.

Although some may take issue with Reiman for depreciating Bukharin's importance as a political figure and economic thinker and for underestimating NEP's potential as a viable system, his book constitutes a significant contribution to the current debate over these issues. Overall, *The Birth of Stalinism* is a valuable complement to such works as Moshe Lewin, *Russian Peasants and Soviet Power* (New York, 1975); Sheila Fitzpatrick, ed., *Cultural Revolution in Russia, 1928–1931* (Bloomington, 1978); Fitzpatrick, *Education and Social Mobility in Soviet Russia* (Cambridge, 1979); and Roger Pethybridge, *The Social Prelude to Stalinism* (London, 1974), all of which focus primarily on the economic, cultural, and social roots of the Stalinist system, as well as Robert C. Tucker's biographical *Stalin as Revolutionary, 1879–1929* (New York, 1973).

Alexander Rabinowitch

TRANSLATOR'S NOTE

With regard to the spelling of Russian names, in the text more familiar and readable forms have been used, without diacritical marks and with *y* rather than *i* or *ii* in the appropriate places. Thus, for example, Grigory Zinoviev (not Grigorii Zinov'ev), Yevgeny Preobrazhensky (not Evgenii Preobrazhenskii), Vyacheslav Menzhinsky (not Viacheslav Menzhinskii), and Yemelyan Yaroslavsky (not Emel'ian Iaroslavskii). Likewise, the *y* usually appears when there is a palatalization between vowels, as in Andreyev (not Andreev) and Ovseyenko (not Ovseenko). Bibliographical items in the notes follow the Library of Congress system, to assist readers who might wish to look them up. Names that appear in both the text and notes are given in the more readable form except in the few cases where they appear in the titles of books or articles. Where possible, first names have been used rather than initials, but when the first name has not been available, initials appear as in the Russian text. Most first names are not Westernized. The exceptions include those best known by the Westernized forms of their names. Thus, Joseph (not Iosif) Stalin, Leon (not Lev) Trotsky, and Maxim (not Maksim) Litvinov.

For administrative units, the Soviet terms *oblast* (province), *krai* (territory), and *raion* (district) have been kept. Similarly, the terms *obkom, kraikom,* and *raikom* refer to the party committees of the respective administrative units. Soviet acronyms or initials for certain official bodies have sometimes been used—for example, Sovnarkom for the Council of People's Commissars, VSNKh (or Vesenkha) for the Supreme Economic Council, and Narkomindel for the People's Commissariat of Foreign Affairs.

Whenever the term Central Committee is used, it refers (unless otherwise specified) to the Central Committee of the Soviet Communist Party. Likewise, Sovnarkom and Central Executive Committee refer to the USSR as a whole rather than to one of the Soviet republics (unless otherwise specified).

PREFACE

At present there are many historical studies that deal in one way or another with the Soviet Union in the 1920s and 1930s and, in particular, with the problem of Stalinism. These works have reconstructed the events of those years in all essentials. Still, the subject can hardly be considered exhausted. Not all the necessary material has yet been circulated through the world of scholarship and some material, particularly in Soviet archives, is not accessible to researchers at all. In addition, the present state of historiography is characterized by a great diversity of views and theories, intensified by the profound differences between East and West in the content and orientation of social and political thought. Thus there remains an ample field for further investigation and discussion.

The idea of writing a book on the birth of Stalinism occurred to me long ago, in the 1960s, when the "personality cult" was being widely discussed among the intelligentsia in Eastern Europe. These questions became a matter of urgent concern in Czechoslovakia, where a reappraisal of the political trials of the 1950s, which had begun in the waning years of the Khrushchev era, became one of the essential impulses behind the Prague Spring.

In 1967 I published a book in Prague, in the Czech language, entitled *The Russian Revolution, February 23 to October 25, 1917*, which evoked quite a strong, though varied response.[1] I intended to follow this work with a study of Soviet history in the 1920s, but I was unable to bring this plan to completion. The changes in Czechoslovakia after 1969 deprived me, along with most historians of my generation, of any possibility of pursuing my profession. I was able to return to my topic only after ten years, and under greatly altered circumstances.

I have limited my subject to the years 1927–1929. There is no need to justify the singling out of these years as a period of special importance—not after the excellent study of the history of the Soviet peasantry by Moshe Lewin.[2] The materials that I have used fully confirm this.

I do not mean to suggest that significant elements, even fundamental components, of the future Stalinist system did not exist in the USSR before 1927. But the social and political system of the mid-1920s, the heyday of the New Economic Policy (NEP), differed substantially from the period that was to follow, both in terms of the content of the system and of the atmosphere and circumstances in which it developed.

In 1969, while working in the archives of the German Foreign Ministry in Bonn, I had the good fortune to come across an entire set of Soviet historical materials from the late 1920s. These included official documents of the highest Soviet party and state institutions and materials by such leading political figures as Aleksei Rykov, Mikhail Kalinin, Georgy Chicherin, Vyacheslav Menzhinsky, Joseph Stalin, Maxim Litvinov, Valerian Kuibyshev, Sergo Ordzhonikidze, Nikolai Krestinsky, and Jan Rudzutak. This extensive set of documents of first-rate importance is crucial for an understanding of the full mechanics behind the rise of Stalinism. Never before published, eleven of them are included as an appendix to the present work. Through these materials I was able to penetrate more deeply into issues and events that had not been treated in the existing literature, or had been dealt with only partially. In this category, for example, we find the 1926–1928 Soviet policy of *dogovorennost* (seeking agreements with the

Western powers) and the Soviet leadership's consideration of steps toward easing the foreign trade monopoly. (For several decades official Soviet publications have categorically denied any such intentions on the part of the Soviet leadership at that time.) Other examples concern conflicts within the party leadership from the summer of 1927 to the spring of 1929; the actual strength of the left opposition and the techniques and mechanisms by which it was suppressed; a detailed account of the origins of the Shakhty affair, the first show trial of the Stalin era, and the struggle over that affair within the top party leadership; the role of the OGPU (Unified State Political Administration—the Soviet security police organization, more commonly known by its last three initials, GPU) in the formation of the Stalin dictatorship and the spread of GPU control over Soviet life in the late 1920s, including control over the ruling party; the question of the social and economic crisis of 1928–1929, its depth, extent, and consequences; and some of the particular circumstances under which Stalin elaborated his own independent political line.

I have also drawn on the abundant but as yet insufficiently utilized materials of the Soviet press of that time as well as the German press, which was represented by a great many reporters and contributors stationed in Moscow, and collections of official documents, especially diplomatic papers, that have been published by a number of countries. Information from the not-very-numerous memoirs of the period has added detail to this material. I have cited information from the Central Party Archive in Moscow, to which I did not have access, on the basis of material from these archives that has been extensively quoted in a number of Soviet historical works.

I cannot, of course, leave unmentioned the fact that the Prague Spring, in which I took an active part, played a major role in the formation of my views on Stalinism, as did numerous discussions I had with friends in Prague and, in earlier years, in Moscow. My many years of daily collaboration and discussion with my father, Pavel Reiman, who instructed me in many things and from whom I learned a great deal, were exceptionally important to me.

I would like to thank the executive board and the administration of the Alexander von Humboldt Foundation and the Volkswagenwerk Foundation and the staff at the Institute of History and Geography of Eastern Europe at Tübingen University, especially Professor Dietrich Geyer, for providing me with the opportunity, after many years, to return to this work and for their day-to-day support. My thanks go also to my wife, Tamara Reiman, who was my first and most attentive reader, and to Dr. V. Schalhorn, who helped me locate the literature and other materials necessary for this book.

Tübingen, September 1, 1979

For this English-language edition of my book, which was first published in Germany in 1979, I have had the benefit of access to unpublished materials in the Trotsky Archive at Harvard University, the Nicolaevsky Archive at the Hoover Institution, Stanford University, and the International Institute for Social History in Amsterdam, as well as a wide variety of published materials. This additional research has enabled me to give a more precise account of the events and of the positions of different individuals and groups.

The Birth
of Stalinism

ONE

On the Threshold of Crisis

I do not hold the view that the rise of Stalinism can be explained by the body of socialist ideas that accompanied the October revolution of 1917 or that the entire history of the USSR, from then on, can be viewed as a linear process leading to the emergence of Stalinism. Certainly Bolshevik theory contained quite a few elements that contributed to the unfavorable direction taken by the Soviet governmental and social structure. In saying this I am not referring to socialist theory or ideology as such, although it undoubtedly contained some elements—especially in its Russian version—which, when stripped of their general democratic content and context, became a point of departure for the establishment of totalitarianism.

The main problem was that in the thinking of the Bolsheviks, the question of reaching socialism became increasingly separated from the question of mature economic, social, and cultural preconditions, so that achieving socialism became almost entirely a matter of using the mechanism of state power. The political dictatorship of the party over society became a principle in itself. The socialization of industry, finance, and commerce was stripped of an essential part of its original social meaning: it was transformed into the construction of an independent economic base for the state. At the same time, extensive administrative interference in economic and social relations, including the use of force, became a standard feature of everyday life.

Nevertheless what was decisive was not this, or rather, not so much this aspect of things. The revolution was accompanied by three years of destructive civil war and foreign intervention, which brought an unparalleled intensification of social antagonisms. The extreme ferocity of the social and political conflicts, which shredded the social fabric of the nation, and the extreme polarization in all social structures were influences that could not fail to have an effect on the character of social thought and social psychology. A new plebeian social stratum came to power, mainly an urban and military social group, in which the cultural substratum of Bolshevism was diluted. This group did not possess the necessary knowledge, experience, or culture to administer or rule. Moreover, the general concept it tried to introduce was not socialist, but the utopian and ultraegalitarian idea of "war communism," which re-

1

flected the backwardness and immaturity of its environment. The normal mechanisms of the market—of money-commodity relations—were rendered inoperative. Production came to a standstill; the transport system totally collapsed; cities emptied; and social distinctions dropped to the common denominator of extreme poverty. Famine and epidemic raged, and the barest essentials were lacking. Human life lost all value. Society continued to function almost exclusively through the use of force and administrative fiat. Repression and terror reached absolutely extraordinary dimensions. Entire social groups were subject to them. The usual form of punishment, even for minor crimes, was death.

The conditions of war communism, far more than the influence of any theory, shaped the conceptions of the new ruling stratum in regard to governmental structure and social life. The conditions of civil war gave the new rulers a taste for the unchallenged use of power and violence and instilled in them an indifference toward human life. Concepts and methods were created that would last for many years, producing a moral and psychological mind-set that served as a highly favorable medium for the later growth of Stalinism.

Still and all, in 1921 a major change occurred: the civil war ended, and it became evident that the concept of universal administrative fiat and the forced imposition of "socialist egalitarianism" were unworkable. Peasant rebellions flared throughout the country. The sailors in Kronstadt, who had been central pillars of support for the Bolshevik government during the revolution and civil war, revolted. Both Moscow and Petrograd were on the verge of major strikes by discontented workers.

On V. I. Lenin's initiative, at the Tenth Congress of the Russian Communist Party (Bolshevik),* a shift was made to the New Economic Policy (NEP). NEP provided for the restoration of market relations, at first to a limited degree but later to an increasing extent, and led to the reawakening of the normal mechanisms of economic life. An economic upturn began, which helped to stabilize social and political conditions. The use of force was substantially reduced in scope and was no longer applied in social and economic spheres. This had an effect on many aspects of social life. Although repression, especially political repression, continued to be widespread, the technique of mass preventive terror was virtually abandoned. A normal peacetime framework of legality and the observance of legal procedures was established. Everyday civilian life reemerged. On the basis of a rising standard of living, which was nevertheless quite impoverished, a differentiation in the degrees of poverty and affluence reappeared. The NEP era's distinctive culture came into its own, with its restaurants, confectioneries, and places of entertain-

---

*Hereafter referred to as the party or the RCP(B).

ment. A richer artistic and ideological life also developed. The numerical growth in the well-to-do layers of the population aroused the discontent of the "lower orders" of society even though the new situation improved their conditions as well. For the first time peasants were able, if only in part, to take advantage of the new system of land ownership. Workers, now that industry was functioning again, actually experienced the positive aspects of the new trade-union laws, labor's new rights, and the freer conditions of supervision in the factories.

The political sphere also changed. The process by which all power became concentrated in Joseph Stalin's hands was clearly observable as early as 1923. Nevertheless, it is significant that this process took place within the context of a moderate policy aimed at consolidating the new situation under NEP.

The strengthening of Stalin's personal power, despite his extreme lack of scruple in party in-fighting, did not bring Stalinism into being as a system as long as functions of violence and repression were being reduced. Stalin's authority was still limited. Although his power was great, it was not unbounded. In a certain sense his move into the political foreground reflected the inevitable realignment of forces with the formation of a new leadership after Lenin's death. Stalin's power depended on certain compromises and agreements by which he obtained necessary support from other members of the party's collective leadership. The preconditions for a de facto division of power within the state were thus maintained. At the same time, the conflict within the party introduced a totally new phenomenon into Soviet political life—the institution of a political opposition. It was an undesirable institution, easily subject to suppression, but because it was linked to the ruling party and because of the authority of its leaders, as well as the strength of party traditions, the opposition was protected from a direct blow by the organs of the GPU and was able to remain in the framework of legality. Its existence could not fail to have an effect on the overall character of the regime.

By the mid-1920s, the new political relationships in the USSR appeared fairly stable. Even foreign observers noted this. Revolutionary convulsions had been left behind. Nothing on the surface indicated the possibility of a sharp change. Certain processes, typical of all preceding revolutions, were under way. Beneath the surface, however, profound new contradictions built up that would change the picture entirely.

The rise of Stalinism cannot be understood without considering the profound social, political, and economic crisis that erupted at the very height of NEP. Most immediately, this crisis was the result of the policy of accelerated industrialization which began to be implemented after December 1925, in line with the decisions of the Fourteenth Party Congress. The real underlying sources of this crisis were immeasurably more complex.

For the USSR industrialization appeared as an imperious necessity.

The most backward of the great powers, prerevolutionary Russia was incapable of providing its population with modern living standards or of defending itself adequately, as was demonstrated by Russia's performance in World War I and the collapse of the old order in 1917. The Russia of old had not been able to withstand the harsh conflicts of the modern era. By 1925–1927, the Soviet Union had completed the phase of economic reconstruction. In terms of real value, the volume of industrial and agricultural production had reached the prewar level.[1] This did not, however, signify a return to the prewar level of economic efficiency. Per capita production remained lower than its prewar standard. Unfavorable structural changes in the economy were also evident. Important sectors of industry (metallurgy, metalworking, sugar, and paper) were not fully restored. Compared to the prewar era, the share of heavy and medium industry in the national economy as a whole declined, and the relative balance between light and heavy industry was thrown off. In general, industry played a smaller part in overall commodity circulation.

The volume of new construction remained inadequate. The number of new or rebuilt factories was small. The overwhelming majority of enterprises were housed in old buildings using wornout equipment that desperately needed replacement.

The USSR had dropped out of the system of international economic relations. Its foreign trade had been sharply reduced and at the same time the influx of foreign technology, equipment, industrial experience, raw materials, and even consumer goods had decreased drastically.[2] The USSR's underdevelopment and total lack of a myriad of important kinds of production were glaringly revealed.

The statistical data on the restoration of agriculture also failed to reflect the real state of affairs. Along with the total destruction of the system of large landed estates and the severe damage suffered by the well-to-do farmers, a large portion of the resources from which modern agriculture and stock breeding drew their sustenance disappeared. This loss was not replaced in any way. The delivery of new machinery— including various types of farm machinery, tools, and fertilizers—which was totally dependent on imports had also fallen off drastically compared to the prewar level. Thus the losses suffered by rural Russia in the preceding years were not made good.

The restoration of agricultural production took place not through any fundamental improvement, but primarily by bringing unused land back into cultivation and by certain changes in the crop structure—greater importance being given to industrial crops and stock raising.[3] The most important sector, grain, was not fully restored to the prewar level.[4] The limits of such an economic revival were quite evident. Production for market, which in the last analysis determined the real share of agriculture in the economic life of the country, amounted to only about half the share held by agriculture before the war.[5]

The needs of the population, which had undergone fifteen years of extreme deprivation, continued to be provided for in an extremely unsatisfactory way. A severe shortage of manufactured goods, the so-called goods famine, became a constant feature of life in those years. Specialists were inclined to explain it as the result of inflation. Hidden behind that, however, was an absolute insufficiency of the most essential goods, a lack intensified by the colossal destruction of material and cultural values in the world war, revolution, and civil war, losses that had not been compensated for in any way.

The weak economy had been unable to accommodate the surplus of available labor power. The problem of rural overpopulation spilled over into the cities, causing a massive growth in urban unemployment. In the second half of the 1920s, unemployment was quickly approaching the two million mark. There was a danger that the number of unemployed would soon equal the number employed in state industry.[6] The unemployed flooded the main cities—Moscow, Kharkov, Leningrad, and Kiev—which had been the strongholds of Soviet power. Their presence exerted a significant influence on the ups and down of political life.

The needs of the army also acquired greater urgency. Before 1927 defense spending was less than half what it had been in prerevolutionary Russia in peacetime.[7] The army and navy, in the quantity and quality of their weapons and technical equipment and in the level of special training and skilled personnel, were very far behind the armed forces of the major industrial powers. They did not have the capability of sustaining the prolonged combat operations of modern warfare.[8]

The Soviet Union urgently needed more rapid industrialization and an overall improvement in its economic situation, but it did not have sufficient resources to accomplish these ends. The influx of foreign capital, loans, and credits, which had been the fundamental lever of industrial growth before the revolution, was almost completely cut off. The economic efficiency of state industry, especially heavy industry, was quite low. It did not produce sufficient profit and often required state subsidies.[9]

Ways of obtaining additional resources from the population were constantly being tried (government bonds, direct taxes, domestic loans, the vodka monopoly, increased prices for manufactured goods, and so on). The government expected most of these funds to come from the rural areas. The peasants sold a considerable share of their marketable output at low state procurement prices while buying manufactured goods at artificially inflated prices. In this way the government obtained food and raw materials on favorable terms and built up reserves for export in order to buy foreign machinery, equipment, and raw materials. At the same time, industry increased its profitability, speeding up the process of capital formation. Taxes and loans from the countryside increased the revenues of the state budget from which industry drew credits and by which industrial construction was financed. These were some of the supplemental techniques that relieved the peasants of their surpluses.[10] It was assumed that peasants would bring their savings to government financial institutions, so that these sums too would be at the disposal of the state.

The government's fundraising plans suffered from certain fundamental defects. The total additional resources that could be obtained for the needs of industrialization were not sufficient in so impoverished a country. There were no large accumulations of wealth in the urban population, and the hopes placed in the countryside were not borne out. The growth of agriculture in the second half of the 1920s proceeded at a slower pace than was necessary to meet the needs of industrial and population growth. The increase in the marketable surplus of grain slowed and then was reversed. It became evident that there were only limited possibilities for the expansion of agriculture while the old economic basis remained. Rural accumulations of wealth went in part to private merchants or simply did not go into circulation. The peasants had no confidence in the stability of the Soviet *chervonets*. They often preferred to store their surpluses or to use them directly for their own consumption or economic requirements.

There were other problems as well. The economic system that took shape in the Soviet Union after the revolution was bureaucratic and not very efficient. Its negative aspects were intensified by the lack of qualifications and experience of most economic and administrative officials. This situation discouraged economic initiative and prevented full utilization of the country's resources. Ever increasing amounts were invested in heavy industry, with no substantial immediate return: positive results became evident only after several years. Construction schedules were overrun greatly, so that new units came into operation only after long delays. The orientation toward economic autarchy, a function of the Soviet Union's complex and unstable international position, required large additional expenditures. Substantial unproductive outlays, particularly to maintain the swollen government and administrative apparatus, devoured considerable resources. Large sums also went for the international schemes of the ruling party, particularly to support revolutionary movements of every variety.[11]

The government sought a way out of these financial difficulties by issuing more paper currency and by gradually allowing a larger economic burden to fall on the population. This course was fraught with serious economic and social consequences, however. Under the existing circumstances, any accelerated industrialization—if the system of economic relations based on NEP were to be maintained—depended increasingly on substantial financial and technical aid from abroad. The Soviet government had tried, since a relatively early period, to obtain such aid by allowing foreign businessmen to operate economic units as concessions. In this way the Soviet government freed itself from the costs of restoring, modernizing, and operating these units. In 1926, a Soviet-German trade agreement was signed, based on existing treaty relations between the two governments. This was an expression—despite the fact that in 1925 Germany began to abandon its one-sided Eastern orientation in foreign policy and from then on established increasingly close relations with the West, even being admitted to the League of Nations in 1926—of the two countries' common opposition to the system of international relations that had taken shape as the result of the victory of the Entente in World War I. The USSR obtained German credits amounting to 300 million marks. Smaller credits were forthcoming from private banks in several other countries. Nevertheless, the scale of foreign aid remained quite modest. Ties had been broken with the major industrial powers after the revolution, and, for many reasons, the Soviet government did not succeed in improving its relations with them, particularly the United States and Great Britain, which had the largest financial resources at their disposal.

The sociopolitical and economic system of the USSR rejected foreign capital. A major obstacle to the attraction of such capital was the Soviet government's monopoly of foreign trade and the complex of economic, legal, and administrative relationships associated with that institution.

The economic situation was a constant source of serious difficulties, in turn producing conflicts within the ruling party. A number of leading political figures and economic theorists, including Leon Trotsky, Grigory Zinoviev, Lev Kamenev, Yevgeny Preobrazhensky, Christian Rakovsky, Karl Radek, and Ivar Smilga, who constituted the nucleus of the opposition within the party, proposed that the country's main forces and resources be concentrated on the rapid expansion of industry, substantially increasing the volume and quality of output and improving the economic indices of production. A major means of pursuing this line of action, in their opinion, was to abandon the autarchic conception of Soviet economic development and involve the Soviet economy, protected by the monopoly of foreign trade, more fully in the world economic system—the worldwide division of labor—which would at the same time strengthen impulses toward technical and economic improvement and enhance the ability of the Soviet economy to compete on the world market. They proposed that part of the resources necessary for accelerated industrial growth could be obtained—and this was said to be in keeping with the existing system of economic relations—by transferring funds accumulated in the private sector, primarily in the countryside, to state industry. One particular aspect of the opposition's proposals was to place the main economic burden on the well-to-do strata, both urban and rural, thus relieving the poorest sections of the population. Such an orientation in economic policy, along with encouragement of democratic forms in government, party, and society, based on class principles, would, it was argued, protect the USSR from the dangers of pursuing such a path.

Countering the proposals of the opposition were the policies of the party leadership—Joseph Stalin, Nikolai Bukharin, and Aleksei Rykov. Within the framework of existing economic and political relations, the party leadership was obliged, to one degree or another, to employ major elements of the economic strategy proposed by the opposition. Nevertheless, its policies differed markedly from that strategy. Citing the need for economic and political independence from the surrounding world, the leadership refused to develop the Soviet economy as a component of the world economic system, preferring the concepts of economic autarchy. Industrial investment was to remain modest in the first phase. The party leadership expected, by using market relations and relaxing central controls in a whole series of ways, to achieve a quick upturn in agricultural productivity. This would strengthen the social and political base of the regime and provide the cities, the army, and industry with necessary food and raw materials as well as increase the overall accumulation of wealth in the country. This was not a fully integrated policy. It was, in fact, a compromise between two somewhat contradictory strategies of economic growth produced by the pressures of existing circumstances.[12]

During the phase of economic restoration, the contradictions in official party theory and conceptions of economic growth were not immediately apparent in day-to-day economic and social activity. Rapid industrial progress, which occurred as the result of the revival of previously existing productive capacity, did not require excessive expenditure and brought tangible results. Successful harvests for two years in a row, 1925 and 1926, strengthened agriculture. The peasants, who sorely needed industrial goods, made use of the relaxation of government controls and responded to the increased flow of industrial goods with increased sales of agricultural surpluses. The party leadership's policies were, to a certain extent, confirmed. Nevertheless, the danger of a crisis had not been overcome. It had simply been postponed.

At the turn of the year, in late 1926 and early 1927, the drama of the situation intensified. It became evident that the leading industrial powers had successfully overcome the postwar economic and social crisis and had entered a new boom period, accompanied by improvements in science and technology.[13] The relative backwardness of the Soviet Union, which had barely managed to restore its economy to full operation, was increasing perceptibly, threatening its position in the world.

The economic boom in the industrial countries, although it was not free of serious international contradictions, some of which were inherited from the preceding era (during and before World War I), gave rise to a desire for greater stability in world political and economic relations. This desire clashed with Soviet policy, which had not freed itself of revolutionary illusions and which still nourished the hope of substantially weakening its potential opponents. China, where a nationalist revolution supported by the USSR was reaching its culmination, became a special source of conflict. The Chinese situation affected what were perceived as the vital interests of several of the major powers. The international position of the USSR deteriorated and the danger of serious international complications arose.

The Soviet leadership could not help but take into account certain aspects of the new world situation. Moreover, with the close of the period of economic restoration (that is, after the previously existing productive capacity had been brought back into operation, as I have described) the rate of economic development threatened to fall off sharply. From the fall of 1926 on—not least because of the pressure of opposition propaganda—discussion began on ways of accelerating industrial development. An especially detailed discussion was held at the Fifteenth Party Conference of October 26–November 3, 1926.[14] The conference emphasized the necessity of mobilizing internal sources of industrialization. It was accepted that the process would be extremely painful and difficult. The country's resources were already greatly strained.

The majority of the leadership felt that expanding foreign economic ties, in particular increasing the volume of foreign trade and securing large new credits from abroad, was the prerequisite for accelerated growth. Radical proposals were heard. Georgy Chicherin, people's commissar of foreign affairs—with the support and sympathy of Rykov, the prime minister (chairman of the Council of People's Commissars)—sought to have a distinction made between Soviet government policy and the policy of the Comintern and to have the Soviet line in China modified. These had been two of the sorest points in Soviet foreign relations.[15] Stalin held the position that the foreign trade monopoly had to be relaxed to make it easier to reach economic agreements with foreign powers.[16] On December 11, 1926, the Politburo passed a resolution orienting Soviet diplomacy toward a "policy of agreement"*—that is, cooperation with the industrialized countries—which was to be embodied in the form of treaties. The resolution pointed to the financial and economic implications of this decision, the need to ensure major foreign credits, and the expansion of the Soviet Union's economic ties with other countries.[17]

In February 1927, the Central Committee plenum made a decision to substantially increase the volume of capital construction.[18] At the same

*Only the German translation of the Politburo resolution, from the German Foreign Ministry archives, is available. The term used there is *Verständigungspolitik*, which, in the Russian original, was probably *politika dogovorennosti*. Hereafter, I will refer to this as the policy of international cooperation.

time, in the spring of 1927, an intensive campaign developed to
strengthen the country's defense capacity and improve the condition of
the army and navy, which had been seriously neglected.[19] The party
leadership nevertheless suffered from a lack of positive new ideas. No
substantial changes were made in its general conception of domestic
policy or its actual conduct of foreign affairs. A profound crisis became
inevitable. It broke out much sooner than might have been expected.

TWO

The Break with Britain

Conflicts in the Soviet Leadership

The immediate cause of the deep and prolonged crisis that arose in the USSR in 1927 was a crisis in foreign relations. Stalin and Bukharin's not very farsighted policy in China, based on the hope that China would remove itself from the "world system of imperialism," and the consequent one-sided and uncritical policy of support for the Kuomintang, which was waging a successful campaign in central China against the Peking government, ended in calamity. The great powers forcefully intervened in China, and the Kuomintang generals, after entering Shanghai, took savage reprisals against the Shanghai workers movement in April 1927, thus breaking their alliance with the Soviet Union. A few weeks later, the left Kuomintang government in Wuhan also broke with the Soviet Union. The left wing of the Chinese revolution began to be hunted down and destroyed everywhere. The consequences of this setback were especially disheartening to the Soviet leadership because, shortly before, it had published triumphant statements hailing the Kuomintang's success.

In May 1927, a new and still heavier blow descended on the Soviet leadership. The British Conservative government was angered by the events in China and by Soviet policy, which aimed at undermining Britain's international position. Guided by domestic political considerations as well—rivalry with the Labour party—the Tories severed relations with the Soviet Union and canceled the Anglo-Soviet trade agreement, which had served as the legal basis for commercial dealings between the two countries.[1]

Great Britain was the Soviet Union's biggest trading partner. British banks had played a central role in the financial dealings of the USSR with third countries, in particular Germany.[2] The Soviet government aggravated the harmful consequences of this diplomatic break when, after a brief internal dispute, it decided to act tough and take retaliatory measures.[3] Direct Soviet trade with Great Britain stopped almost entirely, and Britain's share in the overall turnover of Soviet foreign trade fell to the minimum.

The diplomatic break between Britain and the USSR was bound to affect the entire system of international relations. It abruptly poisoned the atmosphere in which Soviet attempts to achieve a policy of international cooperation were being pursued. Negotiations between the USSR and France, which had been encouraging, came to a halt. The Soviet government had been trying to obtain credits and conclude nonaggression and nonintervention pacts in return for payments on prerevolutionary Russia's debt to French creditors. Additionally, realistic hopes for establishing normal ties with Yugoslavia and Czechoslovakia were dashed.

Still, the Soviet international position was not hopeless. Britain's explanation for its break—the need to stop Soviet and Comintern intervention in the affairs of other states—met with widespread support from the right wing of the European political spectrum.[4] But most European governments acted with restraint; they did not propose to alter their existing foreign policy strategies. Germany, balanced between East and West, was especially troubled. The diplomatic rupture threatened to destroy the system of international ties it had built up and force it into dependence on one of the warring sides.[5] Gustav Stresemann, the German foreign minister, tried urgently to convince his Western colleagues that a policy aimed at isolating the Soviet Union and provoking an internal crisis there would not bring positive results.[6]

The changed international situation critically affected internal relations in the USSR. The authority of the party leadership was severely undermined. Its foreign policy, which had resulted in such serious complications, seemed undeniably bankrupt. Confusion and disorientation were felt in political circles. The party leadership, faced with the collapse of its foreign policy, lost the ability to distinguish clearly between cause and effect in the developing situation and was beset by increasing nervousness and anxiety.

The very first days following the break in Anglo-Soviet relations were marked by distinct changes in the domestic atmosphere. A wave of disillusionment swept over the government's political base. Resignations from the party rose in frequency[7] and the influence of the left opposition grew. A war scare, which was spurred by official statements suggesting that war was imminent, affected broad layers of the population. The Soviet population had not forgotten the bitter experience of hunger and shortages during the long years of world war and civil war. Many rushed to the shops to buy up whatever was available. In the rural areas, too, people began hoarding. Inevitably, the peasants lost their willingness to part with their surpluses. The country's modest reserves of manufactured goods were quickly reduced. The USSR experienced "economic difficulties typical of a country on the eve of war, without there actually being a war."[8]

The new international situation produced abrupt changes in the political conjuncture. Prior to the defeat in China and the break with Britain, the Soviet leadership had not given much consideration to the possibility of war in the near future.[9] The new events shook that confidence. The government could not fail to understand that any serious attempt to wage war on the Soviet Union would have required fairly extensive diplomatic, military, and political preparations, which were not evident. Nevertheless, the statements of the political leaders were permeated with the conviction that such preparations had already begun, that the period of the "peaceful breathing spell" was ending, and that war was inevitable in the near future. It was expected, if not in 1928, then soon after.[10]

This change in the thinking of the leadership necessarily affected its political conception as a whole. With increasing urgency, demands were made for the quickest possible strengthening of the army and the defensive capacity of the Soviet state in general, for a reorientation of the economy and social relations toward a perspective of imminent war, and for more intensive industrialization. Such tendencies were clearly expressed in a number of speeches by government and economic leaders, especially in the early summer of 1927. All economic estimates and calculations existing up until then were brought into the discussion—this certainly did not ease the extremely complex economic situation.*

The Soviet leadership's nervousness was displayed in another connection as well. It was feared that the Anglo-Soviet rupture might spur other forces hostile to the USSR to undertake political or military adventures. In that event, an unwanted, unexpected war might be only a few days or weeks away. Soviet attention focused on Poland, which was seen as the main source of such a danger. The Soviet leaders' apprehensions focused on Jozef Pilsudski's longstanding project for the creation of a Polish-Lithuanian-Ukrainian federation—and on Polish claims to Byelorussia. They found confirmation of their fears in two areas: the conflict between Poland and Lithuania over Wilno (Vilnius), which the Soviet leaders feared might result in Polish annexation of all of Lithuania; and the talks between Polish officials and Ukrainian émigrés. A desire to unleash an anti-Soviet intervention was ascribed to Poland, and suspicions were voiced that it would provoke border incidents or take other actions leading to a generalized military conflict.[11]

A section of the Soviet leadership was inclined toward an ill-considered and unintelligent "policy of strength" posture, which artificially and unnecessarily increased the atmosphere of tension. Such attitudes derived from an oversimplified and schematic conception of the Western powers' motives, but they came to prevail within the Soviet leadership during the first half of June 1927. There followed a flood of official statements, diplomatic notes, and foreign policy maneuvers, which did

---

*This kind of political thinking was displayed especially clearly in a Central Committee statement of June 1, 1927 and was carried even further in a speech by Valerian Kuibyshev at the All-Union Congress of Trade and Industry on June 8 (see *Pravda*, June 1 and 10, 1927).

not improve the Soviet position in any way, but did provoke fears in several countries as to the possible consequences of this activity.[12]

Fairly substantial internal political reasons lay behind the uneasy nerves of the Soviet leadership. The leadership, or at least a part of it, did not believe that domestic stability could be maintained. It was afraid that the government's loss of authority would open the door to increased discontent with the system and heightened activity by its enemies, which could play into the hands of the Western powers and weaken the Soviet Union.

Georgia and the Ukraine caused the authorities particular concern. A marked growth of nationalist sentiment was evident in both republics, stemming from the economic upturn in the countryside, the strengthening of urban middle-class elements, and the NEP-era relaxation of pressure against the intelligentsia. In the Ukraine, nationalist sentiments had even penetrated the ruling Communist Party (Bolshevik) of the Ukraine—a section of that party's cadres resisted Russification of the political and governmental apparatus.[13] Similar sentiments in Georgia drew their strength from the surviving fragments of the social and political structure of the Georgian Republic, which had been crushed in 1921, and from the strongly developed national consciousness of the Georgians.

GPU reports, and analogous information flowing through Western diplomatic channels,[14] spoke of the existence of a highly ramified nationalist underground in both Georgia and the Ukraine, of preparations for armed struggle, and of ties with émigré organizations and British intelligence. Quite an extensive diplomatic furor was raised over the Ukrainian and Georgian questions, in which a number of states had an interest (Poland, Romania, Germany, Britain, France, and Czechoslovakia). The Soviet government regarded such nationalist activity as part of a British plan to prepare for war and eliminate the USSR as a world power.[15]

The extent of the internal danger was obviously exaggerated. The nationalist adversary, who had grown up out of mass discontent and disillusionment, remained nameless and therefore had little opportunity to organize and become a real antigovernment force. Nevertheless, all sense of proportion was lost in the heightened atmosphere of imminent danger. In particular, there was an increasing desire to "show a firm hand." The climax came on June 7. A young Russian émigré named Koverda fired at close range upon P. L. Voikov, the Soviet ambassador in Warsaw, killing him instantly. At nearly the same moment, at a party clubhouse in Leningrad—under circumstances that have never been clarified, outright provocation not being excluded—a bomb was thrown, causing a number of casualties.[16] A wave of mass demonstrations and protests swept the country. Poland was showered with ultimatums and barely concealed threats. The real meaning of these events was revealed two days later. On June 9, the GPU shot, without trial, twenty hostages, prominent holdovers from the tsarist regime. GPU chairman Vyacheslav Menzhinsky commented: "We must show the monarchists we still exist."[17]

The GPU was given emergency powers in violation of normal peacetime legal procedures.[18] After the shootings in Moscow, a wave of arrests, deportations, and executions began in other cities, from the western border to Vladivostok.[19] The country was suddenly thrown back to the repressive practices of the immediate postrevolutionary period of war communism. The instrument of preventive political and social terror, without benefit of law, returned from oblivion; it came back to haunt the consciousness of the politicians and hung menacingly over the entire next phase of development in the USSR.

The resurgence of repressive policy had unexpected consequences. Outside the USSR, a storm of public indignation arose and became a crucial factor in the political situation. "If the Russians had not rushed so hastily into the madness of mass executions in Moscow, England would have found itself in an exceptionally difficult position," French Foreign Minister Aristide Briand commented sadly.[20] The sympathy of a section of Western public opinion for the USSR, a response to the inordinate British diplomatic moves, was dispelled at one blow. It was replaced by a mood favoring a break in relations with the USSR. This mood extended across a broad political spectrum and helped, or in some cases even forced, several governments to change their policy toward the USSR. All this had the effect of a boomerang hitting back at the USSR and its leadership.

A conflict within the Soviet Communist Party leadership began to appear from the very first moment of the international crisis. Stalin and his supporters, feeling the ground give beneath their feet, lurched to the left and began to speak as the most ardent advocates of the hard line I have described. The moderates—Rykov, Mikhail Kalinin, Mikhail Tomsky, Chicherin, and others—did not share the edginess of Stalin and his group, or at least not entirely. Differences of opinion mounted and eventually built up to a confrontation.[21] Within the Soviet leadership a breach appeared that was not to be healed.

Chicherin, the commissar of foreign affairs, returned to Moscow from a lengthy trip abroad about June 19. A joint session of the Politburo and the Council of People's Commissars (Sovnarkom) was held immediately, and there Chicherin informed the leadership of the international situation and the results of his negotiations with government leaders in other countries.[22] His speech, supplemented by a memorandum distributed after the session, came out as a sharp critique of the course pursued by the Soviet Union since the break with Britain, as well as a de facto criticism of the foreign policy of Stalin and Bukharin. Chicherin stated categorically that in the existing international situation he saw no immediate danger of war. The aggressive designs of Poland, he said, should not be exaggerated. British intrigues in the Ukraine and Georgia, aimed at provoking nationalist uprisings and breaking up the Soviet Union, he added, were the only problems of serious importance. The Soviet Union was not threatened by war but by political isolation and economic block-ade.

The United States and Great Britain were the main countries with financial resources at their disposal, Chicherin pointed out. But the United States did not show any special interest in the USSR and the possibilities for economic cooperation with Britain had been ruined by the diplomatic break. The policy of the Comintern was having disastrous consequences. It was impossible to follow one line on the level of official government policy and another on the level of the Comintern. The USSR had gained nothing by its actions in China but had lost a great deal: the policy of international cooperation had been ruined.

The GPU had made the international position of the Soviet Union much worse. The shooting of hostages aroused universal indignation abroad, where people were convinced that the USSR was reverting to war communism. It was necessary to choose: either executions or foreign aid.

The Soviet Union could not withstand an economic blockade, Chicherin argued, but it still had a chance to "slip out of the noose." A quick decision by the party leadership was needed—a decision to con-tinue the policy of international cooperation. An attempt must be made to reduce the severity of the conflict with Britain, while at the same time blocking its activities in the Ukraine, Byelorussia, and Georgia. Comin-tern policy needed to be changed and terror without trials had to be renounced.

Chicherin's speech, backed up with all the authority of his person (including an offer to resign), brought to light a conflict within the Soviet leadership that went quite deep. Those assigned to economic work who spoke in the discussion—Commissar of Finance N. P. Bryukhanov, Com-missar of Trade Anastas Mikoyan, and Kuibyshev, head of the Vesenkha (Supreme Economic Council)—confirmed the danger to the Soviet Union's economic position. Any decision was postponed; the leadership did not have much choice. Stalin had to swallow the bitter pill. He was without doubt the most powerful member of the leadership, but his position was not beyond dispute. The moderates—Rykov, Kalinin, and Tomsky—did not have the fame of Trotsky, Kamenev, and Zinoviev, but they disposed of a much greater share of actual power. Rykov, an open and honest man who did not have Stalin's gift for stacking the apparatus with his own supporters, juggling facts, and back stabbing, was the premier of the Soviet Union and of the Russian republic. The "all-Union peasant elder" Kalinin held the posts of chairman of the Central Ex-ecutive Committee of the Soviets of the RSFSR and of the All-Union

Central Executive Committee, the top parliamentary institutions of the USSR and the Russian republic, which were not yet empty formalities. Tomsky headed the influential trade union organization and enjoyed virtually unchallenged authority within the powerful structures of the trade unions. They were all independent figures, who knew their way around the corridors of power, and each had a fairly large and influential following.

Stalin's position was greatly complicated by the fact that he did not possess all the qualities necessary in a statesman and government leader: the ability to foresee events, to work out a conception of government policy on a grand scale; the knowledge and experience to solve complex international, economic, and social problems.[23] Stalin's closest collaborators also lacked these qualities: Vyacheslav Molotov, a secretary of the Central Committee; Kuibyshev, chairman of the Vesenkha; Lazar Kaganovich, a Central Committee secretary; Mikoyan, the commissar of trade; Kliment Voroshilov, the commissar of war; and Sergo Ordzhonikidze, chairman of the Central Control Commission (CCC) and the Workers and Peasants' Inspection. With few exceptions, these men were capable, diligent administrators and implementers of policy, but only beginners as politicians; they had not yet mastered the intricacies of governmental and economic leadership. Moreover, they were far from immune to the influence of moderate politicians. Stalin remained heavily dependent on the political line put forward by the moderates. His only serious ally, Bukharin, who, with Stalin, bore the main burden for the Soviet Union's international defeats, was not able to give Stalin sufficient support. The nature of Bukharin's theoretical and political conceptions placed him among the moderates, and in fact he was one of the main authors of the moderate economic and social policies. As chairman of the Comintern and editor of *Pravda*, Bukharin did not possess .the necessary complement of real power; he relied mainly on his authority as a theoretician and politician, but this authority had been significantly undermined—even in Stalin's eyes—by the events in China and the Anglo-Soviet rupture.[24]

Stalin retreated, but not without rear-guard holding actions. With Bukharin's support, he stubbornly defended his previous policies, blaming others for the defeats.[25] In the process, he was not averse to taking some discreet jabs at Rykov and Chicherin.[26] Nevertheless, the course of events and the balance of forces within the party imposed a cautious and moderate course of behavior upon Stalin at that time.

At the end of June 1927, the Politburo, followed by the Sovnarkom, modified and approved Chicherin's proposals, which aimed at reducing international tensions.[27] In July, arrests and executions at the sole discretion of the GPU were halted.[28] Diplomatic steps were taken to defuse the extremely tense relations with Poland.[29] Soviet diplomats again tried to promote a policy of cooperation. The most intense phase of the June crisis in the party leadership was overcome, but the source of the conflict had not been removed. The moderates, schooled in the experience of previous internal party struggles, must have realized what a threat Stalin's retention of his post as general secretary was to them. He, in turn, must have seen clearly that the moderates would try to remove him from power.[30]

Meanwhile, events rushed on. The contradictions within the party and government leadership were only one component of the overall political crisis in the country that resulted from the international events. The most striking indication of this was the unusually heated, intense, and persevering struggle of the united left opposition.

THREE

The Opposition Revived

In 1927, the left opposition was not a new phenomenon in Soviet life. It had grown, in the preceding years, in proportion to the concentration of power in Stalin's hands after Lenin's death. During the spring and summer of 1926, an agreement was reached by the two most influential left opposition groups, the Trotskyists and the Zinovievists, both of which had been pushed to the political sidelines by Stalin. They were joined by the Democratic Centralists, a small but radical group led by Timofei Sapronov. It was assumed that an alliance of the three best-known leaders of the Lenin-era Bolshevik Party—Trotsky, Zinoviev, and Kamenev—supported by a large number of important political, theoretical, and practical leaders of the party, would provide the opposition with enough weight to wage a successful fight against the new leadership.

The opposition's main point of attack was Stalin's manner of running the party—his regime within the party—but there were also important differences on questions of economic and social development, which have been mentioned earlier. Thus, the opposition's main blow was divided—it lacked a single focus—and since it aimed at the moderates as well as the Stalin group, it drove the moderates into Stalin's arms, giving him more room to maneuver.

The importance of the left opposition is often underestimated in the literature. It is considered an important current in Soviet ideological and political life, a kind of "revolt of the leaders" in the context of the power struggle with Stalin; and it is cited as evidence that alternate forms of Soviet development were possible. But many authors doubt that the opposition had any substantial influence on the mass of party members and even less on broader sections of the population. One can hardly agree with such views: they seem paradoxical indeed in light of the mountain of ammunition expended on the opposition by the party leadership in those years—the multitude of official declarations, reports, pamphlets, and books, not to mention the mass political campaigns that penetrated even the remotest parts of the USSR.

In the spring of 1926 the united opposition, based on a cadre of old and experienced party leaders, conquered some fairly significant positions. It consolidated its influence in Leningrad, the Ukraine, Transcaucasia, and the Urals region; in the universities; in some of the central government offices; in a number of factories of Moscow and the central industrial region; and among a section of the command staff of the army and navy, which had passed through the difficult years of the civil war under Trotsky's leadership. Repression by the party leadership prevented the opposition from growing, but its influence was still much greater than indicated by the various votes taken in the party cells. Although the top three opposition leaders, Trotsky, Zinoviev, and Kamenev, lost their Politburo posts during 1926, they remained members of the Central Committee along with a number of other opposition leaders. The unresolved economic and social problems did not develop into a major crisis in 1926; in general, the country was still going through a period of relative stabilization and growth. The leadership was able to deal with the situation, which consequently did not prove conducive to success for the opposition. In October, under very heavy political and administrative pressure from the central party institutions, the opposition was obliged to disarm, to renounce any further factional activity. It fell silent, but it had not been broken.

In the spring of 1927, a new stage of the internal political fight began. The foreign policy setbacks of the party leadership inevitably revived the opposition. Events seemed to have fully confirmed its views. In April, at the regularly scheduled plenum of the Central Committee, the opposition leaders presented a series of proposals in connection with preparations for the Fifteenth Party Congress and the Sixth Congress of the Comintern. They also criticized various aspects of the leadership's policies, especially its China policy.[1] Outwardly, the opposition seemed to be advocating an extremely radical course—independence of the Chinese Communists from the Kuomintang, the encouragement of an armed popular revolution, and the formation of soviets (revolutionary committees or councils) in China. In fact, the opposition's policy essentially came down to a demand that the Soviet leadership renounce its adventuristic reliance on an unreliable ally, which was sure to end in defeat.

When the first reports of events in Shanghai came in and confirmed the worst prophecies of the opposition, it was only natural for oppositionists to speak out more frequently, going outside the framework of the party's upper echelons. The opposition saw a real chance to change a policy that, in its opinion, was leading to disaster.

Overcome by nervousness and by fear of a major international conflict, the party leadership responded to the opposition's criticism with threats. The leadership did not want complications inside the party. The opposition continued to speak out, however. A major confrontation took place at the meeting of the Presidium of the Executive Committee of the Communist International (ECCI), held in Moscow in the second half of May 1927. The Soviet party leadership wanted to use the authority of this international body and its official resolutions to cover up its policy

failures. The work of this plenary session proceeded under the humili-
atingly petty administrative supervision of the Soviet leadership. Nevertheless, Trotsky and V. Vujovic, a Serb and former leading figure in the
Communist Youth International, were able to give sharply critical
speeches. Only the representatives of the Thaelmann leadership of the
German Communist Party, which was engaged in a fierce conflict with a
left wing headed by Ruth Fischer, Arkady Maslow, and Hugo Urbahns,
and the representatives of the Far Eastern sections of the Comintern,
lent solid support to Stalin and Bukharin. The delegations from "the
Romance-language countries" (Italy, France, and Belgium) wavered, and
considerable uncertainty could be detected as well in the speeches of the
delegates from the powerful Communist Party of Czechoslovakia, V.
Stern and B. Smeral.

The delegates of the Italian, French, and Belgian parties met with
Trotsky at his apartment. He warned them of the consequences of
supporting the Soviet party leadership: "The Politburo is on the verge of
bloody reprisals against the opposition. I dare say that I know the habits
of our party better than others." The plenum approved Stalin and
Bukharin's foreign policy line, but could not bring itself to accept the
proposal of the Russian delegation to expel Trotsky and Vujovic from
the ECCI and recommend their expulsion from the Soviet Communist
Party. Instead, the plenum confined itself to issuing a "final warning." It
was clear that Stalin and Bukharin's authority had been severely undermined and that openly repressive actions would not have sufficient
support.[2]

Sensing that the leadership was in a shaky position, the opposition
increased its pressure. On May 26, Trotsky, Zinoviev, Smilga, and Grigory Yevdokimov sent the Politburo a declaration signed by eighty-four
prominent oppositionist party members. Among the points made in this
document were the following: events in China had freed the imperialists'
hands for war against the USSR; the party's failures were the result of a
wrong political line, which was contributing to the growth of capitalist
elements in the USSR at the same time that conditions for the workers
and poorer sections of the population were getting worse; rightist forces
were raising their heads, and inside the Communist party itself there was
a growing right wing, while the Politburo was trying to surgically remove
the left opposition. The situation could still be saved, but in order to do
this, repressive measures would have to be renounced, an open discussion permitted, and all decisions arrived at collectively.[3] In private conversations Trotsky was more concrete: the Stalinist parasites would have
to be removed and a healthy regime established in the party; everything
else would follow naturally.[4]

The Politburo, after suffering another heavy blow, the break in relations with Great Britain, lost its usual self-assurance. To risk a split in the
party during a crisis in foreign policy seemed inadvisable. The moder-

ates in the leadership did not fully share Stalin's views and, sensing a
future clash with him, showed no particular eagerness for fighting the
opposition.

The Politburo—according to several sources—decided to negotiate. It
proposed a truce to the opposition for the duration of the diplomatic
break with Britain, promising a future agreement on certain questions
(democratization of the soviets, a change in agrarian tax policies, and a
revision of Comintern policy in China). The opposition—according to
the same sources—responded with counterproposals insisting on immediate changes; they understood very well that the leadership was playing
for time so that its wounds could heal.[5] Meanwhile, opposition activity
was spreading like a river in flood. The opposition organized mass
meetings of industrial workers in Ivanovo-Voznesensk, Leningrad, and
Moscow; at a chemical plant in Moscow shouts were heard: "Down with
Stalin's dictatorship! Down with the Politburo!"[6]

There were rumors of underground strike committees, in which oppositionists were said to be participating, in the Urals, the Donbass, the
Moscow textile region and in Moscow proper—and of funds being raised
for striking workers.[7] The GPU reported to the leadership that it could
not guarantee "order" nor prevent the "demoralization of the workers" if
it was not given the right to arrest oppositionist party members.[8]

Stalin's supporters insisted on repression of the opposition.[9] On June
9, 1927, on the crest of the wave of indignation following the assassina-
tions in Warsaw and Leningrad, a notable event occurred. The opposition organized a meeting at the Yaroslavl Station in Moscow to say
farewell to one of its leaders, Ivar Smilga, whom the Central Committee
was sending away to the remote Siberian city of Khabarovsk, on the
Manchurian border. As many as two thousand people turned out for
this farewell demonstration. Trotsky and Zinoviev gave speeches. Smilga
was borne aloft to his railcar by the crowd. The GPU did not intervene
because members of the party, indeed of the Central Committee, were
taking part in the demonstration. In party circles the incident was described as "an antiparty rally" at a time when there was a direct threat of
war. The foreign press also commented on the incident.[10] The demonstration had a big impact, but the negative interpretation placed on it by
party leaders was clearly exaggerated. It was obvious that a convincing
pretext was being sought for administrative measures against the opposition and intervention by the agencies of repression.

The Central Control Commission took up the case. Hardcore Stalinists raised a fuss behind the scenes, seeking to have Trotsky and
Zinoviev expelled from the party.[11] The situation inside the party became white hot. Aron Solts, a member of the CCC Presidium, one of
many who was touted as "the conscience of the party," began talking
about the history of the French revolution, about arrests and the
guillotine. Among the oppositionists there was serious apprehension

that this was more than rhetoric. Trotsky responded to Solts at the CCC session. It was then that he uttered the winged phrase about "Thermidorian degeneration" of the leadership. Later on he added the point, in a letter to Ordzhonikidze, chairman of the CCC, that the danger of war did not eliminate the need for criticism and that replacement of the leadership might actually be a precondition for victory.[12]

Confusion reigned in the CCC. Its members were certainly aware of the differences of opinion on the Politburo and the growing mood of uneasiness, questioning, and criticism within the party. The number of signatures on the Declaration of the Eighty-Four was increasing and protests by party neutrals were multiplying. The CCC could not agree on immediate acts of repression. It referred the question to the next joint plenum of the Central Committee and CCC, with the recommendation that Trotsky and Zinoviev be expelled from the Central Committee.[13]

The Stalinists did not find this decision especially pleasing. The press adopted an unmistakable tone, publishing resolutions by local party organizations demanding the expulsion of Trotsky and Zinoviev not only from the Central Committee but from the party as well.

The situation did not develop in Stalin and Bukharin's favor, however. The series of failures in foreign affairs that had begun in the spring had not come to an end. The situation in China grew worse with each passing day. The line of the Comintern had been patched up, but, stuck halfway between the conception of the party leadership and that of the opposition, it could not produce results. It also became obvious that the Anglo-Russian Trade Union Committee (established in 1925 after the defeat of the British Labour government and consisting of representatives of the British General Council of Trade Unions and the Soviet Central Council of Trade Unions) faced inevitable collapse. The existence of this committee had been the object of bitter attack by the opposition, which accused the leadership of having made a senseless and disorienting alliance with reformists. The Politburo was obliged to save face by trying to distort the meaning of correspondence between the British General Council and the Soviet trade unions, an exchange that was highly embarrassing to the Politburo. The General Council had made it unmistakably clear that it was taking the initiative in breaking relations.[14] On top of all this, the economic situation grew steadily worse. Here too, the leadership was threatened with a major defeat; the opposition had long predicted that an economic crisis was inevitable.

Disorientation and disorganization found their way into the work of governmental and economic bodies—the result of lack of confidence in the correctness of the general political line. Opposition propaganda steadily grew in intensity. The opposition flooded party units with leaflets, pamphlets, and other materials, contributing to a further decline in the Politburo's authority. To be sure, the official statements of the party leadership contended that the local party organizations supported the measures proposed by the CCC—"not one voice or vote in favor of a softening." Later, it was admitted that the facts were otherwise.[15] A large section of the party took a very guarded attitude toward the organizational measures proposed to counter the opposition; only fear of the consequences prevented many from openly speaking their minds. People began to refer to Stalin—adopting a catch phrase of the opposition— as the "Noske of the Bolshevik Party." Within a couple of months some oppositionists would call him simply "leader of the fascists."[16]

By the end of July, the situation in the party had taken fairly definite shape. The opposition succeeded in increasing its influence; it was beginning to think that a change in the party leadership might be attainable at the forthcoming Fifteenth Party Congress. Against the background of mounting disorientation within the official power structure, the line of the opposition was notable for the clarity of its main positions. In the eyes of contemporaries, the energy, commitment, and enthusiasm of the oppositionists contrasted favorably with the bureaucratic sluggishness of their adversaries.[17] It became clear that Stalin did not have the strength for an immediate, crushing blow against the opposition. The moderates in the leadership did not share his hardened attitude, were reluctant to face further political complications, and did not wish to lose valuable cadres, who, under the existing tense international conditions, were irreplaceable.

Important members of the opposition who had taken responsible positions in the diplomatic service, such as Kamenev, Georgy Pyatakov, Preobrazhensky, and Vladimir Antonov-Ovseyenko, were carrying out the policies of the Commissariat of Foreign Affairs as directed by Chicherin (just as the prominent oppositionists Nikolai Krestinsky and Rakovsky had done before them).* Undoubtedly the relationship of forces inside the Red Army also affected the general situation. Many tried and tested officers belonged to the opposition, and they would be sorely missed in the event of a military conflict. At the same time, there was not much confidence in the ability of the pro-Stalin cadre elements in the Red Army leadership. This was bound to influence the attitudes of some members of the party leadership, as was the fear of having to face Stalin alone some day in matters affecting the party and the Central Committee.

Stalin had not yet recovered from his recent clash with the moderates and could not risk a new conflict with them. He took a conciliatory position, leaving the dirty work to his closest associates.[18]

On July 29, 1927, the Central Committee and CCC convened in Moscow for a ten-day joint plenum. A whole range of political and economic questions were on the agenda, but they were all overshadowed

---

*Trotsky, too, was urged to take up diplomatic duties in this period, but he refused.

by the central question—the fate of the opposition. It was the duty of the plenum to decide on the recommendation that Trotsky and Zinoviev be expelled from the Central Committee. The public, influenced by the newspaper campaign, which was still reverberating, expected reprisals. Many Central Committee members also took an uncompromising stand, after being worked on by Stalin's people in the central party apparatus. In the meantime, the party leaders' intentions had altered; they were now seeking a compromise.

It was not easy for the leadership to reach a compromise. Many of their own supporters had to be hastily cooled down. The opposition, sensing firmer ground beneath its feet, was not inclined to yield. Trotsky and Zinoviev again spoke in a sharply critical tone, with no acknowledgment of "error" on their part. Confusion increased when the leadership adopted many oppositionist positions in the resolutions of the plenum concerning policy in China and Comintern policy in general.[19] By the end of the first week, it became obvious that a compromise was virtually impossible. Ordzhonikidze, chairman of the CCC, presented the opposition with three demands, which seemed to be the minimum necessary to the leadership: (1) to renounce the insulting statements about "Thermidorian degeneration" and Trotsky's thesis that a change of leadership was permissible in the middle of a war; (2) to condemn the German left (the Fischer-Maslow-Urbahns group), which had been expelled by the Comintern but with which the Soviet opposition maintained close ties; and (3) to renounce that tendency in the opposition which, in the opinion of the leadership, was heading toward the formation of a "second party" in the USSR.[20] The opposition rejected these demands. The plenum had no choice but to announce the expulsion of Trotsky and Zinoviev from the Central Committee.[21]

The leadership's response to the opposition's stand was surprising. It continued to search for a compromise. At the same time, the opposition began to realize that a total break was not desirable, that forcing the Politburo to take action would seriously impair its own chances of success. Under pressure from the more fearful and less-principled Zinoviev, who wanted to return to the sphere of "high politics," the opposition decided to smooth some of its rougher edges. It would not seek a change of leadership during wartime, it stated, but even in the event of war it would not abandon its fight to correct the party line; it did not agree with splits in sections of the Comintern and for that very reason would fight to achieve the readmission of the German left to the Comintern; it did not consider factionalism permissible, and attempts to build a "second party" in the USSR were even less so (Sapronov's Democratic Centralists came close to a "second party" position)—but the systematic pressure tactics within the party and distortion of the opposition's views tended to push matters in that direction.[22] The opposition's statement was not at all what the party leadership was seeking, but its small concession was accepted. The plenum added a new resolution to the harsh earlier one condemning the opposition. It sharply censured Trotsky and Zinoviev for "violating party discipline." This was accompanied by lengthy but not very convincing explanations.[23] To calm the situation, the party leadership considered it necessary to make a series of far-reaching pronouncements at party meetings and in the press to the effect that it did not intend in any way to circumvent the decisions of the upcoming congress and was ready to guarantee fully that preparations for the party congress would proceed properly. "Not a single party regulation concerning preparations for a congress will be violated," Rykov assured the party membership.[24]

The mountain had labored and brought forth a mouse. The disparity between the Stalinist fist brandishing and the modest results of the plenum was too obvious. "Stalin, not Trotsky, has had to clip his claws," went the joke.[25] The foreign press became hopelessly muddled in guessing at the reasons behind the unexpectedly soft reprimand. No one thought, however, that the opposition had emerged unscathed from its battle with the leadership. A political crisis was at hand.

Outside the Soviet Union, there was a highly sensitive reaction to the new political situation. Experienced foreign politicians could not fail to understand that the Soviet leadership was in serious difficulty. Speculation began about a change of leadership in the USSR. The Soviet diplomatic corps found this extremely disconcerting.[26] Without having extricated itself from one major crisis in foreign affairs, the Soviet Union was slipping into another.

The consequences of Stalin's hard line during the spring and summer, combined with the uncertainty of foreign governments about the future course of events, resulted in an extremely cautious reaction to all proposals and initiatives by Soviet diplomats. Increased Soviet promotional efforts in the United States, that is, the attempt to interest American business circles in economic ties with the USSR, failed miserably. Already weak ties with Italy and Japan encountered increasing complications. A number of countries developed a desire to take advantage of the difficulties the USSR was experiencing in order to wrest substantial economic or political concessions from it. Relations with France became particularly strained. After the executions in the USSR in the summer of 1927, a wave of anti-Soviet sentiment swept through France, involving a broad spectrum of public opinion. The French government ignored the Soviet Union's increased willingness to make concessions and showed no special desire to renew the economic and political negotiations that had been broken off. In the fall of 1927, Franco-Soviet relations came close to the breaking point. In an effort to demonstrate toughness toward the USSR, the French cabinet categorically demanded the recall of the Soviet ambassador, Rakovsky, a leader of the left opposition, on completely ridiculous grounds.*[27] The Soviet government gave in, complicating its own internal political situation without improving its relations with France in any fundamental way.

Relations with Germany also grew worse, although after the break with Britain, Germany had become the Soviet Union's number-one trading partner. Uncertainty increased in Germany over the course of internal Soviet politics. The German government was annoyed that, in spite of the generally friendly relations between the two countries, the Soviet leadership would not forgo actions or statements that strained relations. Restrictions on German commercial and economic activity inside the USSR were the subject of numerous complaints. These restrictions were the result of the manner in which Soviet authorities applied the monopoly of foreign trade and economic and legal regulations as well as of sheer bureaucratism. The conviction grew in Germany's influential circles that the USSR, under existing circumstances, was ceasing to be attractive as a long-term trading partner. The German government presented its own demands at this point, which although done correctly, tended to worsen the already precarious international position of the Soviet government.[28]

A new political climate was developing inside the USSR. The resolutions of the plenum and the reports on it at meetings of the active party membership, although they contained the usual quota of political accusations,[29] had an undeniably relaxing effect. Fear of repression eased. People began, though very timidly, to conclude that critical activity might produce results.[30] This fed the growth of the opposition.

Precise data on the scale of opposition activity in the fall of 1927 are not available. It is doubtful that such information has been preserved in Soviet archives to any significant degree. After the revolution, conditions for the free expression of opinion were lacking, and the evaluation of the strength of various tendencies was always more a matter of intuition and atmosphere than a comprehensive analysis of facts. Nevertheless, the small amount of existing material gives an impressive picture. Even after the plenum, the party organizations continued to be flooded—especially in the large urban centers and the two capitals—with opposition literature and leaflets. Reports of heightened opposition activity came one after the other from various cities and from entire provinces— Leningrad, the Ukraine, Transcaucasia, Siberia, the Urals, and of course, Moscow, where the greater number of opposition political leaders were working.[31] There was a steadily growing number of illegal and

---

*The French government denounced Rakovsky on the grounds that he had signed the platform of the left opposition, which called on foreign soldiers—and therefore, French soldiers—in the event of a war between their country and the USSR, to refuse to obey their officers and to defect to the Red Army. This was said to be an act hostile to France, incompatible with the status of a diplomat, even though France was not at war with the USSR and, according to official assurances, had no intention of going to war with it.

semilegal meetings attended by industrial workers and young people.[32] The influence of the opposition in a number of large party units became quite substantial. It hampered the former free functioning of the Stalinist party apparatus.[33] The army was also strongly affected by opposition activity. Reports on a significant rise in the authority of the opposition came from the Leningrad military district and the garrison in Leningrad, from Kronstadt, and from troop units in the Ukraine and Byelorussia.

The main problem was not the increase in opposition activity, however, but the overall balance of power within the party. Quite a large number of famous political leaders were on the opposition side. The weakened authority of the party leadership, especially of Stalin and Bukharin, was insufficient to turn the setbacks and failures of party policy into gains. The leadership could not cope with the situation without bringing the GPU into the fight. But until then, GPU interference in internal party matters was strictly forbidden. (A precondition for GPU intervention in political cases was expulsion from the party.) In the upper circles of the party, more than among the rank and file, there was still a powerful fear of the consequences of bringing in the GPU. The experiences of the French revolution, which had been cited more than once since October 1917, were evident to all.[34]

The problem of relations with the opposition was added to disagreements existing in the party leadership. Not all the political leaders, as one might assume, considered the opposition to be excessively dangerous. This fact made itself felt during the July plenum, as I have shown. After the clashes with Stalin in the spring and summer, plans apparently ripened within the moderate wing of the leadership to use the increasingly complicated internal party situation to make fundamental changes in top party posts. The details are hard to determine today. But it remains a fact that rumors were circulating—even reaching diplomatic channels—that in the interest of making peace within the party, Stalin would be replaced in his post by someone else. The name of Tomsky, head of the trade unions, was mentioned.[35]

These plans—even if they were meant seriously—would have been hard to carry through. The opposition and the moderate wing of the leadership were separated not only by deep differences in political outlook but by the accretions built up in the course of a long drawn out internal fight, which affected the attitudes of the forces favoring a moderate policy. The moderates could not try to remove Stalin without placing their own positions in danger.

The political crisis threatened to become a governmental crisis. In early September, the opposition presented the leadership with a programmatic document, the Platform of the United Opposition, which had been written during the summer months. It was intended as the basis for a determined drive to win control of the central party institutions

through the precongress discussion period. It was assumed that twenty
to thirty thousand signatures could be obtained in support of the platform—this in itself testified to the extent of the opposition's connections.[36]

Outwardly, the platform did not contain much that was new; it repeated arguments the opposition had made earlier. It restated the fundamental economic strategy worked out by the opposition in 1925–1926,
and, in some respects, as early as 1923. Predicting inevitable economic
difficulties and a crisis, the opposition proposed immediate steps to
broaden the scope of Soviet foreign trade, using for this purpose an
"administrative loan" of 150 million poods of grain from the well-to-do
rural elements. At the same time, the opposition insisted on a radical
improvement in the structure of the Soviet economy to increase its
efficiency. It also called for a decisive reorganization and reduction of
the swollen administrative and economic apparatuses, which caused
huge losses of national resources because of their costly and incompetent
character.

This was not the platform's only major point. The opposition shifted
the weight of its criticism somewhat away from the failed foreign policy
of the leadership. It attacked the system of internal policy, the way the
NEP was carried out, the expansion of "money-commodity relations,"
and the related growth of the more well-to-do strata in the city and
countryside. It called for a quick improvement in the social conditions of
industrial workers and the rural poor (through such measures as wage
increases, strict adherence to the law on fixed working hours, mean-
ingful assistance for the unemployed, increased housing construction,
government aid and exemption from taxes for the poorer peasant
households, the expansion of poor peasant cooperative farming, and the
organization of the rural poor). The platform also proposed that the
vital core of workers and poor peasants in the party, the soviets, and
public organizations be strengthened and that democracy within the
party and state be expanded as a precondition for the active participation
of working people in public life. At the same time, it urged that increased economic and administrative pressure be applied to the wealthy
layers of the population and that their influence in the society and state
be suppressed.

From this point of view, the platform sharply criticized the "Moscow
centralism" of the party leadership, its crude interference in the national
republics and national regions of the USSR, restrictions on national life,
and instances of national oppression. It proposed the expansion of the
rights and powers of autonomous action for soviet and party bodies in
the union republics and national regions, the encouragement of their
economic development, and a stronger role for the workers and poor
peasants in those areas. At the same time, it demanded that workers of
the Russian national minority in the union republics be protected from

the consequences of the bureaucratic policy of "naturalization," which was used to conceal the real state of affairs.

The opposition extended its assessment of the situation in the society and state to the party as well. It especially stressed the danger of the rightward course, whose main proponents were said to include Rykov, Kalinin, and Tomsky, in the central leadership, and, in the Ukraine, Grigory Petrovsky and Vlas Chubar. In this way an old error of the opposition was not only repeated but compounded: by striking at the moderates, the opposition made things easier for the Stalinists, whom they classified as "centrists."

The platform was far from being an ideal document. It misjudged the real social relations in the USSR, overestimating the wealth and economic power of the better off sections of the population. The implementation of its proposals would undoubtedly have endangered the NEP. In addition, and here Zinoviev's views played an important role, its assessments and recommendations on foreign policy were left-extremist. Nevertheless, it was an integrated political program that reflected fairly accurately the sentiments of a large section of party members and of politically active industrial workers.

There is no doubt that the platform made a fairly substantial impression on the party leadership, particularly—it can be assumed—on Stalin. He had to question the usefulness of Bukharin's political conceptions, which had resulted in serious setbacks. But the leadership, and Stalin in particular, must also have understood what serious consequences— under conditions of intensifying crisis—the circulation of the opposition's demands could have. On September 8, 1927, the Politburo categorically banned the platform. It was determined to do everything in its power to enforce this prohibition.[37]

Other factors affecting the attitude of the Politburo soon made themselves felt. More and more material came into its hands showing the negative international consequences of the internal political crisis. In September, the Politburo was informed of the contents of intercepted dispatches sent by J. Herbette, the French ambassador in Moscow, who was said to have recommended, apparently on the basis of opposition material, that the French government take a hard line in Franco-Soviet relations.[38] The economic situation continued its drastic decline. A number of major planning targets were not met. Economic managers began to speak of an impending disaster.[39] It became obvious that the existing situation in the party could not be allowed to continue; it would simply involve too many risks for the leadership. As always in critical situations, when political means lost their effectiveness, repression came into its own.

Late in the night of September 12 and the early hours of September 13, events occurred that were fated to have momentous consequences for the Soviet future. The GPU raided the apartments of several opposition activists and discovered an illegal "printshop" (an ancient hectograph and some typewriters) where the platform of the opposition was being duplicated. By crude frame-up methods, this "printshop" was linked not only with "certain bourgeois specialists" but also with a "Wrangel officer" (who turned out to be a GPU agent) and with alleged preparations for a "White Guard conspiracy" against Soviet power. Some of the individuals implicated in the case, including the civil war hero Mrachkovsky, were arrested;* others were expelled from the party.[40] Three leaders of the opposition, Preobrazhensky, Leonid Serebryakov, and Y. Sharov, attempted to save the situation by taking political responsibility for the "printshop," but they were also expelled.

It soon became evident that the whole operation had been carefully prepared and planned far in advance. News of organizational measures against the opposition and arrests of its supporters came from all major cities—Leningrad, Kiev, Tbilisi, Baku, Yerevan, Rostov on the Don, and elsewhere. Special "fighting units," organized by the Stalinist party apparatus as early as the summer of 1927, broke up opposition meetings with increasing frequency, turning off lights and creating other disturbances. In many instances, matters came to blows.[41] Almost everywhere, oppositionists were fired and blacklisted, working-class members of the opposition being especially hard hit.

These organizational measures against the opposition moved higher and higher toward its top leaders. On September 27, the Presidium of the ECCI returned to the question of Trotsky and Vujovic's membership on that body. The two were charged with a policy of splitting the Comintern and the Soviet Communist Party, slandering the Soviet party leadership, and supporting underground oppositional activity in association with "alien elements." The Presidium corrected its earlier wavering and assumed the role of agent for the Soviet leadership, on which, in fact, it was totally dependent. Trotsky and Vujovic were expelled.[42]

The decisions of the ECCI Presidium were merely a prelude. After a series of tactical maneuvers, confrontations, declarations, and angry resolutions, on October 21–23, 1927, the question of Trotsky and Zinoviev was again brought before a joint plenum of the Central Committee and CCC. The moderate group in the Politburo, which by then was convinced of the dangerous consequences of the party crisis, abandoned its earlier intentions and retreated all along the line. It became obvious that the opposition, by itself, without the benefit of differences within the leadership, and despite the substantial sympathy and support it enjoyed among the ranks, could not stand up under the fire of organizational measures and repressive acts against its members.

---

*Mrachkovsky was released in time to take part in the opposition's presentation of its case in the discussion preceding the Fifteenth Party Congress. Later, he shared the fate of the other opposition leaders.

The joint plenum proceeded in an atmosphere of white-hot tension. The leaders, Stalin among them, "apologized" to the Central Committee and CCC for their previously soft approach. When Trotsky and other opposition members of the Central Committee tried to explain their position they were unable to speak because of the constant interruptions of rude and hostile remarks. Ordzhonikidze and Bukharin were said to have shouted, "Trotsky's place is in the inner prison of the GPU," and Menzhinsky seems to have accused the opposition of spying—apparently in connection with Herbette's dispatches.[43] Responding to protests by oppositional members of the Central Committee over the arrests of veteran revolutionaries, Stalin made an ominous remark that has echoed down through Soviet history: "Yes, we have arrested them and we will continue to arrest people like them."[44]

Events quickly approached a climax. The opposition, mobilizing its considerable store of influence, tried to make a show of strength to turn the situation to its favor. During Leningrad's celebration of the tenth anniversary of the October revolution in mid-October 1927, the opposition suddenly received impressive support. Trotsky, Zinoviev, and other oppositionists, who found themselves by chance on one of the official reviewing platforms as the workers of Leningrad paraded past, found themselves the object of demonstrative greetings and cheers from the crowd of a hundred thousand.[45] The authorities appeared to be powerless to control the crowd. The GPU reported with alarm, although this was not without a hidden motive, that units of the Leningrad garrison were politically unreliable.[46]

Inspired by this success, the opposition decided on a number of further steps whose purpose was by no means realistic or rational. It tried to organize mass resistance within the party and among politically-minded workers against the offensive of the leadership. In Leningrad, Zinoviev, who vacillated between fits of euphoria and panic, hastily arranged meetings with delegations of Leningrad workers. In early November, the opposition took over the auditorium of the Higher Technical School in Moscow and held a meeting with two thousand of its supporters; representatives of the Central Committee and CCC were not allowed in. Rakovsky, who had just been relieved of his post as ambassador to France and therefore enjoyed an aura of martyrdom, made a speaking tour through the Ukraine. He tried, mostly in vain, to get a hearing before audiences of workers.[47] Beloborodov, people's commissar of internal affairs for the RSFSR, spoke for the opposition in the Urals region. The oppositionists' attention was focused, however, on the November 7 demonstrations celebrating the Bolshevik revolution. They wanted to repeat the experience of October's Leningrad demonstration in all the major industrial centers of the country.

The party leadership was seriously alarmed. If the opposition succeeded, it could destroy many well-laid plans. The leadership was apparently not certain what practical purpose the opposition thought to achieve, or what consequences its demonstrations might have.

The Politburo mobilized not only the party apparatus but also the GPU, with all its resources, against the upcoming opposition demonstrations. Emergency measures were taken in the garrisons of all big cities.[48] Every attempt to hold an opposition demonstration on November 7 was suppressed before it could begin. The Stalinist goon squads ("fighting units") and groups organized by the GPU and party apparatus broke up the opposition columns as they formed and provoked scuffles that developed into full-scale brawls. Opposition leaders were greeted with derisive whistling and various objects were thrown at them; some had difficulty escaping from the violence of the hired mob.[49]

Stalin, encouraged by the successful disruption of the opposition's plans, moved to take command of the situation. He was concerned not only by the opposition but also by the moderate leaders who still objected to direct intervention by the GPU in internal party affairs.

On November 9 and 10, Menzhinsky, as head of the GPU, addressed two secret letters to some members of the leadership.[50] Reliable sources, he said, were reporting that "the opposition's combat organization" had been preparing a coup d'etat for the period of November 6–8. They proposed to occupy the Kremlin, the GPU building on Lubyanka Street, the telephone and telegraph offices, and the radio stations and to sever rail connections between Moscow and the rest of the country. Similar coup attempts were to take place in Leningrad and Kharkov. The planned coup had been aborted owing to the defensive measures taken by the authorities and to the fact that Trotsky had spoken against the plan within the counsels of the opposition. The plan, however, had not been abandoned, merely postponed to a more favorable occasion.

Menzhinsky claimed that the situation was extremely dangerous. Deteriorating economic conditions were contributing to the rapid growth of the opposition, which was becoming the central focus of widespread discontent. Events had shown the unreliability of the Leningrad garrison and its command staff. Vsevolod Balitsky, the head of the Ukrainian GPU, and Iona Yakir and A. I. Kork, commanders of the western military districts, reported low morale among the units in their districts. Voroshilov shared the opinion that the command staff was partly unreliable. At this rate, in two or three months the entire Red Army would be unreliable. Menzhinsky's letters stated that despite his and Ordzhonikidze's insistence, the party leadership had refused to resort to emergency measures. Even Stalin and Bukharin were supposedly against "premature neutralization" of the opposition leaders. Menzhinsky insisted that the opposition leaders had to be "eliminated," without worrying about foreign public opinion, for without them the movement would die. Further delay would be "criminal light-mindedness"; after three or four months the leadership would no longer be strong enough to take such measures.

Today it is difficult to determine whether these reports were the result of a deliberately staged provocation, which sought to affect the balance of power in the party leadership, or the product of the working methods of the GPU, which relied on dubious sources of information.* Be that as it may, Stalin made immediate use of these reports. He sent Menzhinsky's letters to the rest of the leadership with his own covering letter: the opposition was preparing for a coup and had not abandoned the idea for the future. Its ties with counterrevolutionary organizations outside the country had been fully proven; there could be no more wavering; the leaders of the opposition had to be expelled even before the party congress. The opposition had to be eliminated "right away."

The concentrated pressure of Stalin and the GPU, reinforced by Menzhinsky's offer to resign if his proposals were not accepted, could not fail to affect the Politburo.[51] The resistance of the moderate members of the leadership was not entirely broken, however. (The most intensive rumors about suggestions by the moderates, especially Rykov, that Stalin be removed from his post belong to this period.) Apparently, the moderates did not believe Stalin and the GPU's charges of a coup planned by the opposition, but they could not ignore the seriousness of the situation. The moderates' concern was reflected in public statements that the logic of the struggle was leading the opposition toward a coup attempt and in their acceptance of GPU assertions that certain opposition groups were planning an attempt on Stalin's life.[52] Menzhinsky's demand for the "immediate elimination" of the opposition chiefs was not accepted, and the question was postponed until after the party congress.[53] *Pravda* still published the "Counter-Theses" of the opposition in its special precongress discussion supplement. Nevertheless, the leadership, by majority vote, renounced any further adherence to "party legality"; the fate of the opposition was to be decided before the party congress after all.

Events proceeded apace. A Central Committee statement addressed to all party units appeared in the newspapers, publicly appealing for the prevention of all further opposition meetings. The CCC speeded up its procedures in order to expel Trotsky and Zinoviev from the party, and when nine opposition members of the Central Committee and CCC expressed support for the expelled leaders, they in turn were expelled.[54] In view of the serious danger of physical reprisals, the opposition temporarily discontinued its own meetings.**[55]

---

*One indication of the poor quality of the GPU's information is the fact that the party leadership never publicly used this version of events, but spoke only of the anti-Soviet or antiparty actions of the opposition on November 7, 1927.

**The last well-known street demonstration of the opposition was held on November 19, 1927, when several hundred or, according to some sources, two thousand oppositionists marched to the funeral of Adolf Joffe, a prominent Soviet diplomat and opposition leader who had been the de facto chairman of the Military Revolutionary Committee of the Petrograd Soviet during the October insurrection in 1917.

Opposition influence remained strong, but it could no longer exert effective influence on the real relations of power. Party conferences held during November, as well as congresses of the Communist parties of the union republics held the same month, were totally controlled by the leadership. The opposition did not win any elected delegates to the upcoming party congress. The moderate leaders paid a heavy price for this new state of affairs. Against their own better judgment, they publicly stressed Stalin's role as leader of the party and expressed their willingness to defend him against the opposition, even with the help of the GPU.[56]

The Fifteenth Party Congress, on which so many hopes had been pinned, convened in Moscow on December 2, 1927. It could no longer play any role in the fight for an alternative road of Soviet development. Its decisions were predetermined by the narrow circle at the party's top. The congress confirmed the expulsion of the opposition, which in fact had already taken place, and—such is the irony of fate—instead of witnessing a struggle against the leadership, it became the scene of an incipient split between the two original groupings in the opposition, the Trotskyists and the Zinovievists. The Zinovievists were hastily swimming back to the safe waters of party loyalty.[57] Still, the leaders of both opposition tendencies were arrested in the first half of January and deported to remote areas of the USSR. The leadership felt that this method of rendering them harmless was tactically preferable to imprisonment.

The open form of political crisis, seen in 1927, was coming to an end. It was replaced by a hidden crisis, related to the general economic and social situation in the USSR. The resolution of the crisis, as is common in such conditions of society, independently of the wills and desires of individuals, brought about major shifts in political thinking and in the power structure.

Within two or three months of the events of September 12–13, 1927 (the raid on the opposition "printshop"), the basis for the existence of any kind of opposition whatsoever inside the Soviet Communist Party had been destroyed. From then on, opposition was an unequivocal political crime, bringing stern punishment in its train. Resistance to GPU interference in party matters was broken. To reinforce this state of affairs, Stalin presented a number of new proposals to the Politburo before the end of the year: that persons propagating opposition views be regarded as dangerous accomplices of the external and internal enemies of the Soviet Union and that such persons be sentenced as "spies" by administrative decree of the GPU; that a widely ramified network of agents be organized by the GPU with the task of seeking out hostile elements within the government apparatus, all the way to its top, and within the party, including the leading bodies of the party. "Everyone who arouses the slightest suspicion should be removed," Stalin concluded. "Humane considerations have no place here."[58] In the fall of 1927, under the pretext that the army was unreliable, and at the price of conflict with the military command, an intensive reinforcement of GPU troop units began, which were contemptuously referred to in the army as the "Soviet gendarmerie."[59] They were intended to combat the "enemy within."

GPU supervision of and control over the army was strengthened. Menzhinsky engaged in the most complex intrigues against the leadership of the Commissariat of War, seeking, not without Stalin's blessing, to replace the incompetent and conceited Voroshilov, who was totally lacking in authority.[60] The GPU worked its way into every pore of the Soviet state. More and more often the heads of party, government, and military bodies were given instructions to cooperate on one or another matter directly with the organs of the GPU.[61] In order to limit the GPU's unchallengeable autonomy in certain political matters and to subordinate it further to his own personal control, Stalin played a long-range double game. On the one hand, he cooperated with Menzhinsky; on the other, he took advantage of Menzhinsky's serious illness to propose his own friend and front man, Mikoyan, for the post of GPU chairman.[62]

Not all of Stalin's proposals were accepted and not all of them were the product of a precise, carefully worked-out plan. It is important not to make the Stalin of this period into a demon. Still, there is no question that a powerful impulse had been added to the Soviet power structure's general tendency to evolve in a particular direction.

FOUR

Economic Crisis and Power Politics

In the fall of 1927, it seemed to many that the successful outcome of the fight against the opposition would stabilize the internal situation, but no stabilization occurred. Instead, as a result of the contradictory needs of the Soviet economy, an economic crisis quickly developed.

The initial source of the economic difficulties was found in the decisions of the February 1927 Central Committee plenum. It allocated 1.1 billion rubles for the needs of capital construction in industry, especially metallurgy and heavy engineering.[1] On the basis of data presented by Rykov, by mid-year, the economic picture was cause for concern. Total capital investment, which could not be reflected in production during 1927–1928, amounted to more than one billion rubles if spending for the accumulation of reserves was included. The capital spending provided for in the budget also came to about one billion rubles, but it had been necessary to increase that figure by an additional 100–150 million rubles to meet the needs of defense and to renovate the transportation system.[2]* Spending on such a scale exceeded the capabilities of the Soviet economy and financial system.

The party leadership hoped to extricate itself from the situation with the help of supplementary measures: credits from foreign countries, internal loans, and better use of existing resources. But the external and internal political crisis dashed these hopes. Paper money was printed around the clock—a futile effort to stop up budgetary gaps. Strong inflationary symptoms began to appear, since the expanded purchasing power of the population was not backed by goods available for purchase.[3] A shortage of industrial raw materials and a number of seasonal difficulties resulted in the failure of light industry to produce its planned quantities of goods. This deficit had a painful effect on the market,

*By way of comparison: the size of the Soviet budget in fiscal year 1926–1927 was estimated to be about 5.1 billion rubles, and that of fiscal year 1927–1928, about 6.6 billion. Total investment in the industrial sector (state and cooperative industry, transportation, electrification, and so on) was, according to Stalin, about 2.7 billion rubles in fiscal year 1926–1927.

37

which was stripped bare by the buying fever that accompanied the war scare in the first half of 1927.[4] For a number of reasons, the quantity of agricultural products going into general circulation in the Soviet economy was sharply reduced and was insufficient to meet the needs of the country.

From mid-1927 on, the economic difficulties became evident in everyday life. In the countryside, as well as in Moscow and other big cities, a severe shortage of certain basic foods and essential industrial goods was felt.[5] With increasing frequency, the authorities took measures that cut the real wages and social gains of the laboring sectors of the population. Social and political ferment intensified, becoming an important part of the general crisis.

Preoccupied with the fight against the opposition, the party leadership was unable to acknowledge the seriousness of the economic problems. Urgently needed measures were delayed, while the policies that were implemented were not appropriate to the situation.* Within the Politburo, the view was held that after the worst phase of the foreign and domestic political crisis had passed it would be possible to re-establish economic equilibrium and tie up loose ends without altering the established economic conception.[6]

Meanwhile economic difficulties increased. An impasse was reached in the attempt to draft the first five-year plan (1928/1929–1932/1933), which projected a relatively moderate growth rate. The leadership justified the need to revise plans by arguing that the possibility of war and bad harvests in the coming five-year period had not been taken into account in the plans that had been drafted.[7] But this did not change matters. The extreme instability of the economic situation in the USSR was reflected in this very line of argument. It proved impossible to present the Fifteenth Party Congress with a fully worked-out draft of the five-year plan. Instead, only general directives for drafting the plan were adopted. The country remained without a clear and balanced perspective for economic growth.

Starting in October 1927, the economic situation again began to deteriorate appreciably. Insisting on the old conception, the Politburo, whose hands were tied more than ever by the intensified conflict with the opposition, tried to find a solution in the form of increased economic cooperation with other countries. Soviet diplomatic circles reached the

---

*An example of this was the manifesto of the CEC on the tenth anniversary of the October revolution, adopted at the ceremonial session of October 15, 1927, in Leningrad. It proclaimed a number of measures to improve material conditions for industrial workers and poor peasants. The real worth of the manifesto can be judged from the fact that exactly the opposite was occurring in the Soviet Union, that is, material conditions were becoming worse for wide sections of the population. The manifesto was approved despite strong protests by the opposition (Zinoviev and Trotsky) and grave doubts on the part of some Politburo members (Tomsky, Kalinin, and Voroshilov).

conclusion that the worst phase of international tension and complica-
tion had passed; Chicherin therefore reintroduced his proposals for
improving relations with the major capitalist powers. In his judgment,
the best prospects for improved relations were with France. He did not
exclude the possibility of contacts with the United States and improved
ties with Britain as well. It seemed that more of the necessary preconditions for broad economic cooperation existed. In Chicherin's opinion, if
the Politburo changed the way the foreign trade monopoly was handled
in practice, signing economic agreements and attracting foreign capital
to the USSR would be facilitated.[8]

Chicherin's assessment of the situation was hardly realistic, but it
corresponded to an increasingly widespread mood within a section of
the party leadership. Maxim Litvinov, the deputy commissar of foreign
affairs, and Anatoly Lunacharsky, the new Soviet ambassador to Rome,
were sent to take part in the December 1927 international disarmament
conference in Geneva. Their assignment included the development of
more intensive contacts with Western political leaders and sounding out
possibilities for improving the Soviet Union's international position.*

Meanwhile, the Politburo discussed the second part of Chicherin's
proposal: relaxation of the foreign trade monopoly. Stalin vigorously
supported Chicherin, citing proposals he, Stalin, had made at the end of
1926. He stated that the monopoly in its existing form was a relic of the
time of war communism and that refusal to relax its strictures would
lead to a catastrophe.[9]

Resistance to concessions on the foreign trade monopoly was considerable within the party as a whole, as well as within the leadership. Added
to this were fears of possible political consequences; the opposition had
long accused the Politburo majority of wanting to abandon this central
principle of the Soviet economy.[10] However, the party leadership no
longer had a choice if it wished to obtain foreign credits.

Chicherin and Stalin's proposals for the relaxation of the foreign trade
monopoly were approved by the Politburo in late 1927 and early 1928.[11]
In January and February 1928, the Politburo returned to these questions
repeatedly and discussed the possibility of more extensive concessions.[12]
Other steps were also taken. A strict separation between the functions of
Soviet diplomacy and those of the Comintern apparatus was established,
a reaction to foreign accusations of subversive activity by Soviet diplomats.[13]

In February 1928, economic talks with Germany began. The German
government wanted to use the talks to implement its concept of intensified German economic activity in the USSR; the Soviet Union, for its

---

*Litvinov's meeting with Neville Chamberlain dates from this time, although it was
generally unsuccessful and remained without results. It was held at Litvinov's initiative and
was subsequently portrayed as a success for Soviet diplomacy.

part, was hoping to obtain new credits—600 million marks worth.[14] Unfortunately, the path of international agreements, which the Soviet government had chosen, did not produce results. Time was required for success along this path; the Soviet leadership no longer had time to spare.

The Soviet leaders sought foreign aid, based on the assumption that the USSR's economic crisis would develop gradually.[15] At the same time they inevitably felt a certain anxiety. They could not rely on foreign aid, but without it the economic strategy they had chosen would not work. The opposition's proposals to strengthen the "class character" of Soviet economic policy and extract a "loan" from the wealthy peasantry began to attract the attention of a section of the leadership. Beneath the surface there was an increasing differentiation among Politburo members.

Bukharin played the role of trailblazer in this new development. On October 12, 1927, at the Congress of Trade Unions of Moscow Province, he made a statement that had wide repercussions. One phase of the NEP had been completed, he said, and the party was entering a second one, the substance of which would be a "reinforced (*forsirovannoe*) offensive against the capitalist elements, first of all, the kulaks."[16]

When the Fifteenth Party Congress met in Moscow at the beginning of December 1927, the new line still had not been clarified. The leadership, which was interested in the expulsion of the opposition as quickly and with as little friction as possible, mentioned economic difficulties only reluctantly and, it seemed, unintentionally.[17] Evidently, clear statements had not been made in the Politburo; this left the membership to conclude that social and economic policy on the practical level would change only gradually. The report for the Central Committee, made by Stalin, strongly emphasized successes achieved in the economic sphere, further confusing the issue.

The reports on the directives for the five-year plan, made by Rykov and Gleb Krzhizhanovsky, gave as little an impression of a change in principle as Molotov's report on work in the countryside. But an experienced observer could not have missed the shift to the left in the political thinking of part of the leadership. Just before the party congress, the question of speeding up the collectivization of agriculture was presented to the Politburo. It became one of the basic themes of Stalin's report.[18] Obviously, not all members of the Politburo understood the implications of this proposal.[19]

The Fifteenth Party Congress registered a certain ambiguity in the party's political line, allowing different interpretations. The leadership as a whole had no intention of making abrupt changes in practical economic work in the immediate future. It maintained the hope that the next harvest, which the experts estimated would be better than average, would slow the unfavorable economic trends and allow time for the

preparation of new solutions. These expectations were crushed immediately after the party congress. A new factor entered the economic life
of the country with trenchant effect: in October 1927, grain deliveries to
the state abruptly declined.

There is extensive literature on the subject of the grain deliveries in
fiscal year 1927–1928. For a long time the failure to procure adequate
grain supplies was attributed, in the official Soviet version of events, to a
"kulak grain strike," an attempt by the kulaks to force the government to
pay higher prices for grain and to undermine Soviet power.[20] More
objective authors, especially those in the West but some Soviet ones as
well, have pointed to the combined effect of a series of economic factors:
the lag in grain farming, population growth, an incorrect price policy,
insufficient supplies of manufactured goods to the rural areas, and so
on.[21] The real state of affairs has never been fully clarified.

The grain crisis was partly the result of contradictions in the Soviet
economy and partly the result of serious mistakes by the Soviet leaders.
Lulled by previous years of good harvest, they had an overly sanguine
view of the state of Soviet agriculture—as did the opposition, to an even
greater degree. Unsatisfactory conditions in grain farming were con-
tinually disregarded.[22] As early as 1926–1927, in order to supply industry with raw materials and the cities with meat and dairy products, the
government raised prices for industrial crops and animal products,
while reducing procurement prices for other agricultural products. The
peasants' economic interests were thus oriented in a new direction.[23] No
effective measures were taken to stimulate grain farming.

The economic calculations of the Soviet leadership did not take the
serious problems of the countryside sufficiently into account: the growth
of the rural population and the resulting rapid increase in surplus labor
in the countryside; the increased number of agricultural domestic ani-
mals; panic buying because of the war scare; and the peasants' fear of
periodic bad harvests, which always seemed to follow several years of
good harvest in Russia.[24] All these things diminished the marketable
output of grain. In addition, by reducing the size of the agricultural tax
and various other payments made by peasants and not considering the
increasing extent of nonagricultural income in the countryside, the party
leadership weakened the financial incentives for selling grain. Two additional factors have already been mentioned: the constant decline in the
purchasing power of the ruble and a severe shortage of manufactured
goods.

There can be no doubt that under these conditions the peasants,
especially those who were better off, were in no hurry to sell their
surplus grain. They were obviously waiting for an improvement in
market conditions and increased supply of industrial goods. The psychological aspect must not be underestimated either. The peasants assumed, from the experience of the previous several years, that in the

spring the government would raise its procurement prices—1927 was the first year in which the disparity between procurement prices in fall and spring was eliminated. The peasants had not yet grown accustomed to the new situation and therefore expected that the practice of the preceding years would be repeated.

Yet another factor played an important role. Statistics that had been dressed up to please higher authorities gave a false picture of the amount of freely available grain in the silos of the peasantry, as well as the general capacity of agriculture to provide the food supplies needed by the Soviet Union.

The government traditionally used grain exports to earn the means to pay for the imported goods needed by industry, but in 1927–1928 it did not have grain reserves to spare for the export market. It probably could have built up such reserves during the years of good harvests, but had failed to do so.*

Industrial equipment purchased at a cost of tens of millions of rubles (through the sale of export grain) sat and rusted in factory yards for months or was not used at all because sites were not prepared or new construction was behind schedule.[25] As the events of the years 1928 and 1929 were to show, the Soviet Union had not taken sufficient advantage of the possibility of replacing grain with other export items. By having no reserves, the government denied itself the possibility of intervening in the grain market to ward off the crisis in its most serious form.

In the literature, the thesis stubbornly persists that one of the main reasons for the difficulties in grain procurements was the peasants' refusal to sell grain to the state. This account requires careful examination. As early as the Fifteenth Party Congress, Rykov and Mikoyan pointed out that grain procurement difficulties were related to the fact that in the main regions of market production—especially in the Northern Caucasus, the Volga region, Orenburg province, and Kazakhstan—the harvest had been much smaller than in previous years, and in some parts of the country there had been a very bad harvest.[26] Mikoyan cited some interesting details about the procurement campaign: Tataria, Bashkiria, the central Black Earth region, and the Crimea had far exceeded the previous year's grain deliveries to the government; even in the Ukraine more than the expected amount of grain had been delivered. The procurement campaign was lagging badly in regions that had

*Soviet grain exports in 1925–1926 were 147 million poods and in 1926–1927, 185 million poods (in money terms: 198 and 233.5 million rubles, respectively). In 1927–1928 they had to be reduced to almost nothing. The "iron reserve" of grain, a bottom limit established for the needs of the army in 1926–1927, was about 60 million poods (1 million tons). It must be admitted that it was extremely difficult for the Soviet government to reorient itself away from grain exports, not only because the USSR had hardly any other important sources of foreign exchange but also because grain exports, even in the quantities cited above, remained far below the targets set by the plans. (For useful information on this subject, see Paul Scheffer, *Sieben Jahre Sowjetunion* [Leipzig, 1930], pp. 235–238.)

been affected by crop failures or poor harvests—the Northern Caucasus, Kazakhstan, and the Volga region. Besides these, only Siberia and the Urals region were noticeably behind, which was partly because of transport difficulties and because the state apparatus in those areas was not well suited to handling the task of grain procurement.[27] It seems obvious that the causes of the unsuccessful procurement campaign are to be sought, not in this or that detail, however important, but in the general condition of Soviet agriculture and the Soviet economy as a whole.

Within the leadership, the opinion initially prevailed that the difficulties in procuring grain could be corrected through the usual economic measures: industrial goods would be quickly transferred to the rural market, the production of textiles and some other goods would be increased beyond planned quantities, and the work of the procurement agencies would be improved and reinforced especially in those regions where it was not sufficiently developed (Siberia, the Urals).[28]

The difficulties with grain deliveries had an immediate and powerful effect on the entire unhealthy mechanism that was the Soviet economy. The precise data in this regard were carefully concealed by the Soviet leadership and only fragments have been preserved.*[29]

The existing information on the Soviet economy in 1927–1928, fragmentary as it is, presents a rather impressive picture. Grain exports fell off dramatically, and at the same time the Soviet balance of trade became increasingly unfavorable. In November 1927, the trade deficit increased by 8 percent over October and kept climbing steadily after that. The Soviet Union's modest reserves of foreign currency were endangered. To extricate itself from this situation, the government hastily reduced imports. The supply of many goods urgently needed in production was thus cut off, greatly aggravating the shortage of raw materials, especially in light industry. In February 1928, a number of factories were threatened with closure. The metallurgical and metalworking industries experienced serious difficulties. Everywhere the exhaustion of industrial machinery and equipment began to have its effect. In November 1927, industrial production was 18 percent lower than had been projected; in December, 21.4 percent lower. Finances, too, were thrown into disorder. Industry's indebtedness to the state grew, while tax revenues declined. As a result of the greatly expanded issuing of paper money, the value and buying power of the ruble deteriorated. The Soviet Union's internal national debt was growing rapidly.

---

*The figures published monthly on the state of the economy showed a partial decline in industrial production in October 1927 and a major drop in November. In December 1927 and January 1928 they indicated an upturn, followed by a new drop in February. These figures are sharply at odds with the information contained in internal correspondence and in unpublished speeches by leading figures in Soviet economic work.

The supply of goods to the market was in a disastrous state. In the course of a month—from December 1927 to January 1928—it decreased by 15.5 percent. Severe shortages arose, involving an entire range of basic necessities. In a number of provincial cities, supplies fell so low that the needs of the population could be met for only a few days. By the end of January 1928 it was evident that rationing would have to be introduced.[30]

The deep economic crisis, which broke out with unusual speed, caught the party leadership completely off guard. Extraordinary measures were needed to save the day, but the leadership was not prepared to enact them. It was also evident that such measures might lead to momentous consequences—the destruction of the existing economic and social mechanism. The nervousness felt by the leaders increased and with it the potential for sharp disagreement.

Seeking to escape from imminent disaster, the leadership concentrated its attention on grain procurements. Since they were the key point in the economic situation, improved grain deliveries could reduce the tension in the rest of the economy and allow time for the discovery of a more fundamental solution.

The situation was very threatening, however, and time was running short. Spring would turn rural roads to mud, making the shipment of grain from the villages more difficult. In addition, the sluggishness and muddleheadedness of the Soviet apparatus had to be taken into account. The leadership again and again discussed new proposals: to raise procurement prices; to buy grain abroad and use it to intervene on the market, thus forcing the peasants to sell their grain; or to use funds allocated for new construction for measures that would ease the crisis.[31] One after the other these suggestions were rejected. None of them guaranteed quick success and all threatened to undermine the general economic policies then in effect.

Events did not wait. In the period from December 21, 1927 (two days after the end of the party congress) to January 6, 1928, Stalin sent out three directives in the name of the Central Committee to the lower party organizations, demanding that they make a quick breakthrough (perelom) in the grain collection campaign. The third directive was "altogether exceptional both in its tone and in its demands," directly threatening reprisals against local officials if they failed to bring in the necessary amounts of grain.[32] Nevertheless, the situation improved only slowly, if at all.

High-level party officials, including members of the top leadership, were sent out to the provinces, armed with special powers. They were to oversee the "breakthrough" in person. Stalin himself went to Siberia. Exactly how the decisions leading to these events were made within the top leadership is not known. One thing is beyond dispute, however. When Stalin arrived on the scene in Siberia, he immediately bore down on the local party officialdom for slipshod work, for underestimating the danger from kulaks, and for having connections with "kulak and capitalist elements." He recommended the use of Article 107 (of the criminal code of the RSFSR), which permitted the confiscation of grain surpluses from wealthy peasants, and urged the local authorities to purge the party and government apparatuses of "corrupt elements."[33]

Extraordinary measures were applied intensively throughout the country: party bodies and the GPU were given special powers in regard to grain collection, special "troikas" were formed, and thousands of activists were sent into the countryside. An obligatory "agricultural loan" began to be imposed, villages were forced to increase self-taxation for social and cultural needs, the collection of arrears on unpaid taxes and of payments on loans and credits was intensified, and so on. All this was aimed at sharply reducing the amount of spendable money available to the peasants, thus inducing them to sell more grain. However, it also laid the basis for a rapid increase in acts of violence and arbitrariness.

Although the moderate politicians did not like the use of extraordinary measures, the measures, in and of themselves, did not cause excessive disagreements in the early stages. At that time, it was fairly clear that the leadership had no alternative. But Stalin pushed beyond the extraordinary measures, and that brought the differences within the leadership to the fore again. He evidently reached the conclusion that it was impossible to solve the economic difficulties that had arisen while remaining within the framework of the existing economic conditions. Stalin therefore accompanied the extraordinary measures with his own particular interpretation of the line of the Fifteenth Party Congress. He began to describe collectivization, which in the opinion of many members of the leadership could only be the result of long years of persistent effort, as a quick way of replacing "not only the kulaks but individual peasant agriculture [in general] as the deliverer of grain to the state."[34]

Stalin's fundamental reinterpretation of the party's general line was bound to produce discord. The moderate members of the Politburo were angered, it seems, not only by Stalin's arbitrariness but also by the way he circumvented complex economic and social problems by simply shifting the responsibility for solving the difficult situation onto the backs of local officials and activists. An informed Communist contemporary recorded a characteristic detail: "After Rykov had pounded his fist on the table and uttered a truly Russian curse, he left the meeting of the Politburo."[35]

Quarreling continued, even on the commission set up by the leadership to consider the problem.[36] At that point, Stalin was apparently not yet ready to fight. Perhaps he still did not feel confident enough to abandon once and for all the familiar waters of the moderate conception of economic policy. He withdrew the disputed formulations, apologized to the local functionaries for the harsh tone of the directives, and denounced the "excesses" that had occurred during the procurement campaign.[37]

At first, the extraordinary measures occurred as an exception within the general context of Soviet policy, which was to keep searching for a way out of its economic crisis through international agreements. This situation could not last, however. The crisis was affecting the entire economy, and a number of party leaders seriously questioned the idea of making concessions on the foreign trade monopoly. Menzhinsky became the mouthpiece for these skeptics.[38] The main battle was not fought over the concessions, however; it unfolded in an area which, to all appearances, was far removed from economics—the fate of the opposition.

After the expulsion of the oppositionists from the party and after agreement had been reached in principle that the opposition was to be repressed by the GPU, a new divergence of opinion occurred within the party leadership. Some of the leaders—Stalin, Rykov, Kalinin, Chicherin, and possibly a few others—were satisfied with the results achieved. The opposition no longer seemed a serious danger to them. Of course, they did not intend to abandon repressive measures, but they were held in check by possible foreign reaction, as after the shootings in the spring and summer of 1927. They were afraid that if brutality was too open, it could endanger the possibility of international agreements. They were also not quite sure how the foreign Communist parties would react. Although the Soviet leaders had handled the situation in the Executive Committee of the Comintern successfully, they had not forgotten the significant vacillations in the Comintern in the spring of 1927, nor that some important foreign Communists had later broken with the majority, such as Albert Treint in France and Andres Nin in Spain. Stalin, Rykov, and Chicherin therefore preached moderation. Repressive measures should be kept quiet and the possibility of allowing some opposition leaders to return to the party held out—on the condition that they fully capitulate, of course. It is also possible that Stalin was already considering the oppositionists as potential allies against the moderates.[39]

The idea of "restraint" in relation to the opposition encountered both hidden and open resistance. Among its opponents were said to be Bukharin, Ordzhonikidze, and Voroshilov.[40] They were apparently apprehensive over the still powerful influence of the opposition, fearing that the opposition might be able to make a comeback because of the economic difficulties and take revenge for the harsh treatment it had been given. The most adamant opponent of any "softness" was, of course, Menzhinsky. The fight against the opposition had broadened the powers of the GPU. The moment the party leadership gave its consent to GPU intervention in internal party affairs, GPU influence was strengthened. From then on, it was able to maintain surveillance over the activities of state and party bodies from the lowest to the highest level, unmasking "politically unreliable" individuals and proposing measures for purging them. Contemporaries joked ruefully: "Menzhinsky knows the situation in the party better than Stalin does."[41]

In the GPU, it was well understood that if the fight against the opposition were ended, the GPU's enhanced position might be jeopardized. This understanding was reflected in the general approach and particular content of GPU information provided to higher party bodies. The expulsion of the opposition leaders, Menzhinsky reported, did not mean the complete defeat of the opposition. The "Zinovievists" could perhaps be expected to surrender, but the "Trotskyists" would remain irreconcilable enemies. Opposition influence was extraordinarily strong in numerous industrial centers, especially in the Ukraine, as well as in the army and navy. The oppositionists, he said, were receiving support from the German "left." Informational material and leaflets, printed in millions of copies in Germany, were penetrating Soviet borders; the German Social Democracy was apparently supporting the opposition financially. Further measures were necessary: intensification of the purge in the party and state apparatus, an increased number of GPU personnel, expansion of the network of agents in the army down to the regimental level, and confinement of middle-level opposition cadres in concentration camps.[42]

The question of the opposition was gradually transformed into a question of the character of Soviet foreign policy. Everybody knew that one of the main reasons for restraint toward the opposition was the fear that foreign reaction to repressive measures in the Soviet Union might interfere with urgently needed economic agreements.

Bukharin took a not very far-sighted position. He was extremely apprehensive about the situation in the Comintern. Elections were about to take place in Germany and France. Bukharin gave serious weight to the possibility—and the Commissariat of Foreign Affairs was inclined for a while to share the same view—that the Communist opposition groups in those countries might draw enough votes away from the official Communist parties to register some impressive successes. That could greatly strengthen the vacillating elements within the Comintern and weaken the position of the Soviet Communist Party leadership.[43] A major role may have been played by an opposite kind of fear: such a development could serve as an argument in favor of a left course in the Comintern. The foreign Communist parties were flooded with warnings about the opposition—except for the German party, which was energetically doing its part to exaggerate the extent of opposition influence. The official parties were offered large sums of money for the fight against the opposition.[44] These and other considerations decisively influenced Bukharin's position on many questions, particularly the monopoly of foreign trade and Soviet foreign policy.

The denouement was drawing near. At the end of January, the economic crisis plumbed new depths. Kuibyshev, chairman of the Supreme

Economic Council, reported to the Politburo, with some exaggeration, that the economic situation was disastrous and that it was impossible to find a way out with the resources of the USSR alone. Kuibyshev's point of view was shared to one degree or another by all the main economic agencies.[45] On February 8, 1928, the Council of People's Commissars passed a resolution stating that the country was going through extraordinary difficulties in the provision of food for the population and of raw materials for industry. Industrial production was falling. Not only the budget, but foreign currency reserves were in danger. The Council of People's Commissars did not have any means of solving the problem independently.[46] Soviet diplomats were ordered to gather, within the shortest possible time, all pertinent information on the international standing of the USSR and the real possibilities of obtaining foreign aid, even at the cost of further concessions. The odds were highly unfavorable.[47] Foreign governments were very well informed about the nature and extent of Soviet economic difficulties. They were more and more reserved about signing trade or credit agreements. The possibility of a Soviet economic collapse and the consequences of such a thing were being discussed seriously in leading Western circles.[48]

In an atmosphere of imminent disaster, fear of opposition activity increased rapidly. The entire leadership was afraid of the political consequences of an economic collapse. At the same time, it began to consider ways of compensating by administrative measures for the lack of effective economic options, especially by the fullest possible mobilization of the machinery of power and violence. This approach was bound to have major political consequences.

By the end of January 1928, according to documents in the German Foreign Ministry archives, Menzhinsky and Bukharin formed a bloc, whose aim was to change fundamental aspects of Soviet policy.[49] This significantly speeded up the realignment of forces within the leadership. The bloc's main argument was the allegedly dangerous situation in the Comintern and the foreign Communist parties. By the middle of February, Stalin was also leaning in this direction. Apparently he had come to the conclusion that caution toward the opinions of foreign governments and their populations no longer made sense. Concessions on the foreign trade monopoly had not been offered soon enough and could no longer produce significant results. Some stormy leadership meetings took place. Rykov was finally obliged to yield.

Parallel to this conflict of opinion was a dispute over whether the grain crisis could be alleviated by using funds originally earmarked for the development of heavy industry. These disagreements found partial expression in speeches by members of the leadership at the eighth congress of metalworkers in the second half of February 1928. Kuibyshev spoke vigorously for the continuation of industrialization. Rykov, who spoke a few days later and whose speech was viewed by some contemporaries as directed against Stalin, did not oppose Kuibyshev on this point. Mikoyan, the last of the leading political figures to speak at the congress, defended the foreign trade monopoly as a necessary condition for industrialization.*

On February 26, 1928, a decisive meeting of the Politburo was held, with the Council of People's Commissars and the Presidium of the Central Executive Committee reportedly attending. Chicherin spoke against any change of policy.[50] After a long discussion, the Politburo voted for a compromise resolution, which was nevertheless highly characteristic. In accordance with the viewpoint of the moderates, the resolution stressed once again that the industrial development of the USSR was impossible without attracting foreign capital and foreign specialists. At the same time, the fight for the unity of the party and the Comintern against the destructive activity of the opposition and the ultraleft tendencies was proclaimed to be the most important task of the moment.[51] Translated into normal language, this meant that the party leadership had withdrawn the idea of concessions to the Western powers, since such concessions might result in strengthening the opposition.

Literally within a matter of days, the decisions made on February 26 were carried further. On March 2, on the basis of reports by Menzhinsky and Nikolai Kubyak, the people's commissar of agriculture, the Council of People's Commissars acknowledged the existence of a general and extraordinarily serious economic crisis; it ascribed special responsibility for the existing situation to the growing activity of the opposition, which was said to be aimed at disrupting economic development and thwarting the conclusion of agreements with foreign countries. The work of party bodies and organizations was characterized as extremely unsatisfactory. The Council of People's Commissars declared that the government would not hesitate to take any and all measures to "preserve the dictatorship of the proletariat." It would mercilessly punish any form of economic sabotage, not only active, intentional sabotage, but also the "passive," unintentional kind. Special powers were given to the GPU to maintain surveillance over economic life and the activity of party organizations. Any unfriendliness toward the GPU—for example, failure to cooperate with it—would be punished by the immediate removal of the offenders from their posts and the submission of their cases to the Central Control Commission for investigation.[52]

With this, the USSR took a big step toward fundamental change in its internal living conditions and power structure. The entire atmosphere in which economic, governmental, and party work went on was abruptly altered. The GPU had not only succeeded in securing the positions it had won but enlarged them, extending its tentacles ever deeper into the

*Compare *Izvestia*, February 16–25, 1928.

economic and social sphere. The extraordinary measures enacted in response to the economic crisis began to change the pattern of economic and social relations and brought heavy pressure to bear on the very foundations of the accepted economic strategy. The potential differentiation within the Soviet leadership, which had been discernible at the Fifteenth Party Congress, received new impetus. At the same time, a situation arose that allowed Stalin to free himself from dependence on the economic and social conceptions of the moderates.

FIVE

Social Crisis and Social Repression

The extraordinary measures, as the series of leadership decisions at the end of February and beginning of March 1928 are called, were not only instruments for the regulation of a threatening economic situation but also expressions of and products of a deep social crisis, which developed out of the economic crisis. The concept behind the party leadership's method for overcoming the economic difficulties was to keep any reduction in the volume of new construction or the rate of industrialization as small as possible. This probably explains a statistical paradox: that it was almost entirely possible to hide the economic crisis of 1928 behind the long-term trends of economic growth. This also meant that the economic difficulties had to be overcome mainly by administrative measures, that is, by a brutal infringement on the living and working conditions of broad sections of the population. Thus, it is legitimate to say that the economic crisis was increasingly transferred to the social sphere, with the result that all social relations were aggravated in the extreme and severe social tensions created.

The rural population suffered most heavily from the consequences of this policy. Orgies of violent excess occurred in the countryside, bringing a partial return to the conditions of war communism. Incited from above, the power apparatus—a major role being played by the GPU— went after not only the well-to-do peasants but also the middle peasants and often the rural poor as well. The amount of grain to be delivered was set for every household. The agents of the central government went from farm to farm, searching silos and confiscating "surpluses." Often they took anything they came across and left the peasants without enough to meet their own basic needs.[1] They used threats, arrests, and prison sentences to reach their goals. In some villages which had already fulfilled their quotas, requisitioning was carried out a second time.[2] In many parts of the USSR, local markets were closed. On country roads, checkpoints and roadblocks reappeared, as during the civil war, to prevent peasants from taking grain away from the villages. The emergency delivery of industrial goods to the rural market frequently proved a cruel farce, because these deliveries generally consisted of products that were not needed in the rural areas at all. The practice of forced exchange spread: peasants had to pay with grain for industrial goods or, conversely, were paid with manufactured goods for their grain, without regard to the real value of the goods.[3] The agricultural tax was increased by approximately 20 percent for the tax-eligible part of the rural population, with no regard for existing local practices. Added to this was the aforementioned self-taxation of the village for social and cultural purposes. According to a law that had been prepared well ahead of time, in 1927, such self-taxation could be imposed to a level as high as 35 percent of the agricultural tax.[4] Such taxation exceeded the capacities of many peasant households.

The Ukraine, the south of Russia, the Northern Caucasus, and Siberia suffered the most from these arbitrary measures. The regions that mainly produced industrial crops and lacked sufficient food production for their own needs were less affected by these measures. On the other hand, they were soon excluded from the government food-supply system and had to cope with the food shortage on their own.

The government agencies, first of all Rykov's and Kalinin's secretariats, received a flood of complaints about violence and coercive measures. Investigations were ordered, and members of the Central Executive Committee went to the local areas. But this was only a drop in the ocean; it could not alter the policy that led to these incidents. In April, Bukharin involuntarily revealed the true character of the procurement campaign. He explained to a meeting of party activists that a few overly zealous "grain procurers" simply had had to be shot.[5]

The extraordinary measures were certainly effective in their way. In January and February, grain procurements took an upward turn. On the market, a slight improvement began to show. Yet the expected and necessary results had not been achieved. According to official statistics, by the end of 1927 the deficit in grain deliveries from the countryside stood at 130 million poods, which was about 17.5 percent of the target for the second half of that year. In January and February 1928, about 250 million poods were collected, which made up for the previous year's deficit, but was insufficient to meet the new year's targets. Internal correspondence indicates that the real state of affairs was much worse and therefore kept secret.

On the basis of Politburo decisions made in February 1928, the groundwork was laid for new, massive pressure on the peasants. The GPU's intervention in the grain procurement campaign intensified, and preparations were made for the deployment of military units in the villages.[6] On Stalin's initiative—against the resistance of the moderate politicians—an insistent propaganda campaign, which reached substantial proportions as early as May, began urging the peasants to join collective farms (kolkhozy). This campaign, combined with growing administrative pressure, only made the situation worse and aroused fears of total dispossession among the peasants.[7]

It soon became clear that the extraordinary measures could not achieve their purpose. As early as March, the rate of procurements slowed, and in April, it began to fall. No fundamental solution to the food supply problems had occurred and there had certainly been no build-up of food reserves.* Reality had to be faced: the amount of grain the leadership expected simply did not exist in the villages. To provide for its population until the new harvest, the Soviet Union was forced to buy grain abroad.[8]

During March–April 1928, however, another side of the forcible procurement campaign began to show. The grain trade in the villages and the free sale of surpluses decreased considerably. According to Rykov, 800 to 900 million poods of grain were usually traded in the villages and at the bazaars, of which about 100 million poods reached the urban market. The situation worsened in regard to the availability of food for the population. Things were especially hard for the rural poor, who had to buy grain in the spring. Peasant women standing in line in front of city stores became a common sight at the time.[9] Significant numbers of peasants, sometimes entire rural districts, were essentially placed on starvation rations.

A wave of unrest swept through the villages. The GPU noted a rapid increase in "anti-Soviet kulak agitation." In several regions, the peasants sharply reduced the amount of land under cultivation, thereby endangering the year's harvest.** Massive slaughtering of cattle began.[10] Peasant disturbances broke out and were suppressed in some places by force of arms. By the summer of 1928, almost 150 peasant revolts had occurred.[11] Cases in which officials were murdered or beaten increased in frequency.[12] Moreover, the mood in the army became a cause for concern: soldiers were, for the most part, of rural origin and received plenty of mail from their relatives informing them about events in the countryside. Stabilization of the rural situation, which had been achieved with much effort during the years of the NEP, vanished.

The situation in the countryside was only one aspect of the social crisis. Serious difficulties also made themselves felt in the cities, which were traditionally the government's base of support. The urban masses suffered as a result of the severe breakdown in food supply. As early as the end of 1927, major shortages of flour, groats, milk, eggs, butter, and oil occurred in the state and cooperative trade network; soon afterwards bread, meat, tea, coffee, textiles, and a number of other goods also

*In April 1928, under pressure from the moderates, the extraordinary measures were lifted, but after a short time Stalin reintroduced them. The pretext for doing so was that late frosts in the Ukraine and Northern Caucasus made a second sowing necessary, which meant a further loss of quantities of grain.
**The group around Stalin was anxious to suppress any information about the reduced area under cultivation. They engaged in a polemic with the moderates on this issue. According to some sources, the area sown to crops had been reduced by 8 percent or more.

became scarce. Contemporaries tell of long lines of hundreds of people that would start to form in the early hours of the morning and became breeding grounds for open discontent.

The appearance of people from rural and provincial areas on the urban market and the rerouting of industrial goods made previous interruptions in the supply of goods even worse. Limits were placed on the amount one person could buy, and later, rationing was introduced, either openly or in a disguised way. The urban population increasingly found itself forced to turn to the private market, where prices were much higher. In an effort to stop the flow of goods and capital to the private sector, authorities increased pressure on private merchants. Private trading rapidly dwindled. As the situation steadily deteriorated, voices could be heard, "It's like 1919 all over again."[13]

The difficulties with the supply of goods were a highly visible aspect of the broad spectrum of problems causing a sharp deterioration in the urban standard of living. The living and working conditions of industrial workers were under strong attack. Official statistics, of course, showed a rise in nominal and real wages. These statistics are very much open to question, however, because they were based only on prices in the state and cooperative trade systems, ignoring private market prices, which rose to astronomical heights. Nor did they take into account an increase in the intensity of labor, although authorities claimed as one of their major accomplishments the fact that in 1928 productivity increased faster than wages for the first time.[14]

During the signing of collective contracts at the turn of the year 1927–1928, the management bodies and the unions were guided by a directive from the Supreme Economic Council and the Central Council of Trade Unions dated October 29, 1927, and entitled "On Overcoming Low Production Quotas."[15] This directive was applied not only in the form of upwardly revised production quotas, which were introduced everywhere, but also in the transfer of workers to lower qualification categories and cuts in rates paid for particular jobs, resulting in lower pay. This caused great discontent. As early as the end of 1927, orders were sent out that industrial conflicts were to be avoided.[16] The inevitability of such conflicts was rooted in the very policy being implemented. Strikes broke out at Mytishchi and Liubertsy near Moscow, the Putilov works, the Yenakievo metallurgical plant in the Donetsk Basin, Moscow's "Hammer and Sickle" metalworking plant, and other factories in various parts of the country.[17]

The seven-hour day, decreed in the Central Executive Committee's manifesto on the tenth anniversary of the October revolution, resulted in the introduction of a three-shift workday at many textile mills. In addition, one worker had to operate several machines without a corresponding wage increase. Because most machinery was old and worn out, the increased intensity of labor led to a very large number of accidents.

As if to mock the seven-hour day decree, a number of factories continued to require overtime, resulting in a workday of up to twelve
hours.[18] Most work places were in unsatisfactory condition—an old
evil—making the observance of elementary safety and hygiene rules
impossible. The rate of tuberculosis and other diseases associated with
poverty was quite high.[19]

The situation of the unemployed was especially desperate. Restrictions
were placed on the payment of unemployment benefits in 1927, so that
many people who had fled to cities from the poverty and extraordinary
measures in the countryside found themselves practically without any
means of subsistence. There was a further problem: by 1928 many
workers had already been unemployed for more than two years and
were therefore in danger of losing their unemployment benefits. As a
result of the crisis and the precarious situation in the countryside, the
rate of unemployment took a sharp upward turn, then continued to rise
more slowly. In big cities, the unemployed came to form a mighty
army.[20] Here was an enormous reservoir of social ferment.

On top of all this, people had to put up with living conditions that
were extremely difficult and constantly deteriorating. The housing situation grew worse every year. It was one of the main reasons for an
extremely high labor turnover. No funds remained for housing development, so that construction projects were delayed from one year to the
next. Workers were crammed into squalid, barrackslike quarters that
were often located far from the factories, which made the workday
incredibly long. In the winter months, this led to high rates of illness and
absenteeism. Alcoholism, prostitution, "hooliganism," and crime assumed frightening dimensions, amounting to a veritable social disaster.

The social crisis produced its own kind of political reaction. Some
contemporaries claimed that anti-Soviet sentiment was not significant, at
least not among the Russian part of the population. Although such
statements should not be taken literally—there was no alternative political force able to voice the sentiments of the masses—they certainly
mirror the psychology and habits of thought that had developed during
the years of revolution and civil war and been strengthened thereafter
by education and propaganda. Capitalism as a social system had been
discredited, and few wished to return to it. Because of this, discontent
assumed more complicated and contradictory forms. In the period immediately after the Fifteenth Party Congress, sympathy for the opposition persisted among a section of the working population. Certainly the
influence of the opposition was gradually waning; it was fragmented by
repression (arrests, exile, and imprisonment), which denied oppositionists the chance to carry on large-scale agitation and propaganda.
Nevertheless, the influence of the opposition was a noticeable factor in
political life and remained fairly strong until fall 1928 or spring 1929.

The majority of workers reacted in other ways. Deprived of any opportunity to organize themselves independently and voice their opinions, they expressed their discontent in the form of sharp condemnation of the economic situation, lack of interest in the political and social measures proposed by the authorities, and reduced productive effort.

The political mood in society showed a growing antagonism among the various social groups and nationalities. The most characteristic expression of this was the growing alienation and even mutual hostility between city and countryside. This tension was nourished by official propaganda, which blamed the economic difficulties on "sabotage by the peasantry." The workers had a certain interest in the official operations to extract food from the countryside: not everybody understood the real reasons for this policy, nor its harmful consequences. On the other hand, the peasants could not help but blame the city in general—and the workers in whose name the authorities acted—for the misfortunes that had befallen them. Each form of discontent, rural and urban, remained isolated from the other, but the existence of both intensified the general atmosphere of conflict.[21]

In the cities, antagonism between workers and the narrow well-to-do strata intensified. The declining social position of the workers and urban poor made them extremely sensitive to any differences in wealth and general cultural level, as well as to personal enrichment, speculation, and corruption, all of which were quite common among officials and merchants. Distrust also spread to the factories. It resulted in an increase in concealed animosity, and sometimes open hostility, between workers on the one hand and, on the other, engineers, technicians, administrators, and managers—those who carried out the government policy of increased pressure to raise labor productivity.

Anti-Semitism, which is typical in such social situations, also spread quickly. Several times in 1928, the Ukraine was on the verge of openly anti-Semitic street disorders.[22] The situation was also quite serious in Byelorussia, as well as in Russian cities, including Moscow and Leningrad. A contemporary has passed on a form of "greeting" common at the time: "Bud' zdorov, bei zhidov" (Keep healthy and beat the Jews).

Anti-Semitism also spread to the party organization; it penetrated the GPU and other parts of the power structure and threatened to turn into an official policy of persecution against the Jews. Contemporaries suspected that the party leadership supported anti-Semitism in order to use it as a safety valve for discontent and as a tool in the fight against the opposition, which had many Jews among its leaders. The anti-Semitism of some representatives of the regime cannot be doubted. Evidence of it is given by contemporaries.* But it is difficult to argue that this was

*The suspicion that the leadership, especially Stalin, was using anti-Semitism in the fight against the opposition was aroused at a rather early date. Trotsky first spoke of it in the first half of 1926.

official policy. Bolshevik party tradition was an obstacle to that, as was the national composition of a fairly substantial section of leading party cadres. The party leadership surely realized that a growth of anti-Semitism would, in the long run, turn against the government itself, which was called "Jew Bolshevik" in Russian and Ukrainian nationalist circles. Therefore the leadership sounded the alarm. Anti-Semitism was made a special point on the agendas of Politburo meetings. Attempting to halt anti-Semitic activity, Stalin blasted the base-level party organizations in extraordinarily harsh letters, threatening them with the severest punishment, up to and including executions.[23] But this was not effective. Anti-Semitism was too deeply rooted in Russian and Ukrainian society, and it continued to grow.

The situation in the national republics also degenerated. In Transcaucasia, especially Georgia, and in the Ukraine, a new upsurge of nationalist sentiment became evident; the impetus for it came from the troubled stirrings in the vast sea of the peasantry as well as the discontent in the cities. Both inside and outside the Soviet Union, various nationalist political groups became active, a development encouraged by the spread of the notion in Western Europe that an economic collapse of the USSR, and consequently its political collapse as well, was possible in the short run. Again rumors circulated—about increased activity by the British secret service, an increased French interest in Transcaucasia, and Polish plans for annexation of the Ukraine and establishment of a Polish-Ukrainian federation.[24] The GPU reported the existence of a widely ramified anti-Soviet underground, as well as strong nationalist tendencies in the Ukrainian Communist Party.[25] The situation in the Ukraine was actually extremely complicated. The growth of nationalist sentiment there clashed with leftist moods among the substantial number of Russian-speaking workers, who had nothing in common with the Ukrainian nationalist movement and sympathized with the demands of the opposition. This introduced curious and contradictory twists into the situation, which could not be calculated exactly by the authorities.

The spreading social crisis did not yet represent a direct threat to the government, but it greatly complicated the situation, causing the leadership to fear for the future and hindering the implementation of the policy course that had been chosen. Voices were heard within the leadership to the effect that the Soviet Union had not experienced such difficulties since the civil war.[26] A search began for possible ways to relieve social tension. These conditions lent additional force to certain events that were to play an exceptionally important role in giving the Soviet system a new shape. I am referring to one of the most disgraceful and scandalous judicial cases in the Soviet Union in the 1920s—the trial against a group of engineers and technicians in the coal industry, which became notorious as the Shakhty case.

The early stages of the Shakhty affair remain obscure. Like many other occurrences in this period, the Shakhty trial was not the result of a carefully thought out plan. No outward appearances indicated that such a trial could occur. Specialists, especially prerevolutionary specialists, enjoyed the support of Rykov, Kuibyshev, Jan Rudzutak, and all people's commissars responsible for economic matters, without exception. Other members of the Politburo, Stalin and Menzhinsky among them, also shared the opinion that in the face of the extreme lack of qualified forces, it would be impossible to cope with the tasks of economic development without the "specialists from the old days."

Some contemporaries believed that the initial stages of the Shakhty case were mainly the work of the local GPU agencies; apparently they were correct.[27] It is appropriate to look for the causes of the Shakhty case in the specific conditions of the coal industry in the Donetsk Basin (the Donbass).

At the beginning of 1928, coal production in the Donbass was 30 percent higher than before the war, according to official statistics. The coal industry was one of the sectors of industry that managed to cope fairly well with the economic crisis.[28] The growth of production in the Donbass was accompanied by a series of extremely complicated problems. Because of the shortage of capital and equipment, production efforts were concentrated in those mines where high output could be expected. A number of mines were closed, with the expectation that they would be reopened at a later time.

The equipment in the working mines was very old and worn out, the influx of new equipment totally inadequate. The Donbass had one of the highest accident rates in the USSR, including fatalities.[29] The organization of production was grossly inadequate. Labor turnover was extremely high in the Donbass, and the skills of those working in the mines was correspondingly low. Alcoholism, fights, and knifings were very common. Because of the shortage of trained personnel, engineers and technicians were overburdened.

At the end of 1927, the Donbass was in a state of severe and nearly constant unrest. Labor disputes and wildcat strikes broke out again and again.[30] Great bitterness was expressed against the administration of the mines, the engineers, and the technicians. The unions, instead of performing the functions for which they were intended, collaborated with management. Within the party, the leadership's policy during the fight against the opposition had resulted in a total stifling of party life and the frequent promotion of unscrupulous individuals to leading posts.[31] Some workers, losing hope that the outrageous and disorganized state of affairs, especially the accidents, could be corrected in any other way, turned to the local agencies of the GPU.[32] For its part, the GPU found itself unable to handle the wave of disturbances and was apparently ready to seize any opportunity to offer the workers a scapegoat, some particular target that could be blamed for all their grievances.

The first known reports of an investigation into a counterrevolution-ary organization "engaged in wrecking activity" date from the fall of 1927.[33] Apparently, by the spring of 1928 a certain number of cases had accumulated in which engineers or technicians were being investigated by the GPU because of instances of neglect of duty or disorganization in the mines. Nothing is known about the results of these investigations, but it can be assumed that the investigators were not satisfied with banal explanations. After all, they were dealing with "alien class elements" and assumed from the start that counterrevolutionary intentions were in-volved.

Yet the GPU was not given the "go-ahead" immediately: the direction of the investigations was at variance with the policy of the party lead-ership. Furthermore, the investigating bodies were trying to implicate some German engineers and technicians who were working on the installation of imported equipment in the Donbass. This threatened to draw a great deal of public attention to the matter and cause serious international complications.

The subsequent course of events is known only in part. According to the best known version, Yefim Yevdokimov, the man in charge of the GPU in the Northern Caucasus and in whose administrative district the town of Shakhty was located, is said to have appealed directly to Stalin after failing to obtain approval from Menzhinsky. At least part of the available information raises questions about this version; it ascribes the chief role in the events, not to the GPU of the Northern Caucasus, but to the Ukrainian GPU and its leader, Balitsky. At any rate, there is no question that it was Stalin who authorized the arrests.[34] He was appar-ently tempted by the chance to provide some release for social tensions in the Donbass. He undoubtedly understood that a major case involving "wrecking activity" would reinforce an atmosphere supportive of the extraordinary measures and the use of force to overcome the economic crisis. In any case, at the beginning of March, when reports about arrests in the Donbass reached Moscow, only part of the leadership was in-formed about the affair, and not even the GPU Collegium had sufficient information at its disposal.[35]

Stalin's high-handedness and the events in the Donbass greatly irri-tated the moderate politicians. They insisted that the Donbass matter be taken up in the Politburo.[36] The session took place, by all indications, on March 5. We can deduce from some of the available information that the confessions of the twelve arrested men were presented to the Politburo. There was talk of German engineers and technicians' involvement in the affair, of other foreign involvement (by former mine owners and "coun-terintelligence"), of "wrecking activity" to prepare the way for the defeat of the USSR in a future war, and of shocking treatment of the workers. Rykov expressed doubts about all this; he was supported by Kalinin, Chicherin, and, apparently, Kuibyshev.[37] Menzhinsky is said to have guaranteed the accuracy of the GPU's information. Unexplained acci-

dents and fires at other large industrial installations were also mentioned. The Politburo decided to hold a major trial, one that would
justify the arrests and investigations to foreign public opinion. Stalin (or
one of his allies) made a clever move, suggesting that the chairman of the
Council of People's Commissars, Rykov, be the one to inform the public.
Rykov agreed reluctantly.[38] Thus implicated, the moderates' line of
retreat was cut off.

In his speech at a meeting of the Moscow Soviet on March 9, 1928,
which was later published in the press, Rykov reported the "uncovering
of a conspiracy." On March 10, *Pravda* joined the campaign of denuncia-
tion over the Shakhty "conspiracy"; the rest of the press followed suit.
Mass meetings to express public indignation occurred at virtually every
factory, office, or other workplace. Much of this anger was genuine,
reflecting the strained relations between workers and specialists.

As early as March 12, a major dispute over the Shakhty affair erupted
within the party leadership. Rykov was informed that in the opinion of
the Procuracy (Public Prosecutor's Office) the material of the Ukrainian
GPU could not stand up under criticism. He wrote Menzhinsky a very
sharply worded letter, speaking of arbitrariness on the part of local GPU
agencies and impermissible sabotage of government policy—in effect
laying responsibility on the GPU Collegium for an incorrect understanding of the party line.[39] On March 13, Chicherin also sent a letter to
Menzhinsky. He pointed to the serious effects the Shakhty affair could
have on the Soviet Union's international position, especially its relations
with Germany, and suggested that the charges be considered very carefully before they were made the subject of a trial.[40]

The case was reconsidered by the party leadership. In top party circles
the rumor circulated that the GPU had been the victim of "provocation
by the opposition."[41] Andrei Bubnov, head of the Political Directorate of
the Red Army, was sent to the Donbass as an official emissary of the
Central Committee.[42] At about the same time, the leadership released
two of the five German engineers and four Soviet specialists.

The Shakhty case had already become an extremely serious international political issue. The German government, under heavy pressure
from public opinion and business circles infuriated by the arbitrary
actions of Soviet authorities, decided on March 15 to discontinue Soviet-
German economic talks.[43] This step was applauded in other Western
countries, where the wave of arrests in the Donbass was seen as further
proof that it was impossible to collaborate fruitfully with the USSR.[44]
The international atmosphere was increasingly reminiscent of the situation after the executions of summer 1927. Relations with France again
deteriorated abruptly, following the trend set by Germany. France revived its demand for the return of French gold that had been held by the
Soviet state bank since the revolution, demonstrating its lack of interest
in improving Franco-Soviet relations.[45] The isolation of the USSR deep-

ened, and a new danger arose—destabilization on the Soviet western border. Poland, aware of relaxed Soviet and German pressure to its east and west, sought to take advantage of the situation to further its own political aims. Rumors of the possibility of a new Polish-Soviet war circulated again in Western Europe.[46]

The international repercussions of the Donbass events greatly troubled the moderate politicians. They exerted more and more effort to prevent international complications. Primarily, this meant limiting the scope of the Shakhty affair. But attempts in that direction met with resistance from Stalin: scaling down the affair was tantamount to admitting that its pursuit was a political mistake. While willing to make concessions on matters of detail, Stalin countered the moderates by arguing that the prestige of the USSR was at stake. He pointed to the economic quarantine of the USSR by the Western powers, contending that it doomed the policy of international cooperation to failure. With this argument, he played upon the disappointment in Soviet political circles over the insignificant results of the Soviet-German economic talks.[47]

After two weeks of the propaganda campaign over the Shakhty case, Stalin's intentions became more evident. The immediate internal political effect of the events was unquestionable. The attention of a significant section of the working class had been distracted from the mistakes and failures of the leadership. A lynch mob atmosphere directed against the technical intelligentsia had been created. Engineers and technicians in factories were called "Shakhtintsy" or "Donbassovtsy" (Shakhty-ites or Donbass types). Their situation became extremely difficult, if not dangerous. The technique of solving social problems by repression had won new ground. Stalin now implied that "wrecking" by old specialists was a major problem affecting the entire country; it was no longer just a regional matter. And, he argued, solving this problem was crucial to finding a fundamental solution to the economic difficulties.[48]

The conflicts within the party leadership grew sharper. Relations between Narkomindel (the Foreign Affairs Commissariat) and the GPU, and between Chicherin and Menzhinsky, became extremely tense.[49] But the moderates did not have the means to influence the course of events in any decisive way. Because they had initially agreed to make a major public issue of the case, their hands were tied. The alleged findings of the investigation also served as a major weapon against them. By a decision of the Politburo as a whole, individual members of the Politburo were forbidden to interfere in the work of the GPU. Exertion of Politburo influence on the GPU was permissible only as the result of a collective decision.

Stalin maneuvered cautiously. Understanding that a premature confrontation with the moderates was not to his advantage, he concentrated his attention on preparing a plausible version of the Donbass events—a version that could effectively influence opinion in the party as a whole—

for presentation to the Central Committee plenum that was to meet in April 1928. While the moderates—Rykov, Kalinin, Tomsky, and Kuibyshev—made soothing statements, Stalin engaged in feverish activity behind the scenes. On March 23, 1928, Ordzhonikidze, people's commissar of the Workers' and Peasants' Inspection and chairman of the Central Control Commission, agreeing with the GPU, sent instructions to local authorities on the attitude to be taken toward specialists. He called them masked enemies of Soviet power who wished to restore capitalism. Local authorities were categorically ordered to establish strict surveillance over specialists, both at work and in their private lives, and to report any suspicions immediately to the GPU.[50] The Bacchanalia of arrests intensified considerably, affecting not only the coal industry but other branches of the economy as well. A commission of the Central Committee headed by Yemelyan Yaroslavsky, a supporter of Stalin and chief of the party collegium of the CCC, arrived in the Donbass.[51] The commission's task was to investigate the political work of local party bodies. Such a commission might have represented a threat to Stalin. In fact, it enabled him to claim the initiative in exposing deficiencies in party work. Not only could such deficiencies no longer be used against Stalin; they became an additional weapon in his hands.

Under these conditions, a joint plenum of the Central Committee and the Central Control Commission (CCC) met in April 1928. Two points were on the agenda: grain procurements (which implied a review of the domestic economic situation as a whole) and the Shakhty case.[52] The existing political conflicts did not come to the fore under the first point. Prior to the plenum, an agreement had been reached within the leadership that the extraordinary measures would be approved as unavoidable and that the moderates would be compensated for this approval by a strong condemnation of "excesses" and the abandonment of further compulsory measures.*

The plenum focused on Shakhty. A report was given by Rykov: he spoke mainly about the economic and organizational aspects of the affair, defending the specialists, especially the foreigners. Two information reports ran counter to his position: one by Yaroslavsky, who outlined the results of the investigation into party work in the Donbass; and one from the GPU, probably written by Menzhinsky. The GPU report was based on quotes from documents and correspondence, which had supposedly been confiscated during searches by the GPU, as well as on prisoners' confessions. A contemporary, who heard about it second-hand, states that the impact of the GPU report was staggering; listeners were stunned by it. After all, those at the session were not legal experts nor were they able to check the validity of the facts presented.

---

*At this time, the extraordinary measures were virtually ended under pressure from the moderates, as mentioned earlier.

Stalin used the situation to strengthen his position. He argued that the Shakhty case was proof of economic intervention by the Western powers against the USSR and attacked his opponents for "thinking that we can pursue a liberating foreign policy and at the same time succeed in winning the praise of . . . the capitalists of Europe and America."[53] Stalin then not only proposed that "the old specialists" be closely monitored and quickly replaced by "red specialists" and that a purge of "hostile elements" be carried out; he also called for a general campaign of "self-criticism." At first sight, his proposals appeared democratic. The slogan of criticism "without regard to the standing of the person crit- icized" (ne vziraya na litsa) was put forward, along with the demand that the masses be involved in party, trade union, and governmental work on a broad basis. The hidden motif of these demands, however, was "in- creased vigilance" based on "the lessons of Shakhty." Stalin sought to make his social maneuver more effective by allowing certain lower levels of the apparatus to come under fire. The outcome of the Shakhty case had essentially been predetermined.

The trial opened on May 18 in the Hall of Columns of Moscow's House of Trade Unions. It lasted about six weeks, until the beginning of July 1928. The special session of the Supreme Court of the RSFSR was chaired by Andrei Vyshinsky, rector of the First Moscow State Univer- sity, a former Menshevik. Two Old Bolsheviks, M. I. Vasilyev-Yuzhin and V. P. Antonov-Saratovsky, served as judges in the case. The prosecution was represented by Nikolai Krylenko, deputy prosecutor of the republic. The charges read were "economic counterrevolution," "wrecking," ties with former mine owners and foreign intelligence organizations, and preparations for armed intervention against the USSR. Fifty-three per- sons were indicted—employees of various local Donbass mine admin- istrations, the central administration of the Donugol' coal-mining trust in Kharkov, and the central offices of the coal industry in Moscow. Three German specialists were also among the defendants.

Widespread international publicity—for months the Shakhty case was featured regularly on the front pages of the foreign press—the repeated sharp representations of the German government, and conflicts within the party leadership itself resulted in a quick completion of the investiga- tions. Of the fifty-three persons in the case, only twenty acknowledged full guilt, ten pleaded partly guilty, and twenty-three denied any guilt whatsoever.[54] During the trial, some defendants retracted their earlier confessions.

In the 1980s, nearly sixty years after the Shakhty trial, no doubt exists as to the unfounded and politically provocative character of the indict- ment's main charges. Parts of the indictment against certain individuals may have been justified: charges of corruption, disregard for safety rules, harsh treatment of workers, and similar things. Yet any objective court would have exonerated the defendants. During the investigations, illegal methods were employed: the "conveyer belt," that is uninterrupted interrogation lasting for hours while interrogators relieved one another; "vystoika," in which prisoners were kept in a standing position for hours; detention of prisoners in cells with hot or cold floors; threats of execution, and other psychological pressure tactics, including taking advantage of prisoners' illnesses.[55]

The Shakhty trial was the first of its kind, and the GPU was not yet experienced in staging public show trials. The prosecution was virtually unable to present convincing expert testimony. Things did not go well in the matter of documentary evidence either. As was to be expected, the searches and seizure of materials produced nothing substantial. Most of the documentary evidence was presented by the defendants and their lawyers, a fact that Krylenko found extremely irritating. There were not many witnesses: no one could claim to know about someone else's "wrecking activity" without risking indictment himself for "failure to report," or some greater offense (such as acting as an accomplice). The prosecution called working-class witnesses, but they were not competent in the complicated technical and economic questions raised in the indictment. Those specialists who appeared as witnesses, on the other hand, mainly gave evidence in favor of the defendants.[56]

The prosecution faced even greater difficulties regarding the charges against foreign governments, companies, and specialists. On the one hand, the prestige of the Soviet government was involved in these charges (the authorities could not admit that they had arrested foreign citizens without good reason); on the other hand, the prosecution was supposed to help prove Stalin's contention about "economic intervention" by foreign powers. In reality, the investigation had not produced any credible evidence; its only ammunition consisted of the forced confessions of the defendants. The naming of foreign companies, especially German ones, which occurred repeatedly during the trial, caused a wave of indignation abroad. In the end, the leadership felt obliged to announce publicly, through Kalinin, that the charges were not directed against foreign companies or institutions, but exclusively against individuals.[57]

The entire trial was based on the confessions of a group of defendants, mainly officials of the Donugol' administration in Kharkov and of some local Donbass mine administrations, who had been broken by the pretrial interrogation and were willing to collaborate with the prosecution. The majority of the defendants firmly rejected parts of the indictment or even the indictment as a whole. In the courtroom real verbal duels took place between defendants and the prosecutor. The defendants fought back stubbornly against the absurd, incompetent, and insulting assertions made by Krylenko, who was worsted in these exchanges more than once. In and of themselves these setbacks tended to call the indictment into question, and therefore the validity of the trial as a whole. By the end of the trial, no thinking human being could any longer doubt that its real purpose was not to establish guilt or innocence but to meet a certain social and political need.

At its end, the trial seemed to have been a big failure for those who organized it. Yet, paradoxically, this seeming failure turned out not to be decisive, because the crucial factor was its general internal political effect. For a large number of workers, who were not very familiar with the subtleties of jurisprudence, the trial was a sufficiently convincing confirmation, especially as presented and interpreted by the Soviet press, of the correctness of their own antipathy toward specialists and toward management in the factories as a whole.

The affair came slowly to an end. On June 26, Krylenko gave the final speech for the prosecution. In flagrant disregard of the actual course of the trial, he demanded the death penalty for twenty-two of the defendants.[58] The degree of punishment was apparently discussed at a Politburo meeting on June 27 or July 2. Relations between Stalin's supporters and the moderates were extremely strained at this time. Stalin himself did not speak in favor of the death penalty; he preferred to leave this unseemly task to others.[59*] Krylenko's demands were modified. The court handed down eleven death sentences; six of them were "provisional" and were later reduced by the Central Executive Committee. The German defendants were released.[60] Nevertheless, even in this form the verdict was outrageously severe.

Blood had to flow, it seemed, to bring the judicial ritual to its conclusion. In Moscow, rumors circulated—apparently they were not unfounded—that a commutation of all the death sentences was imminent. Such a step—its initiators would not have been hard to find—would have implied that the entire trial was questionable and would have been a painful blow to the prestige of the GPU.[61] In this strained atmosphere, a bombing occurred at the GPU headquarters in Moscow, the Lubyanka. Contemporaries spoke of a provocation organized by the GPU itself. There is no way of verifying this.[62] The five sentenced to death were executed immediately.[63] With this tragedy, the Shakhty trial came to an end.

The economic and social crisis in the USSR had borne its fruit. In addition to the use of force and administrative measures to solve social

*According to the text of the conversations between Bukharin, Kamenev, and Grigory Sokolnikov of July 11, 1928, a text whose meaning or accuracy is not completely clear, Stalin proposed that the death penalty not be imposed. Bukharin, Rykov, and Tomsky voted against this proposal. If this information is correct, it represents an artful new maneuver by Stalin, who forced his opponents to vote this way in order to deflect charges of being "rightists." At the same time, it is important not to lose sight of the different positions held by individual figures. There can be no doubt that Rykov was critical of the Shakhty affair as a whole, while a number of sources fail to mention Bukharin among the critics of this trial.

problems, methods that made their appearance very quickly from the beginning of 1928 on, a new element entered Soviet history: the public show trial. Certainly, the Shakhty trial had its predecessors in a series of smaller trials in preceding years.* What was new about the Shakhty trial was its dramatization, the fact that it was played up as an event of prime importance for the country as a whole. Thus, it had a major effect on aspects of the political line in general and on the entire political situation.

A characteristic feature of the Shakhty affair was not only and not primarily its intimidating effect. It served as a means—and in this it became a model for future trials—of relieving excess social and political tension while providing justification for an increased use of administrative and repressive methods by the authorities. An entire system of measures was developed resulting in a new situation in Soviet society. This could be seen in the basic restructuring of relations in industry and the penetration of the GPU very deeply into this area, and in the slogan of "self-criticism" raised by Stalin in April 1928. This slogan was made official on June 3, in an appeal from the Central Committee of the CPSU "to party members and to all workers."[64] For months thereafter it was the subject of an intensive nationwide campaign. The discontent of broad layers of the working class over the general situation in the country was now directed against the lower ranks of management. The centers of political power were raised above society and above their own apparatus, gaining greater room for maneuver and greater possibilities for arbitrary and oppressive rule. A special mechanism began to take shape that would allow a high degree of social tension to persist for a prolonged period without exposing the system as a whole to the danger of immediate collapse.

*The major trial against the Socialist revolutionaries in 1922 had already been forgotten; it belonged to a different period of Soviet history. But it was significant that Krylenko referred to it in his final speech.

SIX

Intermezzo at the Top

The Crisis Continues

Despite the importance of the Shakhty affair, and of all the changes in the structure and nature of power that derived from it, these developments did not play a decisive role in and of themselves. The overall content of party policy remained the basic problem, preventing any fundamental solution to the USSR's economic and social crisis.

The events of the first half of 1928 shook the foundations of the social and economic strategy being pursued by the Soviet leadership. It seemed that, within the framework of the system of relations established by NEP, the increased targets for economic growth could hardly be met while relying upon the resources of the USSR alone. Moreover, these targets—as the failure of the original draft of the five-year plan had already demonstrated—did not satisfy all of the Soviet Union's pressing needs. The Soviet leadership found itself at a crossroads: a need for fundamentally new solutions was emerging. The policy course pursued by Stalin in January and February 1928 entered the picture as a new factor with its own dynamic.

Bukharin once made an assertion that has gained wide currency in the historical literature; the changes in Stalin's political views were the result of his efforts to do away with the moderates and to seize total control of the power structure.[1] Bukharin's account seemed convincing: the considerations of the power struggle played no small part in Stalin's activities. Nevertheless, this factor was secondary.

The economic crisis that followed the series of setbacks in 1927 apparently had a strong impact on Stalin's political thinking, causing him to doubt seriously the value of a continued alliance with the moderates. Of course, he could not totally renounce cooperation with them at that time: the moderates possessed an important reservoir of experience and had a good grasp on practical ways of solving economic and political problems. To Stalin, however, their proposals must have seemed fraught with the danger of new economic and political setbacks. A potential basis for a split in the party leadership had arisen.

In steering toward a break with the moderates, Stalin placed himself in a difficult position. At that time, as I have said, he did not have his own independent socioeconomic plans and concepts. Within the party leadership—in contrast to previous years—there remained no significant political group with whom he could ally himself to fill this gap. His attention was inevitably drawn to the proposals made earlier by the defeated opposition. The authority of these proposals was underlined by the fact that the opposition had foreseen the economic difficulties from which the USSR was suffering.

The influence of the opposition's views on the formation of Stalin's new political line is hardly open to question. His new opinions on the decisive importance of rapid industrial growth to overcome the Soviet Union's economic crisis and his proposals that the peasants must pay "tribute" to finance industrialization were obviously inspired by the opposition's platform. Even Stalin's new vocabulary was borrowed from the opposition—such as the call for a "reinforced offensive" (*forsirovannoe nastuplenie*) against the kulaks and other capitalist elements.[2]

Stalin's inspirational sources were an open secret in the party as early as the first months of 1928: the moderates were talking almost openly about his plagiarism from the opposition's platform, and many members of the opposition felt it acceptable to state that the "party line" was now moving closer to their political conceptions.*[3]

Nevertheless, Stalin's line was not identical to the opposition's. Stalin borrowed primarily the external aspects of the opposition's ideas; he left out the core—the opposition's orientation toward improving the material conditions of the workers and poorest sections of the rural population and increasing their actual participation in public and political life. Stalin's idea was bureaucratic, based on the use of force and violence: "Even in the heat of debate, who among us would dream of canceling NEP in the countryside?" Lev Sosnovsky, one of the leaders of the opposition demanded.[4]

Stalin's political course intensified the conflicts within the leadership and quickly overshadowed disagreements on other important questions, in particular, the urgent matter of the Shakhty case. The moderates, increasingly convinced that the extraordinary measures created a threat to the fundamental orientation of the party, pressed for their cancellation and for a return to the ordinary instrumentalities of NEP. Stalin, supported by his alter ego Molotov, resisted. To acknowledge that the extraordinary measures were a mistake or had failed would have been a serious defeat. Again, as in 1927, rumors began to circulate in Moscow about strained relations between Stalin and Rykov, and Stalin's impending departure from the post of general secretary.[5]

---

*Several oppositionists, including such prominent leaders of the "Trotskyist" wing as Antonov-Ovseyenko and Pyatakov, not to mention the "Zinovievists," used Stalin's "left turn" to justify their own break with the opposition. Even Trotsky initially overestimated the "leftism" of Stalin's course.

The conflicts did not remain behind the closed doors of the Politburo. An anonymous, but nonetheless sharp, public polemic developed. The main question in dispute was not mentioned, but it was obvious enough. The moderates insisted that the need for the extraordinary measures arose as a consequence of errors in planning, prices, tax assessments, and provision of goods to the market. The use of the measures was, therefore, not "obligatory" and could not be cited as an argument against the existing economic strategy as a whole. The moderates refused to recognize the extraordinary measures as a fully valid and permissible means of solving the economic crisis. It was not the mistakes of the local organs but the very essence of the extraordinary measures, their function as extraeconomic means of constraint, that was to blame for the radical increase in "excesses."[6]

Stalin did not hesitate to respond to these attacks. He sought firmer grounds for substantiating his actions. The grain crisis, in his opinion, was caused not by one or another mistake of the leadership or the planning agencies but by the objective condition of agriculture and its severe lag behind the needs of industry. He doubted the capacity of the individual farm to achieve rapid progress: "Our agricultural system is a petty peasant economy that lends itself to improvement only with difficulty."[7] Stalin—although he did not say so openly—viewed the extraordinary measures as more than a temporary expedient; they represented a necessary feature of Soviet economic life for a relatively protracted time to come. Forced to justify the recourse to extraordinary measures, Stalin insisted that they were purely anti-kulak in nature; thus, he condemned his opponents to the role of defenders of capitalist elements. In Stalin's opinion, the conditions for a definitive restoration of the normal state of the country's economy involved not just a return to NEP but a rapid reorganization of agriculture based on collective farms and state farms. Such a reorganization, even over the course of three or four years, would necessarily result in a change in the entire structure of the economy and meet the country's need for marketable grain.[8]

There was a great lack of candor, and many verbal compromises, in the arguments made by both wings of the party leadership. The moderates, in opposing the extraordinary measures, granted that they were unavoidable in the first phase of the grain procurement campaign of 1927–1928. Stalin, in turn, dissociated himself from any plan to reintroduce war communism and stressed the importance of NEP, while interpreting this policy as an offensive against capitalism.[9] No substantive changes were made in actual practice. In this area, Stalin maintained the upper hand.

Meanwhile, the general situation in the USSR was becoming more and more difficult. Members of the leadership received an ever increasing number of letters and reports about trouble in the countryside and discontent among the peasantry. Moreover, the practical effect of the extraordinary measures, as already mentioned, had been reduced to a minimum. Supplies were in a bad state again. Waiting lines were turning into large crowds of desperate people, capable of the most unforeseen reactions. Food riots broke out in a number of towns. At the end of May, they even spread to Moscow.[10] Stalin's policy had apparently reached an impasse.

Passions became inflamed, and the tension produced a new political alignment. The moderates were supported more and more firmly by the Moscow party leadership, headed by Nikolai Uglanov.[11] Serious developments were ripening within the Politburo itself. The economic situation pushed Bukharin into the moderates' camp. As early as April 1928, he attacked those—it wasn't hard to guess whom he meant—who refused to understand the temporary nature of the extraordinary measures and who were drawing up plans for collectivization "virtually on the model of the allocation system" [*chut' ne po razverstke*—a reference to *prodrazverstka*, the "surplus grain allocation system" used under war communism for requisitioning grain from the peasants.—Trans.].[12]

Stalin responded with caustic remarks at the Komsomol congress and a new polemic against the "pleaders for the peasants' cause" (*radeteli za krest'ian*), who were trying to expand market relations and who underestimated the danger of the kulaks.[13] A split occurred: Bukharin spoke of Stalin with hatred; it must be supposed that Stalin paid him back in kind.[14]

In the Politburo, a moderate "group of five" (*pyaterka*) was formed: Rykov, Kalinin, Tomsky, and Bukharin, plus Voroshilov, who joined the moderates out of concern over the condition of the army and because of the unceasing intrigues around the War Department. Following the lead of the five were three candidate members of the Politburo: the Moscow leader Uglanov, mentioned above; Grigory Petrovsky, chairman of the Ukrainian Central Executive Committee; and for a while Andrey Andreyev, party secretary for the Northern Caucasus region. Other members of the party leadership wavered: Kuibyshev, Rudzutak, and Ordzhonikidze. Several of the people's commissars supported the moderates, and they had supporters in the GPU: Menzhinsky's deputies Genrikh Yagoda and Mikhail Trilisser. The central party press, *Pravda* in Moscow and *Leningrad Pravda*, and the influential trade union press leaned toward their views.[15]

Stalin's supporters complained to some oppositionists in an attempt to win them over: "We have no press. It's in Rykov's hands. We have no cadres; they're partly with Rykov, partly with you. We haven't yet solidified our own forces sufficiently. We need our own press, to keep from being censored."[16]

As Stalin's support within the party leadership slipped, he resorted more and more often to making decisions unilaterally or after consulting only with his own group. He sought to create a situation that would allow him to make personnel changes and dislodge the moderates from their positions.[17] A conflict was soon provoked. The occasion for it presented itself in the middle of June. The deputy commissar of finance for the USSR, Mikhail Frumkin, lost his patience. After receiving the draft of the new industrial and financial plan, which in his opinion exceeded the country's capabilities, he appealed to the party leadership in a letter, which was essentially a sharp attack on Stalin. It alleged that the grave international position of the Soviet Union was a consequence of the undermining of the country's economic and political forces. The causes lay in the extraordinary measures, the disruption of proper relations with the peasantry, the orientation toward accelerated expansion of collective and state farms, and the inadequacy of capital investments. Frumkin called for a return to the policies of the Fourteenth and Fifteenth congresses, which were in keeping with NEP.[18]

Frumkin's letter was a significant event in inner-party life; it became known to a fairly wide circle. Stalin insisted that the Politburo reply. The Politburo was willing to go along with Stalin, but it declined to pass immediate political judgment on Frumkin's letter. Without waiting for the Politburo to compose a collective statement, Stalin wrote his own and sent it out as the Politburo's position. A scandal erupted.[19] In two letters addressed to Stalin, Bukharin demanded that certain general questions of party policy be taken up at the next Central Committee plenum. He declared that there was "neither a common policy nor a common opinion" in the leadership; that the Central Committee apparatus was pursuing a policy "different from the line of the Fifteenth Party Congress"; and that it was "disorienting the party ideologically."[20] The question was referred to a Politburo session. Here, Bukharin read a declaration setting forth the joint opinions of Bukharin, Rykov, and Tomsky: relations between the working class and the peasantry were on the verge of a split; there was an urgent need to revoke the extraordinary measures and the constraints on the market; the focus of the party's attention ought not to be on collective and state farms, for which the material preconditions did not exist, but on effective support and incentives for the individual small- and medium-sized peasant farms.[21]

The session was stormy and filled with sharp personal attacks. Molotov, nicknamed "stone bottom" by his colleagues in the Politburo for the peculiarity of his intellectual stamp, was not overly tactful. He gave Bukharin's declaration a hostile reception, calling it an "antiparty document." The more sober Stalin, however, soon realized that he should not insist on the extraordinary measures.[22] The alignment of forces in the leadership was unclear—the advantage might go to the moderates. To cause a new inner-party split not quite six months after the crushing defeat of the left opposition hardly seemed expedient. The whole matter was referred to a subcommission. Stalin came to the next meeting of the Politburo, on July 2, 1928, with his own draft resolution: he accepted a number of the moderates' demands (cancellation of the extraordinary measures, a partial increase in farm prices, a repeal of the constraints on rural trade, and backing for individual small- and medium-sized peasant farms), while reserving for himself the opportunity to defend the fundamental provisions of his own policy. The moderates' offensive petered out. The wavering Stalinists were satisfied, and the moderate "group of five" broke up: Voroshilov and Kalinin obviously preferred a bad peace with Stalin to a good war.[23]

The next plenum of the Central Committee met in Moscow on July 4, 1928. The moderates, who had not yet grasped all the consequences of Stalin's latest maneuver, tried to carry their success further and shake Stalin's position. On the eve of the plenum, *Pravda* printed articles by editors D. Maretsky and V. Astrov, containing attacks on Stalin's political course.[24] The discussion on domestic policy began on July 9, with the moderates on the offensive. Mikoyan read aloud the draft of a compromise resolution.[25] Moderate speakers followed one after another. Rykov was the principal figure. He characterized the situation sharply, and talked about the danger of a "civil war" with the peasantry.[26] The moderates were aiming for a complete rejection of the extraordinary measures, a substantial increase in farm prices, effective backing and encouragement for individual small- and medium-sized peasant holdings, and the extension of NEP.

Initially, it seemed that the moderates' attack might be successful. Stalin's compromises, however, strengthened his position: the compromise draft resolution predetermined the results of the discussion. Stalin had protected himself from the essential danger and sensed the support of a number of *krai* and *oblast* leaders, who, with him, held joint responsibility for the direction of the party's work. Stalin mobilized his forces. He not only defended himself; he counterattacked.

Central to Stalin's argument was the defense of high rates of industrialization. He rejected all attempts to demonstrate the seriousness of the situation as "capitulationism" and "alarmist moods." While recognizing, just as before, that agriculture was seriously lagging, he denied that the extraordinary measures had had harmful results. A substantial increase in agricultural prices was unacceptable to him; such an increase, in his opinion, might divert resources needed for industry. Stalin supported proposals concerning the primary importance of heavy industry with the slogan "a *smychka* [alliance, or 'bond'] with the peasantry not only through textiles but also with cast-iron," arguing that the goods famine, which had an unfavorable effect on relations between town and country, would be made up by industry through deliveries of machinery.

A belief that the peasantry had to make sacrifices for the sake of a faster rate of industrialization continued to play a large part in Stalin's conceptual system. Though forced by necessity to renounce the extraordinary measures, he did not rule out their use in the future. At the same time, he insisted adamantly on the accelerated construction of grain-producing collective and state farms, pointing out not so much their great productive capacity as their increased yield of marketable output—that is, a greater degree of alienation between the peasant and the fruits of his labor.

Stalin's proposals meant continued disruption of normal relations with the peasants. He could not have failed to understand this; increased pressure on the peasantry was part of his plan. The problem was that Stalin could not openly acknowledge the nature of the policy he was proposing. Instead, he introduced the theory that the class struggle would inevitably grow sharper as the country came closer to socialism. This concept, which subsequently stimulated the most diverse discussions, originated as nothing more than a casuistic device branding the struggle of broad sections of the peasantry against the authorities' use of force as a struggle by capitalist elements against the Soviet regime. Stalin was justifying in advance not only the permissibility but even the desirability of severe repression.[27]

Discussions at the plenum grew heated; Stalin's speech had been rather blunt. Bukharin again attempted to emphasize the serious nature of conditions in the country: "yawning holes and gaps" in the economy had become evident; the economy had "reared up" (*vstala dybom*) and was threatening to "make [all] the classes [in Soviet society] rear up too" (*postavit' dybom i klassy*).[28] It was impossible to achieve success simultaneously in all directions—the forces for that were lacking.[29]

Open clashes followed. Tomsky attacked Molotov, and Stalin came down on Tomsky. The Stalinists acted with unconcealed rudeness, counting on the effect of intimidation. Relations within the party leadership were totally spoiled; the more farsighted politicians could not doubt that the compromises agreed to were only temporary.[30]

It became clear, toward the end of the plenum, that the moderates were not strong enough to weaken Stalin very seriously. Fearing the consequences of his continued strength, they decided on a risky step. There were persistent rumors within the party that Stalin, aiming to achieve a solid preponderance over the moderates, was negotiating with the leaders of the opposition, including even Trotsky, who was then in exile at Verny (Alma Ata).[31] By this time, several opposition leaders who had capitulated earlier were back in the party and were collaborating with the Stalinist party apparatus. On July 11, 1928, while the plenum was still going on, Bukharin, with the consent of Rykov and Tomsky, met with Kamenev, who had just been readmitted to the party and had returned to Moscow. With exceptional frankness, Bukharin related to Kamenev the main developments occurring within the party. Among other things, it was his intention to stave off the danger that Kamenev

and Zinoviev would make an alliance with Stalin and to draw them as far
as possible over to his, Bukharin's, side.*[32] This was not a sensible move.
The moderates could not have prevented an alliance between Stalin,
Kamenev, and Zinoviev, if Stalin had considered such an alliance desirable. A record of the conversation, made by Kamenev for Zinoviev's
information, did not remain a secret from other opposition leaders.
Stalin subsequently used Kamenev's notes as a major weapon to discredit
the moderates.[33]

It might have seemed to the uninitiated that the July plenum was a
success for moderate policies. Stalin's position actually did become more
difficult—he was bound by the character of the decisions adopted. Rykov
gave a report on the results of the plenum at a meeting of party activists
in Moscow, in which he set forth his version of the reasons behind the
economic and social difficulties without concealing the serious errors
made by the leadership. His speech differed notably in its tone and basic
content from the one Stalin delivered in Leningrad.[34] In a private
conversation, Uglanov is said to have declared: "Stalin is straddling the
party's back, but we will pull him off."[35]

Practical steps followed. On July 14, *Pravda* announced publicly: The
"party is definitely lifting" the extraordinary measures; they had been
temporary in nature and were becoming a burden to further growth. All
methods of forced extraction of grain from the peasants were immediately prohibited, the restrictions on markets and trade within the
village were canceled, prices for cereal grain and forage crops as well as
fodder were raised, and the implementation of measures for the timely
provision of industrial goods to the countryside was announced.[36]

The concessions won by the moderates were actually rather modest.
Prices were raised by roughly 15 percent (later, in connection with
regional differences in prices, the increase proved somewhat greater).
Offsetting this increase, however, was a previous decision to increase
agricultural taxes both in terms of percentages and in total amounts.
Notwithstanding the arguments of the Stalinists, the higher taxes affected not only the interests of the well-to-do strata but the middle
peasants as well.[37]

As before, the measures proposed by the moderates were carried out
without any reduction in the volume of capital investment or in the rate
of industrialization.[38] The country's financial position was still over-
strained, and the foreign trade balance remained unfavorable. The
balance was restored only by the increased dumping of a number of

*On June 22, 1928, forty prominent members of the opposition who had capitulated,
among them Zinoviev and Kamenev, were readmitted to the party by the CCC. Formally
speaking, this measure was based on the decisions of the Fifteenth Party Congress, which
permitted the reinstatement of expelled party members after six months. However, at the
time, this action hinted that an alliance between the Stalin group and the former oppositionists might eventually be possible. (See *Pravda*, June 29, 1928.)

export goods (oil, timber, furs and so on).[39] Besides, major additional expenditures had to be provided, because in the summer of 1928 the Politburo and Council of People's Commissars approved an extensive program to develop and redesign a modern war industry intended for the conduct of war under conditions of economic blockade. The budgets of all the commissariats and even of the Comintern were cut back.[40]

The national economy had almost no reserves at its disposal, either financial or material. Any additional financial obligations placed on the population raised an immediate threat of a general strike. The situation became complicated due to unchanging social conditions. The living standards of wide sections of the population remained extremely difficult. The "outburst of war communism" in the first half of the year severely undermined confidence in the authorities' new measures, which on the whole did nothing to better the moods of the masses.

The moderate politicians were looking for possible ways to alleviate the situation, if only in part. But any reduction in the pace of economic development was blocked by the resistance of Stalin and his supporters. Once again, the path of international agreements, foreign credit, and capital investment seemed the least unhealthy choice. The international situation, however, was in no way reassuring. The repercussions of the Shakhty trial had not subsided, continuity with earlier economic negotiations had been broken, and any confidence other countries had in the possibility of cooperation with the Soviet Union had been seriously undermined.

The attention of Soviet diplomacy was focused on the United States. The presidential elections were at hand, with the possibility of a change in the administration. Hopes rose that American policy would begin to change.[41] Such a development might also affect the positions of other governments.

In an effort to reduce the Soviet Union's dangerous international isolation and sound out the real chances for cooperation, the Soviet leadership demonstrated its interest in participating in the international conference in Paris in August 1928.[42] The conference was being held to ratify a pact on the renunciation of force as an instrument of national policy, proposed by United States Secretary of State F. B. Kellogg, and was one link in a chain of attempts to ease tense relations among the Western powers. Ratification of the pact without participation by the Soviet Union would have deepened Soviet isolation. The Soviet government kept a watchful eye on all efforts by the Western powers to reach common agreements, considering any such agreement an essential step toward the formation of an anti-Soviet united front.

The moderate wing of the Soviet leadership attempted once again to broaden the basis for economic negotiations. As early as July 24, two weeks after the conclusion of the Central Committee plenum, the Sovnarkom authorized a change in the concessions policy and approved a long list of enterprises that could be taken over as foreign concessions.[43] It was proposed that foreign entrepreneurs might take over not only small business operations but also large-scale enterprises in the major branches of industry, as well as municipal ventures in many cities; proposals were made to ease a number of regulations governing concessionary activity and to make the terms of sale of the product more profitable to the concessionaires. The plan was aimed at relieving the Soviet Union's straitened financial condition and at hinting to foreign governments that major concessions might be had if sufficiently lucrative offers were made.

A muted struggle within the Bolshevik leadership accompanied this foreign policy initiative. Only fragmentary information about it has become known. Certain proposals were again introduced by Chicherin, who was trying on a limited scale to continue the course approved at the turn of the year, in late 1927 and early 1928. Chicherin's proposals were supported by Rykov, Kalinin, and other members of the party leadership.[44] Nevertheless, the mood was one of restraint. The members of the Politburo could not help but understand that the chances for quick success were slight. The leadership as a whole feared that an expression of inordinate interest in international economic agreements might bring about increased pressure from the Western powers.

It was no accident that Chicherin sought to dampen any eagerness among Soviet diplomats with the assertion that the Soviet Union had at its disposal the means for an independent way out of the crisis (nor did he do so, apparently, on his own initiative).[45] There was great significance, however, in the fact that the moderate line of foreign policy was now both secretly and openly being torpedoed by Stalin. He had sufficient grounds to be convinced that foreign policy related directly to internal affairs. Stalin began to resist any relaxation of the monopoly on foreign trade and leaned toward the idea that the Soviet Union's independence from fluctuating foreign economic ties and foreign financial and economic aid had to be maintained.[46] This struggle within the Soviet leadership acquired a rather exceptional significance. It predetermined not only the possibility of an immediate solution to the economic difficulties, but the entire future direction of domestic policy as well.

The Soviet proposals, as one might expect, produced nothing more than gradual shifts in the attitudes of the Western powers. Soviet participation in the Paris Conference was rejected by the West. (The Soviet Union ratified the Kellogg-Briand pact later on.)[47] Serious changes in the international climate developed only several months afterward. Even the proposed modifications in Soviet concessions policy produced no visible results. (They were not published until after the end of negotiations on the Kellogg pact—typical of the situation inside the Soviet leadership.)[48]

Germany remained the only important economic partner of the Soviet Union. It is true that the conclusion of the Shakhty affair provided the opportunity for the resumption of Soviet-German economic talks, but this did not especially improve the Soviet Union's position. The Shakhty affair left a deep imprint on German public opinion, particularly in business circles. The Soviet Union's weakened position in world affairs also greatly influenced the German government. German diplomats were instructed to avoid the question of granting new credits to the USSR; the outcome of the economic talks as a whole was made conditional on the Soviet government's payment of the first two installments on the three hundred million marks it had received in credits in 1926. For the USSR, this was a painful additional financial burden.[49]

The limited openings available to Soviet diplomacy in the late summer and early fall of 1928 shifted Soviet foreign policy onto a new track. The USSR took the road of "financial self-defense," of relying almost exclusively on its internal resources.[50] Instead of the policy of accelerated industrialization that Trotsky once suggested, a policy requiring the all-around integration of the USSR into the international division of labor, and instead of the policy of industrialization within the framework of broad financial and technical cooperation with the non-Soviet world, which was the essence of the moderate policy course, the Soviet Union ended up with a policy of accelerated industrialization based on isolation imposed both from without and from within—that is, by the Soviet government itself.

Having failed to ease economic pressures, the moderates from the very outset were greatly limited in their chances of realistically changing the economic practices introduced in the first half of the year. The cancellation of the extraordinary measures evoked powerful resistance from the political leaders in Stalin's camp. They interpreted it as "the sacrificing of the working class" and had little faith that it would produce positive results.[51] They were dominated by fear that a display of "weakness" would totally enervate those in the apparatus of power. On July 31, 1928, Menzhinsky presented his objections in a letter to the party leadership: the situation in the countryside was difficult and attitudes were hostile there; he would abide by party discipline, but he could not help pointing out the danger represented by the decisions that had been made and hoped that the Central Committee would not regret those decisions.[52]

The new line did not have much effect on the work of the apparatus on the lowest level. Local officials, accustomed to applying administrative measures implacably during the half year that had transpired, resorted once again to forced exactions of grain, the use of roadblock detachments, a prohibition against grinding grain locally, and refusal to pay peasants the higher prices set by the government.[53] Abuses in the levying of local taxes reached huge proportions: the authorities sought to reduce the strain on the industrialization budget and at the same time to supplement local budgets.

The moderate leaders tried to forestall such developments. Official statistics, distorted to suit Stalin, indicated a fairly good harvest, one supposedly larger than the year before. The only negative note was sounded in reference to the Ukraine and Northern Caucasus, which were said to have suffered from spring frosts. It was again necessary to rely on grain deliveries from distant locations; therefore delays in its reaching the market could be expected.[54]

The real situation, however, was menacing. Almost everywhere the harvest was poor; later, more exact figures spoke of a harvest that was at most "one-half or one-third of normal" (sam-dva, sam-tri).[55] Not only the Ukraine and the Northern Caucasus suffered from a poor harvest but other regions as well, especially northwest Russia (the Leningrad region). The yield of the basic crops, rye and wheat, was particularly poor—the consequences of Stalin's policy. The poor grain harvest was combined in some areas with low yields of another very important crop—potatoes.

The grain procurement campaign did not go well in July, or in August, or in September.[56] The peasants, deprived of most of their surpluses and even their reserve supplies in the preceding year, had little grain to spare. Not only did they not wish to sell their grain; they had none to sell—or hardly any. Anxiety mounted among the apparatchiks of every kind. With their procurement zeal held in check by the urgent warnings of the party leadership, which had given in to the moderates on this point, local party workers redirected their attention more energetically to permitted areas: tax policy and the formation of collective farms. (There were exceptions of no small significance, to be sure, and they were later branded as "right deviation.") As early as September, "excesses" reached quite exceptional proportions. In some provinces, agriculture was taxed two or three times the usual amount, and individual farms five or six times over. Increased individual taxation, which by law was supposed to apply to 3 percent of the most prosperous households employing hired labor, was imposed on other types of households as well. Things were carried to tragically absurd lengths: in some places, those who owned a radio, a sewing machine, a phonograph, or simply metal spoons (!) were subjected to the increased tax. The struggle was waged against the entire cultured layer of the middle peasantry. Households with many mouths to feed, whose nominal gross income was higher, were also taxed excessively. Strong pressure was exerted on the nonagricultural income of the rural population. This pressure was extremely intense even when such income was the main source of livelihood. The cottage industries, which provided work for millions of people, suffered severely. More and more frequently, in order to pay their taxes, peasants sold their livestock or equipment. Instances of outright dispossession of kulak households also occurred.[57]

There was a mounting campaign for peasants to join collective farms (*kolkhozy*). A steadily growing number of peasant households, threatened with ruin by extremely heavy taxation, did join. This means of escaping the authorities' pressure had been known in earlier times as well. Peasants would return to their individual farms after taking advantage of collective farm privileges, waiting out the bad times as kolkhoz members. Now, however, circumstances had changed: the authorities took measures to protect and preserve the collective property of the kolkhoz (the "indivisible fund" of land, equipment, and livestock). A peasant could leave the collective only at the price of losing much of his property.[58]

Stalin's supporters talked about the beginning of a breakthrough in the collective farm movement, claiming that the middle peasant was being attracted to the kolkhoz.[59] A large number of sober-minded contemporaries pointed out that the growth of collective farms implied the peasants' loss of interest in independent productive labor, which no longer produced positive results. By October 1, 1928, the number of collective farms had reached 35,000, and they accounted for 1.7 million hectares of the total area under cultivation. Simultaneously, mass complaints by peasants against the kolkhozy increased, and peasant delegations followed one another without a break in Kalinin's reception rooms.[60]

The old rural structure was being destroyed. Prosperous farms were completely undermined. The great mass of the middle peasantry lost all interest in expanding and improving production. The area sown to crops continued to decline, and the size of the cattle herd shrank. According to official figures, which no doubt were greatly embellished—though Stalin later disputed them—the area sown to winter crops (*ozimoi klin*) decreased on the average by 3 percent and in the fertile regions of the Ukraine and Northern Caucasus, by more than 10 percent.[61]

From all quarters of the Soviet Union, reports poured in of mounting unrest, increased hostility among the peasants toward the towns and town residents, and the murders of Communists and other representatives of authority. (Mostly they murdered "their own"—locals—because "a commissar is a plague, but he will leave.")[62]

By October, the real harvest results became clear. It was evident that even a massive tax squeeze would not fundamentally improve grain deliveries. Supplies were in a critical state. Some thought had to be given to surviving the winter and spring of the year to come.

Within the party leadership, particularly among the Stalinists, attitudes favoring the reinstitution of extraordinary measures were on the rise. In the middle of October, the question was submitted to a joint session of the Politburo, the Sovnarkom, and the Presidium of the Central Executive Committee. The pressure exerted by Stalin's supporters was massive, and any alternative solutions were blocked. Kalinin vacillated. Referring to the views of the rest of the party leadership, he recommended—with all the authority he had as the reputed defender of the peasants—the use of all available measures to obtain the grain that was lacking.[63] Moreover, such recommendations came not only from him as chairman of the Central Executive Committee. Menzhinsky had been authorized to act as he saw fit; he ordered local GPU units to help ensure that grain was delivered and taxes were collected.[64] A new order followed several days later. It confirmed a menacing growth in the number of attempts on the lives of representatives of authority. The guilty were to be sentenced to death, immediately and unconditionally; appeals were not allowed, and sentences were to be carried out in the period prescribed by law.[65] In its way, this was a prototype of Stalin's notorious decree on dealing with "terrorists," issued December 1, 1934, after the murder of Sergei Kirov.

By the fall of 1928, the organs of the Finance Commissariat, the Commissariat of Agriculture, the GPU, and the Workers' and Peasants' Inspection were acting, for the most part, with a complete lack of mercy. The official use of force occurred on a vastly increased scale, effectively negating the decisions of the July plenum. Procurements, as in the preceding year, took an upward leap for a short time. The peasants in the eastern and southeastern regions suffered especially heavily: in the middle Volga region procurements increased by 195 percent; in Siberia the increase was 107 percent and in Kazakhstan, 252 percent.[66]

In order to "meet" the demands of the moderates (Rykov, Kalinin, Bukharin, and others) that the law be observed, more and more elaborately disguised and refined methods of pressuring the peasants were devised. The total agricultural tax collected exceeded the prescribed limit of 400 million rubles and continued to grow steadily. In a number of cases, local areas were forced to tax themselves, and various new ways of extorting additional taxes were devised. Later, it would be established that a further 165 million rubles were extracted from the peasantry by such methods.[67] Peasants were forced to sign agreements making loans to the government, a campaign was carried out to speed up peasants' payments of shares to cooperatives, and there was much broader use of a wide variety of articles in the criminal code of the RSFSR, especially articles 107 and 61 (which carried penalties for refusal to perform tasks of general importance to the state.)[68] A particularly refined mockery of the peasants was the introduction (chiefly in Siberia, the Urals, and Kazakhstan) of the so-called "Urals-Siberian method of procurement," in which the extraordinary measures were introduced through "public procedures" (*obshchestvennym poryadkom*): at village assemblies the peasants themselves were forced to determine the size of the harvest, how much marketable surplus the village would have, to draw up a local plan for grain purchases by the state, and set the dates for grain deliveries. Against those who were "negligent" in meeting these obligations, sanctions were applied, including refusal to issue documents required by the government, denial of admission of children to school, denial of medical assistance, denial of permission for priests to administer religious rites, and refusal to sell certain manufactured goods.[69] A folk saying was born: " 'Soviet power is firm,' said the peasant—and wept."[70]

There was no end to the torments. The countryside's resistance grew—in spite of the arrests, the show trials, and the sharply increasing number of "terrorists" executed. In most cases, murders remained unsolved; the villages carefully concealed the guilty ones, for they had taken vengeance on the peasants' persecutors.[71] The authorities talked about the menacing growth of the "kulak counterrevolutionary movement." Local units of the GPU in the countryside were reinforced and expanded.[72]

By the end of the year, grain procurements had reached 61 percent of the annual target; this was somewhat higher than the level during the preceding year of crisis.[73] This success was more apparent than real, however. Deliveries of the main grain crops, rye and wheat, were substantially in arrears. Moreover, since autumn, procurements had been made by taking grain needed by the peasants themselves. Consequently, the demand for food supplies in rural regions rose enormously. A large amount of the procured grain made a return trip to the countryside in devious ways. Even the postal system was flooded with packages of bread or flour being mailed to peasant families.[74]

There was no more grain in the villages for meeting the remaining 39 percent of the annual goal for procurements.* The terrible spectre of approaching famine was growing in the country. The calendar year had not ended before the Sovnarkom was forced to release some of the country's reserve funds to seventy-six southern districts (the Ukraine, which was in a particularly threatened position, Odessa, Kherson, Nikolaev, and so on). The total released was wretchedly small, only 34 million rubles. By modest calculations, a minimum of 200–280 million rubles was needed to stave off famine not only in the Ukraine but in other parts of the Soviet Union as well.[75] The Soviet budget did not have such funds to spare.

Implementation of the July plenum's decisions was frustrated not only by the situation in the countryside. Difficulties also increased because of urban and industrial conditions. Food supplies, which did not improve in any fundamental way even with the coming of the new harvest, dwindled gradually to a point below the level of the previous hunger-plagued spring. Prices rose not only in the reduced private sector but in government and cooperative trade as well. High prices were not com-

---

*By Kalinin's admission, made in July 1929, 7.62 million tons of grain were procured in 1928–1929, as opposed to 10.24 million tons in 1927–1928. Therefore, by comparison with the crisis of 1927–1928, the shortage constituted 2.86 million tons. Since the official data indicated that by December 25, 1928, 5.7 million tons had been collected, in the remaining six months of 1929 only 1.92 million tons were stockpiled. According to the reduced annual plan it was proposed, however, to collect 4.2 million tons.

pensated for by increased wages—the government did not have the
resources to raise them. The chronically severe shortages of raw materials and the need for financial resources caused interruptions in the
operation of industry. In the summer of 1928, industrial output again
declined, aggravating the already severe goods famine.[76]

With all its resources tremendously strained, industry could ease the
economic situation only by improving its qualitative indices. A new
factor, however, began to make itself felt: the results of the social crisis.
Under the influence of Stalin's policies, and the Shakhty affair in particular, these social consequences were expressed in highly concentrated
form in a decline in labor discipline, which threw industry into complete
disarray. Workers refused to carry out the orders or requests of administrators, engineers, and technicians. Measures aimed at increasing production and raising the intensity of labor were regarded as counterrevolutionary. In turn, the specialists, finding themselves between two
fires—the workers and the administrators—and living in constant fear of
the GPU, showed no initiative on the job and limited their efforts to the
absolute minimum. Disorganization increased.

These basic circumstances were soon supplemented by others: work
stoppages, absenteeism, shirking of responsibilities, drunkenness—even
drunkenness on the job—assumed enormous proportions. Labor productivity plummeted.[77] By August 1928, the situation in the industrial
centers in many of the country's oblasts—in the textile industry of the
central industrial region, the Urals, the Ukraine, and even in Leningrad,
famous for its high level of culture—had become extremely alarming.
The Donbass, in the wake of the Shakhty affair, suffered a profound
breakdown in production, endangering the country's coal supply.[78]

Neither Stalin nor Menzhinsky had expected their maneuver in the
realm of social policy to produce such "side effects." The hostility and
indiscipline of the workers created an extremely awkward and difficult
situation. The workers, despite all the burdens imposed on them by the
policies of the Soviet government, remained its fundamental base of
support: government propaganda was directed first and foremost at
them; the outward appearance of a privileged position was created for
them. To confront this social milieu, which was already in turmoil, with
undisguised repression and administrative pressure, without first laying
the groundwork for it, would have been a very risky step. The Shakhty
affair, too, remained an object of great controversy within the party
leadership, which at that time was still trying to work out its basic political
positions.[79]

The authorities sounded an alarm. Interminable meetings began to be
held, and an avalanche of directives and instructions were issued. The
trade unions, the government, and the party all studied the industrial
chaos. In a letter addressed to his subordinates and circulated on August

11, Menzhinsky asserted that the Shakhty case had been "incorrectly understood." The situation in industry had become intolerable, he said, and could be compared only with the chaotic years immediately after the revolution. Local GPU units were ordered to immediately stop any activity among the workers aimed at "unmasking specialists."[80] A whole series of similar instructions followed. As early as September 1, Menzhinsky accused not only the workers but some GPU operatives themselves of not abiding by the decisions of the party leadership.[81]

It was not easy, however, to stop the raging element. It fed on the workers' unceasing resistance to the lowering of their living and working conditions. On September 3 and 4, the Council for Labor and Defense noted a steep decline in labor discipline and productivity. The government hastily ordered specially empowered commissions and representatives to the industrial centers. The "red directors" of industrial enterprises were charged with lack of energy and unsatisfactory work. Threats of removal from their posts and even prosecution were directed at them.[82] On September 11, the Politburo took up the question, obviously not for the first time. It demanded the fastest possible breakthrough. At the beginning of October, Jan Rudzutak, deputy chairman of the Council of People's Commissars and the Council of Labor and Defense, repeated these instructions, referring to the serious threat of a general economic breakdown.*[83]

The measures that were taken improved the situation somewhat, but the breakdown in labor discipline, combined with the other economic problems, had already borne fruit. In October 1928, the general financial situation and the need to raise the level of production forced the Sovnarkom to reduce or restrict industrial credits and suspend a number of new construction projects. The country's largest industrial operations were affected by these measures, among them Yugostal', Donugol' Azneft', the metallurgical plants in the Urals, and the northern and southern chemical trusts.[84] Further implementation of the policy of industrialization was threatened. Industry, too, now found itself the object of a system of "extraordinary measures." The application of administrative measures of every possible kind intensified sharply. Directors of industrial enterprises again began to receive orders to collaborate as closely as possible with the GPU.

The situation in the Soviet Union had become fairly clear: the moderates had failed to win the battle over economic strategy; their policy had

---

*The officially published monthly conjunctural reports, unlike the information found in internal correspondence, failed to show the substantial drop in production. Such a decline was recorded only in November 1928, and again in February 1929. The publication entitled "Control Figures for 1929–1930," however, admits that "the year [1928–1929— M.R.] began under extremely unfavorable conditions, with considerable disorganization and slackness of labor discipline." (p. viii)

not effectively influenced the practical course of economic and social affairs. By contrast, Stalin's policy during the first half of 1928 reproduced the conditions necessary for the continued existence of that policy. Another clash at the top became inevitable; it was necessary to determine the entire character of the Soviet Union's future development.

SEVEN

Defeat of the Moderates

After the July plenum a unique condition of unstable equilibrium arose in the Bolshevik Party. Both the moderates and the Stalinists considered it necessary to assert that there were no disagreements on questions of principle in the Politburo. They even protested against "rumors" of such disagreements.[1] Stalin, of course, had a certain advantage. As before, the decisive elements of political power were in his hands. It was not easy for him to use this advantage, however. Stalin had formulated the basic direction of his independent policy in the preceding period; he had to expand it into a solid concept for the future development of the Soviet Union. He could no longer limit himself merely to general theoretical and political postulates; his policy also had to be expressed in the realm of practical economic and social planning. At the same time, the key levers of economic life continued to rest in the hands of the moderates. In general, it was difficult to get around such a major fund of knowledge and practical experience on the Soviet economy as the moderate Rykov.

In the fall of 1928, economic and social developments in the USSR were proceeding contrary to the ideas of the moderates, but they were not propitious for Stalin either. A number of contemporaries believed that, because of the extent of economic and social difficulties, a full renunciation of Stalin's course toward industrialization was only a matter of weeks or even days away.[2] Such a way out, however, was to all appearances already closed to the Soviet Union. The process that was destroying the economic and social relations of the NEP period was already far advanced; a return to the original position was hardly possible. There was a huge shortage of goods and food; to overcome this shortage, time, resources, and great effort were required. The authorities did not have the material means at their disposal to effectively defuse social tension. The retreat from the extraordinary measures, and with it the inevitable disorientation, disorganization, and weakening of the coercive machinery of the state, seriously threatened to increase popular resistance and open the doors to growing discontent and rebellion. Additionally, the constantly accelerating pace of technological development among the Western powers created apprehension among Soviet leaders. Stalin spoke of this openly enough: "Look at the capitalist countries and you will see that technology there is not merely progress-

ing but racing ahead, leaving behind the old forms of industrial technology. . . . It is impossible to defend the independence of our country
without a sufficient industrial base for defense. It is impossible to create
such an industrial base without technology in industry. . . . Either we
acquire it or we will be wiped out."[3]

The situation once again approached an impasse. Stalin could no
longer back down without suffering a fatal defeat. The decisions he had
made in the spring of 1928 and their consequences predetermined his
position. He concluded that the Soviet Union's international and internal
situation made an increase in the rates of industrial growth desirable. In
Stalinist circles a new slogan gained popularity: the economy could not
be equated with its "bottlenecks."[4]

Stalin made a decision which, in the Soviet Union's circumstances,
seemed like pure madness: he decided to save himself with a leap
forward. Such a decision was not devoid of political reason; there was a
certain boldness and revolutionary quality to it. Nevertheless, Stalin's
boldness and revolutionism were of a special kind. In a situation of very
severe economic and social crisis, which had already brought unbelieva-
ble deprivation to broad layers of the population, his program inevitably
showed a total disregard for the human factor and human needs; it did
not hesitate to accept any moral, material, or human loss regardless of its
extent. Stalin's economic and social concepts, aside from his personal
aims or ideological motivation (he was rather ignorant on many social
questions), sank to a level of thinking common to any exploitative system
that is not forced to allow for the corrective effect of public resistance to
government action. This was a complete break with the meaning and
essence of the social doctrine of socialism.

Given the real situation in Soviet society, it was impossible to justify, let
alone defend, Stalin's political decisions. A discussion of maintaining
high rates of industrialization would have been impossible if the real
state of society were openly acknowledged; it would have been necessary
to talk about something the Stalinists preferred to pass over in silence—
the cost of the Stalinist course. Such a discussion would have been
extremely compromising. Therefore, Stalin and his supporters, particularly Molotov, not only hushed up and distorted important facts of
economic and social life, a tactic the Bolshevik leadership had resorted to
frequently in the past, but also constructed an arbitrary picture of society
as a whole. The discrepancy between the economic plans and the material prerequisites for those plans became one of the most characteristic
traits of Stalinist policy. A simple statement of the actual state of affairs—
even behind the closed doors of the highest party and government
bodies—became, in the eyes of Stalin and his supporters, an "antiparty
act" that deserved the most rigorous censure and punishment. The
foundation was laid for a system of political relations that was subsequently characterized, highly inaccurately, as the "cult of personality"—

that is, a system of undebatable, consciously arbitrary personal and group judgments and decisions.

It was extremely difficult to involve the moderates in projects involving this kind of methodology; the two groups in the Central Committee were speaking different languages. The moderates constantly avoided making an evaluation of the real situation in society and the limits it imposed. Stalin was able to develop his own line by merely assuming the responsibility for working out concrete statistical plans for economic and social development.

In the summer and fall of 1928 the apparatus of the Central Committee was feverishly active. Economic specialists were sent for and received orders for their expert opinions on the economic situation.[5] Stalin mobilized his supporters in the agencies of economic management. The Supreme Economic Council (VSNKh), headed by Kuibyshev, one of Stalin's highly placed protégés, became the definitive center for drafting economic plans. It was counterposed to the more sober State Planning Commission (Gosplan).[6] Primary work was focused on the control figures for the development of the Soviet economy in 1928–1929, which was also the first year of the not yet existent five-year plan.

In the summer of 1928, both planning centers, Gosplan and the VSNKh, submitted their proposals for rates of industrialization to the party leadership. The proposals were examined in August. Both Gosplan's rough drafts and the VSNKh's indices, which projected higher rates, were deemed inadequate. The Politburo, undoubtedly under pressure from Stalin and Molotov, demanded a further increase in the rate of industrialization.[7]

One of the main arguments for raising the planned rate was that in preceding years the pace of industrial growth in the USSR had exceeded the expectations of the planning agencies; figures supporting this were cited.[8] Thus, instead of a realistic tabulation of the country's resources, the essential role in the drafting of the plans was an estimation of need, of the so-called deficits in the economy.[9] Another factor that became an important element was the need to reduce dependence on foreign countries, that is, a decrease in the volume of imports and the satisfaction of a number of previous import requirements by domestic industry.[10] It was on this basis, then, that economic priorities were determined, in particular the allocation of capital investments to particular branches of industry and the desired rates of increased production.

Such a system for drawing up a plan should not in itself be considered bad. It was a step forward to establish the needs of the Soviet economy. The problems lay in the balance between the needs that were established and the country's actual resources, and in the balance between production requirements and the consumption needs of the population at large.

The planning bodies (primarily the VSNKh) based the established rates of growth of production in 1928–1929 on official data from the plans fulfilled the preceding year. Outwardly, this might also appear justifiable: the planning agencies based their proposals on what had already been attained. The statistics indicated a production increase of 22.5 percent in large-scale government industry, with somewhat higher percentages in light industry and somewhat lower in heavy industry.*[11] The increase in output projected for large-scale industry was therefore set at 21.4 percent for the new fiscal year, and for production as a whole, at 18.4 percent (compared with 21.6 percent in 1927–1928). This was unquestionably a very substantial increase. The planned growth rate for heavy industry and the flow of capital investment into heavy industry were to exceed those for light industry. Consequently, an increased amount of capital would be frozen in construction projects for a number of years.[12]

Stanislas Kossior, who had just been transferred to the Ukraine from a post as secretary of the Central Committee, was already reporting to the VSNKh on the preliminary outlines of its plan. He spoke of the plan's "maximal character."[13] The plan was inadequately provided for by the output of metal** and raw materials. It also displayed a profound disparity between the projected growth of capital construction (22–23 percent) and the growth of the construction materials industry (14.7 percent).[14]

The proposed control figures for 1928–1929 fully revealed the nature of Stalin's decisions. The demands made on the budget, despite some reduction in the initial proposals, significantly exceeded the demands of the previous year.†

The redistribution of resources in favor of industry increased sharply (from 477.3 million rubles to 819 million rubles, according to data from

---

*The verification of Soviet statistical data is not one of the tasks of the present work. It should be noted, however, that the data from the Soviet leaders' internal correspondence, a portion of which I have quoted, has not in any way confirmed the claim of brilliant successes by the Soviet economy in 1927–1928. The official conjunctural reports published monthly recorded a partial or general decline in production in October and November of 1927 and in February, April, June, and July of 1928.

**According to data given by Kuibyshev, the "deficits" in ferrous metallurgy included the following: a 33.7 percent shortage of cast iron, 34 percent shortage of iron in bars and ingots (zagotovki i bolvanki), 26.9 percent in structural iron (sortovoe zhelezo), and so on. (Pravda, November 27, 1928.)

†Statistical data varied significantly from document to document and from speech to speech, reflecting both the concrete course of fulfillment of the plan and the struggle within the central institutions. Kuibyshev (Pravda, September 12, 1928) initially spoke of demands on the budget of 1,300 million rubles as compared to 700 million rubles in 1927–1928 and of the need to lower this to 1,000 million rubles. A resolution of the November 1928 plenum of the Central Committee spoke of capital investments in industry in the amount of 1,650 million rubles as against 1,330 million rubles in 1927–1928, which, of course, also included investments not from the budget. (See KPSS v. rezoliutsiiakh, vol. 4, p. 133.) Finally, at the same November plenum, Stalin spoke of the VSNKh's request for 825 million rubles for the needs of capital construction, Gosplan's request for 750 million rubles, and the Commissariat of Finance's proposed figure of 650 million rubles. In agreement with Stalin, the Central Committee reached a decision in favor of the sum of 800 million rubles (Soch., vol. 11, p. 276.) Other variants on these figures also exist.

the Commissariat of Finance).[15] Pressure was intensified on the basic sources of revenue for the budget: excise and other taxes, loans to the government, the monopoly on the sale of vodka and other distilled liquor, and, of course, the continued excessive issuing of paper currency.[16] Nevertheless, there were not enough resources to guarantee the proposed rates of industrial growth. The planning agencies therefore decided on a not entirely customary measure: to balance the plan by means of resources that the economy did not yet have at its disposal. A reduction in the cost of production was projected at 7 percent (initially at 8 percent), reduction in the cost of construction at 15 percent, and an increase in the productivity of labor at approximately 17 percent (thanks to a projected increase in wages of approximately 7 percent).[17] The effect of this projected improvement in the basic indices of production was included in the financial plan for industry, but in fact Soviet industry never achieved such fine results. It was not provided with the means to do so, neither by an adequate influx of new technology and equipment nor by the actual situation in the factories.

Agriculture was planned in a similar manner. The premises on which the plan was based were even more flimsy in this area because Stalin and his supporters denied the real state of affairs in the countryside and greatly exaggerated the results already attained. Disregarding the actual reduction of the area sown to crops and the visible decline in the peasants' interest in working the land, the plan projected an increase of 7 percent in cultivated area, with a growth in yield of 3 percent (initially, a 10 percent increase in the grain harvest was proposed).[18] In practice, this could mean only that, under this economic plan, grain procurements and the provision of agricultural products to the country as a whole would be based not on what was actually attainable but on an imaginary harvest. The implications of such planning were clear. The fulfillment of the plan depended directly on a very brutal attack on the living and working conditions of industrial workers and the rural population. The plan remained extremely unstable. Any fairly substantial divergence from the planned indices or any fairly serious change in economic conditions threatened to disrupt it. The plan left almost no maneuvering room for the economic agencies and organizations, nor did it leave any resources or reserves to ease the difficult economic conditions that had already been created for broad sections of the population. This was a plan of organized poverty and famine.

Stalin's entry into the arena of economic planning inevitably intensified the conflicts within the party leadership. The moderates, having lost the initiative in this area—formerly a vital base of support for their activities—did not find an effective way of defending themselves. They were forced to follow a policy of merely correcting the Stalinist plans. This placed the moderates at an extreme disadvantage.

The tactics selected by the core of moderates on the Politburo were unfortunate. While continuing to stress the absence of disagreement on questions of principle, the moderates, doubting their own strength, reinforced their objections to the Stalinist plans with an attack on "Trotskyist super-industrializing"—by which they meant Stalin's new course. Thus, the moderates diverged into an area that was not their strong suit, and could not be. Moreover, this move facilitated a certain rapprochement between Stalin and the capitulationist wing of the left opposition—something the moderates initially had wished to avert.[19] Trotsky, in Alma-Ata, had been considering the desirability of a provisional alliance with the moderates against Stalin, but now found himself isolated on this question even among his close collaborators.*[20]

Under these conditions, at the end of September 1928, Bukharin made an attempt to turn the Stalinist plans into the object of broad inner-party discussion. He published his article "Notes of an Economist: At the Start of the New Fiscal Year" in *Pravda*, causing a major sensation.[21] In its external form this article was also a criticism of "Trotskyism." Constrained by the decisions of the Politburo, Bukharin outwardly accepted the framework of the Stalinist proposals. But he made the question of the proper proportions of economic growth a central topic for discussion. The cause of the Soviet Union's serious economic and social difficulties, according to Bukharin, lay in the fact that accelerated industrial development ran up against limiting factors: a strong lag in agriculture, particularly in grain production; lack of development in the metallurgical and construction materials industries; inadequacy of raw material supplies; and an unsatisfactory situation in foreign trade. From this point of view, in Bukharin's opinion, two economic problems came to the fore: capital construction and improved performance in agriculture.

Bukharin attached exceptional significance to the problem of an economic upturn in agriculture. He proposed—this was a concession to Stalin—that serious attention be paid to the development of collective farms and state farms, but at the same time he stressed the importance of price policy and of stimulating small and medium-sized individual peasant farming.

Bukharin's attitude toward the problem of capital investment was quite a different story. While fully acknowledging the importance of capital investment, particularly in the lagging branches of industry, he tried to give Stalin a real battle on this question. Bukharin declared that attention to capital construction did not mean investing all resources in industrial development. It was necessary to establish limits for accumulation, to create reserves, and to balance supply and demand; construction

---

*It should be noted, incidentally, that Trotsky obviously recognized the generally prevailing attitude within the opposition on this question; in all his published statements of this period he sharply attacked the moderates, showing a preference for Stalin.

projects had to be provided not only with financing but with materials as well. It was necessary to avoid tying up too many resources in large-scale, long-term construction projects. Bukharin warned against racing ahead too fast in industrialization; to do so would result in failure.

Bukharin's article was not consistent. He did not say everything he had in mind; he could not bring himself to speak out full force against Stalin's idea of a leap forward. This was typical of all the tactics used by the moderates. Clearly, the moderates were seriously considering the possibility of a substantial reduction in the pace of development; Bukharin and Rykov spoke openly of the permissibility of a retreat.[22] On this point, they were sharply at variance with Stalin and his supporters.

The moderates made a serious tactical error by coming out against Stalin under the banner of "the fight against Trotskyism." By doing so, they carried the struggle into Stalin's favorite area. While agreeing with the moderates that the struggle against the left was necessary, Stalin added that a struggle against the right was also necessary. But for Stalin this was only a transitional formula. Within a very short time he was posing the question quite differently: the danger from the left had been sufficiently exposed; the chief danger was from the right, from the "capitulators" who were under the thumb of the kulaks and capitalist elements.[23]

Stalin interwove these general political exercises—it was still necessary to reorient the party to the unaccustomed struggle against the "right deviation"—with preparations for directly administrative measures. He moved gradually, taking the time to differentiate among his various targets. He concentrated pressure on Bukharin, who was laying most of the groundwork for the moderates' views. As before, Bukharin held no significant personal power and was not an eminent figure in the implementation of practical economic and social policies. In July 1928, at the Sixth Congress of the Comintern in Moscow, which had been delayed for two years, Stalin, who had been relegated to the background by the moderates—the Comintern was Bukharin's domain and the moderates skillfully made use of this—nevertheless conducted refined intrigues. Contemporaries spoke of the "congress in the corridors." Behind the scenes, Stalin launched an attack from the left on Bukharin's theses on the international situation. These theses were already fairly far to the left but still reflected the Soviet Union's international isolation. Then Stalin managed to have the Comintern adopt a resolution on the struggle against the "right danger."[24] Making good use of this slogan, Stalin gradually expanded the struggle against those leaders of foreign Communist parties who were politically allied with Bukharin. A particularly intensive struggle was waged in the most influential section of the Comintern, the Communist Party of Germany (KPD).[25] At the same time—while Bukharin was occupied with the Comintern Congress, followed by a vacation—Stalin moved in on Bukharin's position at *Pravda* by having the moderates Maretsky and Astrov dismissed from its editorial board and his, Stalin's, supporter Garald Krumin appointed as executive director. (Krumin had the dubious fame of being known as "the lead dog of the pack.")[26] By the fall of 1928, troubling rumors had already begun circulating in the Comintern: Bukharin was to be replaced in his post as the head of the Comintern by either Molotov or the well-known Czechoslovak Communist leader, Smeral.*[27]

Important events were about to unfold in the Moscow organization of the Soviet Communist Party. The plenum of the Moscow Committee and the Moscow Control Commission, which took place in the middle of September, provided the impetus. Uglanov's report referred to the extremely difficult living conditions of the Moscow workers, and the perversions of the tax policy in the countryside. Uglanov defended the need for a more intensive development of light industry and the upgrading of agriculture and put heavy stress on the struggle against the danger from the left.[28]

Uglanov's report took a moderate line, which was understandable within certain limits: light industry prevailed in Moscow, and industrial workers there still had close ties with the villages. The report did not exceed the limits of what was then considered permissible in the party. Nevertheless, it worried Stalin. The Moscow organization was a significant base of support for the moderates. Decisions by the Moscow Committee became the basis for decisions by all the party organizations in the capital. Also, as a rule, they had a strong influence on party bodies making similar decisions in other parts of the country.

Stalin sought to disavow the policies of the Moscow Committee and to change the balance of power in Moscow. For the time being, however, there were insufficient grounds to justify this: there was no hope that the Politburo, where the forces remained in equal balance, would sanction organizational measures. Not wanting to risk a premature clash, Stalin conducted a game behind the scenes. Officials of the Moscow party organization were individually called in to the Central Committee offices, where it was suggested to them that the policies of the Moscow City Committee were "antiparty" in nature. Masterful use was made of personal conflicts and policy disagreements.

The results of this effect soon materialized: a whole series of statements by party "activists" protesting against the policies of their leaders appeared.[29] One after another, the Moscow district committees passed resolutions dimissing secretaries who supported the moderate political

*It is impossible to verify the authenticity of these rumors. The plans for replacing Bukharin with Smeral, if they were serious, were unrealizable. In the Czechoslovak party, Smeral was under heavy attack by Klement Gottwald's left-wing group, which described Smeral as a primary source of the "right danger."

course. Demands were made for an emergency plenum of the citywide Moscow Committee.[30] The party organizations were disoriented; many thought that what was involved was a faction fight against the leaderships of the district committees and the Moscow Committee.[31]

The events in Moscow seriously alarmed members of the Politburo. Stalin feigned lack of interest.* By a decision of the Politburo, the situation was examined at a joint session of the Central Committee Secretariat and the Moscow Committee Secretariat. On October 18, 1928, the results of this session were submitted directly to the Politburo. In a special message to the Moscow organization, the party leadership, confronted by accomplished facts, sanctioned the changes that had been made in several district committees; at the same time, however, it emphatically defended the Moscow Committee, declaring that "on the whole the Moscow Committee and the nucleus of its leadership have carried out and are carrying out the party line and are indisputably carrying out the decisions of [higher] party bodies." The party leadership demanded an immediate halt to the conflict within the Moscow organization.[32]

The Politburo's decisions were clear: it did not want to untie Stalin's hands. Nevertheless, Stalin continued his game. A broad campaign against anonymous "rightists" unfolded in the party press. An emergency plenum of the Moscow Committee and Moscow Control Commission, convened on October 18 immediately after the Politburo session, proceeded under the banner of continuing struggle. Stalin, speaking at the plenum on October 19, dissociated himself, it is true, from the attack on the Moscow leadership, but at the same time he backed the general tendency of the plenum.[33] Many leaders of the Moscow Committee and Moscow Control Commission, seeing that they were not being defended in any effective way, resorted to "self-criticism." Despite the Politburo's resolution, the decisions of the plenum made reference to errors by the Moscow Committee and the Moscow Control Commission; in addition, further personnel changes were made.[34]

The campaign against the right now took hold throughout the country. The party apparatus, mobilized by Stalin, Molotov, and Kaganovich, passed resolutions in oblast and city committees that backed the actions of the Stalinists in Moscow.[35] Repression against the right began in a number of party organizations.[36] In order to affect a greater change in the alignment of forces, Stalin made use of a method tried and tested in the struggle against the left opposition: he started rumors about the danger of an armed putsch by anonymous "rightists."[37] Orders for a

---

*Stalin's "lack of interest" was deliberately underscored by the fact that he remained away from Moscow on vacation until October 3 while all the dirty work was being done by the Central Committee Secretariat, where Molotov played the key role in Stalin's absence. In this way Stalin also retained the possibility of further maneuver.

new purge of the army's command staff and surveillance of the army by the GPU were hastily isssued.[38] The GPU made arrests.[39]* In November 1928, Stalin, no longer feeling constrained, removed Uglanov and his deputy Vasily Kotov from their posts in the Moscow organization. The moderates did manage to have Uglanov appointed to the post of People's Commissar of Labor (with the help of the All-Union Central Trade Union Council),[40] but this did not alter the state of affairs. Stalin had, for all practical purposes, achieved what he wanted. The influence of the moderates had been weakened, while the personnel changes and campaign against the right laid the groundwork for their total defeat.

The alignment of forces in the country as a whole was changing more and more in Stalin's favor; in the Politburo, however, the situation remained complex. Conditions in the countryside once again pushed Kalinin toward the moderates. He actively opposed a number of Stalin's measures. In informed circles, the impression began to form that Kalinin, not Rykov, was the leading figure in the moderate section of the party leadership.[41] Even Voroshilov began to waver. Stalin, who had obviously considered him a firm ally since their clash in the summer of 1928, carried out a number of individual transfers in the Red Army.[42] The insulted Voroshilov presented the Bolshevik leadership with information about the grave situation in the army, which was a result of rural policy. He also gave vent to this criticism in a public appearance before the workers of the Krasnaya Presnya district in Moscow. Stalin demanded reprisals, but the Politburo did not agree.[43] Kalinin mediated between Voroshilov and Stalin. The situation eased somewhat, but the threat of a restoration of the moderate "five" in the Politburo was undeniable.[44]

Stalin's position in the party leadership became more and more difficult. The next Central Committee plenum was drawing near; it had to approve the Stalinist economic plans definitively. The open eruption of conflicts, however, would make some compromises obligatory. Compromises certainly could blunt the edge of Stalin's schemes. The lesson of the July plenum was instructive enough in this regard.

Stalin had to take evasive action. The principal report on the control figures for the economy was offered to Rykov, whose objections to them were well known. This maneuver was well considered. Rykov would supposedly be defending a point of view common to the whole leadership, but in fact Stalin's proposals lay at the basis of the report. In formulating his own corrections and comments. Rykov laid himself open to the Stalinists' criticism. It was not Stalin's proposals but the moderates' counterproposals that became the subject of polemics. A heated conflict

---

*The tenseness of the situation at that time produced a flood of rumors in Moscow, for example, that Stalin had carried out a coup, that Uglanov had been arrested, that Tomsky was to be banished to Narym and Rykov to Turkestan.

erupted. The draft resolution prepared by Rykov went to a Politburo commission, composed almost entirely of Stalinists, which declared it unsatisfactory.*[45]

The discussion was carried over to a meeting of the Politburo. Attention was centered on the actual situation in the countryside and in agriculture generally. Kalinin apparently supported the moderates, and several other top party and government leaders may have as well.[46] No one wanted a split, however. The Stalinists made some concessions that softened the tone of the draft resolution[47] without changing its substance. This satisfied the majority. The moderates, realizing that Stalin's offensive had already gone rather far, raised the question of his arbitrary activities. They demanded a halt to the campaign against the "right deviation" as practiced by Stalin, the cancellation of several appointments and personnel changes, an end to the struggle in the Moscow organization, and respect for the Politburo decisions in that regard.[48] Stalin, trying to avoid a new discussion in the leadership, succeeded in having the question referred to a committee that he had no intention of convening. At this point, the moderates decided on an extreme step: Rykov, Bukharin, and Tomsky handed Stalin their resignations. This was a gesture of despair, meant to mobilize support in the leadership. Stalin, however, was in command of the situation. The rest of the leadership did not want to break lances at the plenum after agreement had been reached on the economic questions. Stalin made new concessions, or rather, promises of concessions. The moderates, without winning anything of substance, backed down.[49] As Stalin wished, the conflicts did not go beyond the leadership bodies. He could now count on the unimpeded approval of his political and economic course by the plenum.

The Central Committee plenum that took place in Moscow, November 16–24, 1928, presented a strange picture. The members of the Central Committee were, of course, fairly well informed about the conflicts of principle in the leadership. Rykov and Stalin, however, announced that no disagreements existed.[50] The announcement could be interpreted in only one way: the moderates refused to defend their views openly. This gave an extraordinary lift to the Stalinists' spirits. In the corridors they commented: Stalin is "a genius, Lenin's equal, if not greater."[51]

The moderate point of view was presented weakly at the plenum. Bukharin and Tomsky, realizing that they had lost the opportunity to speak out effectively, were mainly absent.[52] The other moderates on the Central Committee likewise refused to say anything of significance. Frumkin was the only "daredevil"; the avenues of retreat were closed to him after his clash with Stalin in June. Rykov reported the agreed-upon

*The commission was made up of Bukharin, Krzhizhanovsky, Kuibyshev, Mikoyan, Ordzhonikidze, Rykov, and Stalin, and functioned for the most part with Bukharin absent, since he was on vacation.

decisions to the plenum, pointing out, however, the critical condition of the economy and the dangerous situation in the countryside. He warned that an increase in the number of collective and state farms could not, for the time being, replace the individual farm and that the government's modest aid to the countryside could not equal the weight of peasant self-interest or the mobilization of the forces of private peasant agriculture.[53]

Even weak hints, such as Rykov's, concerning the nature of Stalin's plans, however, met a hostile reception. Central Committee members from among the *obkom* and *kraikom* secretaries and officials of the central party apparatus, who were not at all constrained by the agreements in the Politburo, openly attacked Rykov. A firm belief in the salutary nature of forcible methods now held sway in this milieu. Those who spoke demanded full recognition of the thesis concerning "the intensification of the class struggle," that is, that the increased use of force was necessary. A contemporary recorded typical statements of the Stalinists in the corridors at the plenum: "Nicholas II would not have fallen if the apparatus of force had acted more ruthlessly."[54]

At the plenum, Stalin presented his views on the need for high rates of industrial growth. Held back by the agreements made in the Politburo, he was unable to attack the moderates directly, but he came down on the only openly oppositional speech, Frumkin's, whose views were declared to be typical of the "right deviation." Organization of a broad ideological campaign against this deviation was proposed. Yielding to the moderates, Stalin still dissociated himself from the use of organizational measures, without rejecting their possible use in the future. He also urged his supporters to keep in mind the experience of the Moscow organization: "Members of the party have the right to remove their leaders democratically."[55] The Central Committee approved a resolution "On Recruiting Industrial Workers and Regulating the Growth of the Party." It ratified the idea of a party purified of "corrupted" and "rightist" elements.[56] The anonymity of the campaign against the "right deviation" could be used for nefarious purposes: any party official or party member was potentially the object of attack. There arose an atmosphere of political terror against anyone who thought differently. Stalin obtained a powerful weapon not only in the struggle against the moderates but also in the struggle for the suppression of any form of disagreement—active or passive—with his policies. Despite the compromises in the leadership, the plenum became an important success for Stalin.

Events were coming to a head. Although he had secured support for his political course, Stalin must have understood that matters had not yet been resolved once and for all. The composition of the party leadership remained unchanged; the economic and social crisis continued to build, making new outbreaks of inner-party struggle probable, even inevitable. Stalin quite naturally wanted a guarantee against such developments. He increased the pressure.

Stalin's first blow was directed at the remnants of the left opposition, which had ceased to be necessary to him as a means of making the moderates nervous. The possibility of an alliance with the capitulationist opposition leaders was dropped from consideration. Stalin spoke of this with cynical frankness: "To enlarge [their] rights means to make a bloc [with them]. And a bloc means a division in half. There is nothing for me to divide."[57] He no longer dissociated himself from the campaign against Trotskyism unleashed by the moderates: this campaign now became a convenient means of deflecting the charge of "super-industrializing" from himself.

The campaign against Trotskyism was significant in other ways as well. Stalin could not ignore the fact that the left opposition still remained a potential nest of serious resistance. The overall deterioration of urban conditions had led to a growth in political activism. Once again, opposition leaflets were being distributed widely, and members of the opposition had penetrated the workers' ranks, helping to organize their social struggle. Trotsky's articles, letters, and notes, illegally obtained from Alma-Ata, were circulating among party members.[58] On the anniversary of the October revolution in 1928, the opposition once again tried to organize street demonstrations.[59] Trotsky's popularity was growing. "His firmness and courage are patently impressive," noted a contemporary.[60] For many, the name "Trotsky" became a symbol of consistent and open struggle against Stalin's policies.

It would be an overstatement to say that in the fall of 1928 the left opposition had become as strong an adversary of Stalin as it had been in 1927.* But its existence did complicate the situation. The opposition's activities preserved an awareness of the possibility of a political alternative to Stalin from the left and in general created more room for inner-party differences. This situation was becoming unacceptable to Stalin. In a secret letter, he informed the party organizations that any "liberalism" toward the opposition was intolerable, that the "Trotskyites" had completed their evolution into "an underground anti-Soviet organization."[61] The GPU received orders to increase repressive measures against members of the opposition, to arrest and exile them. Not only the political but also the physical defeat of the left opposition was imminent.

The blow to the left opposition was only a secondary matter; Stalin's

*In addition to the capitulators I have named, many former leaders of the opposition were leaning toward capitulation, including Radek, Smilga, and others. Increasingly, the leading place in the opposition was reduced to two men, Trotsky and Rakovsky.

primary attention was fixed on the need to hamstring the moderates' resistance. Relations in the party leadership were still tense. The rapidly deteriorating conditions in the USSR provoked renewed conflict. As was to be expected, the unrealistic proposals for improving the quality of industrial functioning (reducing costs of production and construction and raising labor productivity) could not be carried out.[62] Gaps kept appearing in the plans for industry, and reserves had shrunk to the minimum.[63] In spite of the critical condition of the countryside—I have mentioned that famine was an imminent threat in several regions—the pressure on the peasantry was not eased.

In following the political course he had chosen, Stalin tried to rely on sheer force. He called for "the work" to be intensified, for new administrative measures. Opposition from the moderates increased, however. The All-Union Central Trade Union Council (VTsSPS) refused to sanction any further attacks on the workers (such as making collective agreements more disadvantageous, increasing the rights of management, or waging an administrative struggle for "labor discipline").[64] At the Eighth Congress of Trade Unions, held in December 1928, there was a clash. Stalin passed a resolution in the Politburo on strengthening the VTsSPS with new staff members. In practice, this meant that Kaganovich was placed in the union officialdom with the powers of "leader number two," alongside Tomsky.[65] Tomsky, making use of the support of the trade union leaders in the industrial regions of Moscow, Leningrad, Nizhny Novgorod, Tula, and elsewhere, resisted and on December 28 submitted his resignation to the Central Committee.[66] His resignation was refused by the Politburo. The oblast party committees, undoubtedly acting on Stalin's instructions, began to "mobilize" rank-and-file unionists and remove uncooperative trade union officials from their posts.[67] Tomsky refused to return to work, seeking to achieve a fundamental resolution to the conflict.

In the Politburo the "five" were activated once again as a result of their joint opposition to Stalin's policies in the countryside. Kalinin, pointing to Voroshilov's report on conditions in the army as well as the national movements in the Ukraine and Byelorussia, insisted on a change of course, threatening, otherwise, to speak out publicly in December at the session of the Central Executive Committee.[68] At the last minute, Stalin agreed to form a commission to review tax policies.[69] As usual, however, the matter was not carried very far.

On January 21, 1929, in connection with the fifth anniversary of Lenin's death, Bukharin gave the official speech. His remarks, programmatic in nature, were rather categorical: there was no need to fear admitting that the stabilization of capitalism in the industrial countries was a long-term condition; the Soviet Union could hold out if proper relations were maintained with the peasantry; it was impossible to industrialize on the basis of unwise expenditure of reserves, issuing worthless money, and taxing an already overtaxed countryside. The only correct path was a qualitative rise in national labor productivity and a decisive struggle against unproductive expenditures.[70] It seemed that a decisive offensive against Stalin had begun. At that moment, however, the moderates received a blow that they could scarcely have foreseen.

It is difficult to reconstruct precisely what occurred in the party leadership in the middle of January 1929; it is difficult even to determine the exact sequence of events. But the basic facts are beyond doubt.

It seems that in December 1928, Stalin brought the question of deporting Trotsky from the USSR before the Politburo.* Stalin's proposal was part of the campaign he had launched against the opposition. Deprived of its leader, the left opposition was sure to lose its strength rapidly, and Trotsky's presence abroad would surely provide pretexts for compromising him and help undermine his influence and authority.[71] Stalin's schemes ran into resistance in the Politburo. Trotsky was therefore presented with an ultimatum: to end his "counterrevolutionary activities" or be completely isolated from the country's political life. When Trotsky, as was to be expected, rejected this ultimatum, Stalin was able, without too much difficulty, to obtain a definite decision from the Politburo in the middle of January 1929—despite objections from Rykov, Bukharin, and Tomsky.[72]** All these goings-on were secret; nevertheless, they became known to a certain circle of party functionaries, including some members of the opposition.[73]

At about the same time, Stalin, made a sudden about-face on the question of his policy in the countryside. He unexpectedly admitted what he had previously denied: overtaxation of the peasantry, the enormous scale of "excesses," and the danger that agricultural work as a whole could break down. The Politburo unanimously passed a resolution on tax relief for the middle peasantry.[74] It provided a significant decrease in the total agricultural tax and additional relief for peasants who made improvements on their farms and increased the area they cultivated.[75] Violations of the law were condemned harshly and threats of punishment poured forth.[76] Urgent steps were taken to ensure the spring sowing campaign and to save the harvest of 1929.[77]

---

*Evidently the English-language publication, by Trotsky's American ally Max Eastman, of *The Real Situation in Russia*, which included the opposition's 1927 platform, served as the pretext for raising this question in the Politburo.

**It was proposed that Trotsky be exiled to Turkey, with whom the Soviet Union had good relations. Trotsky resisted. In an attempt to comply with his wishes, expressed even though he was in a hopeless situation, the Soviet government at the last minute tried to arrange Trotsky's exile to Germany. The question was discussed at a meeting between Maxim Litvinov and Herbert von Dirksen, the German ambassador. Dirksen originally viewed the request favorably, but the German government decided otherwise, fearing that Trotsky's arrival in Germany would, in the final analysis, damage Soviet-German relations. Trotsky was then forcibly deported to Turkey.

At first, the moderate policy appeared to have won. This evidently accounted for the victorious tone of Bukharin's speech in connection with the anniversary of Lenin's death. Almost simultaneously, however, there occurred an event that immediately reduced the moderates' chances to nothing: the left opposition distributed a leaflet in Moscow with the text of Bukharin and Kamenev's conversation during the July 1928 plenum of the Central Committee.[78] This leaflet contained explosive material. Bukharin and Kamenev were immediately summoned to appear before Ordzhonikidze at the Central Control Commission, where they were obliged to confirm the accuracy of the text. Stalin had obtained what he needed: proof of the moderates' "factionalism," even though they had been trying in every way possible to avoid factional activity.[79]

The story of this provocation cannot be considered fully explained. The left opposition did not deny that the text was published by its supporters. The opposition even argued that its aim was to disrupt collaboration between the moderates and the Stalinists.[80] However, a fairly wide circle had known about the text of the Bukharin-Kamenev conversation and for a fairly long time; one may safely assume that the GPU and Stalin were also aware of its existence. After all, the GPU had an extensive network of agents among the oppositionists. The coincidence of the publication of this text with the decision on Trotsky's exile and the preparation of measures for the complete repression of the opposition must be noted. Stalin was the sole winner in this matter, and this inevitably raises many serious questions.

At any rate, the first result of these events was a crippling blow to the opposition. The leadership as a whole was enraged by what had happened and immediately sanctioned all possible measures for suppression of the opposition. Some members of the leadership apparently hoped to distract attention from the moderates and prevent the worst.[81] The press reported the uncovering of underground "Trotskyist" organizations.[82] A spreading wave of resolutions demanded harsh measures, and soon hundreds of oppositionists filled the prisons. The opposition departed from the scene once and for all as a serious factor in the country's political life.

The situation also changed abruptly within the party leadership: Stalin was now on the offensive. His concessions had already had their effect, enabling him once again to drive a wedge between Kalinin and Voroshilov, on the one hand, and Rykov, Bukharin, and Tomsky, on the other. At a session of the Politburo and the Central Executive Committee on January 30, 1929, the qustion of Bukharin's conduct was brought up; Rykov and Tomsky were also criticized:[83] the now famous conversation between Bukharin and Kamenev was used as a pretext. Bukharin tried to direct the question of his conduct back to the original source of the disagreements: he declared that industrialization was being carried out through a policy of "military-feudal exploitation of the peasantry," that in the Comintern a policy of "shaking up" the different sections was being pursued ("splits, breakaways, and factional groups, without a trace of [concern for] the concentration of forces"), that democracy had been eliminated in the Soviet party and a bureaucratic system of local secretaries appointed from the center had been imposed. Rykov and Tomsky supported Bukharin's statement, but the rest of the moderately-minded members of the leadership apparently held their tongues: Stalin had too many trumps in his hand.

A commission formed at the January 30 session of the Politburo proposed that Bukharin acknowledge the error of his conversation with Kamenev—Stalin was still making a sham display of softness—and renounce the statement he had made at the session. Bukharin would not agree to this. Such a solution would not improve the existing situation, but it would give Stalin the opportunity to totally restrict the activity of the moderates and take reprisals against them later on. At the next session of the Politburo and Presidium of the Central Executive Committee, on February 9, Bukharin, Tomsky, and Rykov repeated in detail their charges against Stalin. Bukharin and Tomsky refused to work further under Stalin's political course. The Stalinists were able, without any real difficulty, to pass a resolution referring the matter to the next Central Committee plenum. The position of the moderates was characterized as a "right deviation," and Bukharin's conversation with Kamenev was declared factional and "contrary to the elementary demands of honesty and simple decency." Bukharin and Tomsky's refusal to work was sharply condemned. Rykov, meanwhile, remained apart: his authority was still strong, his knowledge and experience essential. The moderates had suffered a defeat that sealed their fate.

An important phase of the inner-party struggle was over. Now Stalin not only had his own political line but had assured himself a predominant position in the party leadership. The way was open for destruction of those elements of the separation of powers that, up to that point, had characterized relations in the Politburo and provided a base for opposition to the Stalinist course.

EIGHT

The Stalinist Regime
Takes Shape

To a great extent, the events of early 1929 determined the subsequent development of the Soviet Union's political system. Stalin still faced the challenge of consolidating the fruits of his victory, but his opponents had been reduced to impotence. It is doubtful that Stalin consciously intended to create the social and state system so inseparably associated with his name. A pragmatic response to particular social situations continued to play a large role in his actions, but—because of certain features of his personality and the vast extent of his actual power—his pragmatism was now freed from many previously restraining influences.

The basic elements of the new situation, as I have shown, had already taken shape. The connecting link among these elements was Stalin's social and economic conception.

In December 1928, Kuibyshev informed the public of the proposed details of the revised five-year plan. Industrial production was to increase 250 percent by the end of the plan, reaching a level three times that of the prewar period. High rates of growth were also set for agriculture, transportation, energy, raw materials, and fuel.[1]

These proposed goals, in and of themselves, decided many things in advance. They not only reproduced but firmly entrenched Stalin's idea of a "leap forward," the main premise of his economic and social thinking. The draft five-year-plan proposed that the annual rate of increase in industrial production be maintained at the level of 1928–1929, that is, at more than 20 percent, for the entire duration of the five-year-plan.[2] Such growth rates had not been achieved for a very long time, in prerevolutionary Russia or in any other country.

A drastic increase in capital investment was projected. Compared to the preceding five years, overall investment would more than double (going, in absolute terms, from 26.5 billion rubles to 64 billion, according to the final variant of the plan), and in industry a fourfold increase was projected (from 4.4 to 16.4 billion rubles).[3] As before, the situation was further aggravated by the fact that a substantial enlargement in heavy industry's share was envisaged: the bulk of the proposed investment in industry (as much as 78 percent) was to go to heavy industry.[4]

The magnitude of capital investment unavoidably became a serious strain on the budget. It was estimated that financing the economy while increasing outlays for defense, cultural, and social purposes would swell the budget to four times its previous size.[5] Although the planning bodies expected a considerable increase in revenues from the expanding economy, there could hardly be any thought of reducing those sources of budget revenue which caused the population's standard of living to remain low. Still, all this could not produce a sufficiently large budget. Thus, a method tested during the drafting of the control figures for 1928–1929 was used again—the financial plan included high rates of improvement in the qualitative indices of production (higher productivity of labor, lower costs of production, and so on).[6] In addition, the agricultural plans were based not only on a substantial projected improvement in the material and technical base (traction power, machinery, implements, synthetic fertilizer, and so on) but also on a rapid increase in the number of state and collective farms. By the end of the planning period, they were expected to include as many as 21 million persons and 27 million hectares of cultivated land (16 percent of total grain output and 43 percent of marketable grain).[7]

The planning agencies, which employed quite a few qualified economists, must certainly have understood, at least in part, the specific consequences of the plan. They placed their hopes on certain mitigating factors. In 1928 and 1929 more and more new factories went into production and the renovation of old factories increased considerably.[8] More preconditions had come into existence for placing projected increases in output and labor productivity on a healthier foundation. High rates of growth for capital investment were projected mainly for the first years of the five-year plan; thereafter the rates would be lowered, thus reducing financial pressure on the population.[9]

At the same time, international relations were taking a new turn. In particular, relations with Britain began to improve; diplomatic relations were soon restored and a number of economic agreements signed. Economic ties with the United States also expanded, and trade talks with Germany produced results. A trend toward improvement was also observable in relations with France. The Soviet Union's tense foreign policy situation relaxed, and cracks appeared in its financial and economic isolation.[10] The ruling circles in the industrial countries, who only six months earlier had refused to lend their support to the possible victory of a moderate course in the USSR, were now ready—such is the irony of fate—to finance Stalin's despotism. The planning bodies could count on international economic cooperation on a larger scale.[11]

These mitigating factors (many of which never or only partially materialized)* did not change the basic character of the five-year plan, which firmly established an exceptionally high rate of alienation of surplus

---

*The mitigating factors did not become operative, mainly because of a feature built into Stalinist policy: the plan's targets were constantly raised; success was to be achieved

value and exploitation of labor power, along with very difficult living and working conditions for broad sections of the population. The projections, especially for the first two or three years, went beyond the bounds of what was actually possible. They ignored the USSR's extremely difficult conditions at the point when the plan went into operation.

In the last quarter of 1928 and the first quarter of 1929, despite the high degree of pressure, industry and agriculture failed to reach the targets set by the plan, nor were the goals met for the qualitative indices (higher labor productivity and lower production costs). The budget was in a difficult situation, and the provision of financial means and credit to industry was extremely irregular, with delays in the payment of wages and social benefits (although this was not a new phenomenon in Soviet life).[12] All this was worsened by the catastrophically inadequate food situation that I described earlier.

To insist on the projected targets of the five-year plan meant to assume that the rate of growth would accelerate considerably during the second half of the year. This contradicted years of experience in the Soviet Union (the second half of the year was generally marked by lower economic indicators). It was evident that even if the material resources and financial means could be found for this kind of industrial development, it would increase social tension and the use of force and coercion on such a large scale that a definite imprint would remain; not only social existence, but the public and political structure of the entire country would be permanently affected.

The character of the draft five-year plan and the reality embodied in it must have caused serious concern among the managers and officials of the central institutions. Deprived of the possibility of effective political resistance, they concentrated on making practical objections. Rykov, who had not yet lost all influence, was especially active. The State Planning Commission worked out two versions of the plan—a basic, or initial (*otpravnoi*), version and an optimum version. Both versions were oriented toward industrialization of the USSR at an accelerated (*forsirovannoe*) pace, but the basic version gave more consideration to the difficult economic situation and the especially difficult social situation in the year of transition, 1928–1929. The difference in the rates of growth was approximately 20 percent. This actually meant a delay of about one year, which was necessary in any case to avoid extraordinary difficulties.[13]

From the very beginning, the basic version was condemned to play the role of a control version; the pressure from Stalin and his supporters was extremely strong, and a number of their proposals went even beyond the

through coercion and administrative pressure. Stalin ultimately called for fulfillment of the five-year plan in four years, totally invalidating the draft of the plan, which had been worked out with much difficulty. The economic crisis that broke out in the West in the summer of 1929 again complicated the Soviet Union's economic relations with the industrial countries and at the same time increased tension internationally.

bounds of the optimum version.[14] Rykov therefore concentrated on working toward a compromise. With full justification, he warned that great caution was required during the first two or three years of the plan. He urged that those aspects of the plan essential to overcoming the economic crisis be singled out and especially favorable conditions for meeting those targets be created. This meant focusing on the achievement of a rapid upturn in grain farming and the development of those sectors of industry that could ensure the technical and agrotechnical reequipment of agriculture. Furthermore, Rykov suggested that favorable conditions be created for seriously deficient sectors of industry. Those sectors, first of all metallurgy, would be developed according to the optimum version. Other sectors could grow more slowly: using the initial version as a basis, planners could be guided by conjunctural economic conditions. Such an approach, in Rykov's opinion, had two advantages: rapid moderation of the most threatening economic disproportions, and provision of some maneuverability to the economic planning agencies—even in the event that an extremely compressed plan were adopted—thus reducing the pressure from the plan on wide sections of the population.

Like Bukharin before him, Rykov linked achievement of a substantial rise in the social productivity of labor to fundamental changes in industrial technique and technology, to raising the cultural level in production and the general level of culture and civilization in the country as a whole. He considered it most important to improve the skills and cultural qualifications of Soviet industrial workers and to bring culture and modern methods of farming to the countryside. It was only natural that science, scientific knowledge, and the work of the scientific and technical intelligentsia acquired great importance in the overall context of Rykov's thinking. After the experience of the Shakhty trial, the opinions he expressed and the instructions and orders he issued on such matters again reached the level of frank and open opposition to Stalin.

One entirely new feature appeared in Rykov's proposals. He was the first Soviet political leader to seriously consider what shape the system of national economic management should take under the conditions of an integrated, unitary, long-term plan. Rykov's thinking consisted essentially in the idea that the centralization of economic management was a condition of the period of Soviet development marked by scarcity of resources and limited, small-scale planning. With a single, well-developed plan as a basis it would become possible to relieve the all-union and union-republic planning agencies of not only a mass of minor detail but also a major part of their operational functions. These functions would be transferred to factories and local areas, freeing the hands of the central planners and allowing them to solve the fundamental questions of economic growth. In Rykov's view, the establishment of a cheap and efficient management system, reducing nonproductive administrative expenditures to the minimum, would be one of the fundamental preconditions for the success of the plan.[15]

Rykov's efforts to achieve modifications in the plans did not win substantial support within the leadership; Stalin and his supporters offered active resistance. Stalin totally rejected the essential substance of the moderate economic conception. He was not particularly inclined to listen to rational arguments even if they did not contradict the general framework of his own approach. Here another peculiarity of Stalin's political thinking became apparent: it was narrowly fixed on achieving a set goal. From his point of view, achieving the maximum version of the plan was merely a question of mobilizing material and financial resources. Since Stalin had accumulated extensive experience during 1928, when he intervened forcibly in economic and social life, he lost all respect for the mysteries of the economic process. He openly expressed his contempt for the "fetishism of doctors' robes and hidebound [zakostonelykh] textbooks".[16] In his thinking, Stalin put one factor first, one he understood and was familiar with: the "will of the party." What could be done economically was decided in a totally new way (although the war communism of the first years after the revolution served as a model)—through total mobilization of the machinery of administration and repression.

There is good reason to believe that Stalin was determined to carry out the optimum version of the plan no matter what, even to exceed it, as early as January 1928, when he was still making concessions to Kalinin and the others. Not quite two weeks after the defeat of the moderates in the Politburo, Stalin's victory was made public at the regional party conferences leading up to the all-union Sixteenth Party Conference scheduled for April 1929. Bukharin, Tomsky, and Rykov were openly and bluntly portrayed as "the main bearers of the right danger," the "right opposition" within the party.[17] In the middle of March, an unbridled press campaign against the "rightists" began, lasting a month and a half and reaching previously unparalleled proportions. The papers were filled with dozens of "very important" articles that didn't really say anything but succeeded in creating a highly charged atmosphere. The campaign quickly escalated, extending to literature, the arts, academic research, and other fields.[18] Everywhere "rightists," "traitors," and "supporters of hostile ideology" were sought and found. The term "hostility toward the party" was interpreted in an extremely loose way, even by Soviet standards; almost everything could now be subsumed under it— an unsuitable practical proposal, insufficient enthusiasm on the job or in party work, even a modest display of ordinary human decency toward victims of social discrimination.

Appearances might have indicated that this campaign was simply an

unusual method of attacking the moderates to ensure a definitive decision in Stalin's favor at the next Central Committee plenum, to which the
dispute in the Politburo had been referred. But the extent and ferocity
of the campaign revealed Stalin's true intentions. Such a widespread
campaign was not needed to permanently suppress the already weakened moderates. The campaign fit in and blended organically with the
general line of Stalin's policies. Within the context of an extremely tense
social and political situation, it made clear to the broad masses of the
population that there would be no relaxation, that the party would
remain relentlessly hard.

For an entire year there had actually been two political lines within the
Soviet Communist Party. Not only the large number of divergent interpretations of party policy but also the numerous compromises served as
visible signs of this situation, which was bound to leave its traces in
general public opinion. From Stalin's point of view, those traces had to be
wiped out and the undivided authority of his policy course asserted.
Otherwise, mobilization of all the means of administrative pressure,
discrimination, and violence would not be possible.

The effect of two party lines was inevitably reflected in intellectual life
as well. Stalin's theoretical authority was never very high during this
period; among the initiated his theoretical pretensions were noted with
irony. This corresponded to the actual state of affairs in the party. In the
eyes of most party members Stalin was an important "organizational
man" (*praktik*) and the most powerful member of the party leadership.
But the overall course of policy and its theoretical foundations were set
by Stalin's allies in the Politburo. Stalin was forced not only to tolerate
their theoretical and political authority but also to support it. Now the
situation changed completely: Stalin assumed personal responsibility for
the elaboration of the party's political line. He had an urgent need to
claim authority in his own right as a theoretician and politician; the
theoretical and political authority of his previous allies was harmful and
dangerous to him. Thus, the campaign against the "rightists," which now
supplemented the years-old campaign against the "leftists," from the
very start took the crude form of personal attacks aimed at undermining
the authority of Stalin's former allies. Much of the campaign was directed at Bukharin, whose merits in the field of theory were highly
valued by the party membership. The Central Committee apparatus
quickly surrounded Stalin with the halo of the infallible party theoretician and politician.[19] Thus, the foundations were laid for a system
featuring one sole ideological-political authority within the Soviet Communist Party, something the party had not previously known.

The methods of threatening to remove people from their jobs or put
them on trial, of monitoring party, government, and other bodies by the
GPU and the Workers' and Peasants' Inspection were more and more

universally employed. Special GPU powers were expanded to include a very broad spectrum of social life: industry, agriculture, trade, the army, and so on.[20] But even that was not enough: the campaign against "rightists" was linked with a party purge, put into effect on the basis of the decisions of the November 1928 plenum of the Central Committee and Central Control Commission. On the surface, problems of "corruption," "degeneration," and bureaucracy remained in the foreground. There was renewed discussion of the cases of drunkenness and debauchery in the party organizations of Tula, Smolensk, Sochi, Artemovsk, Kushva, and elsewhere, which had been disclosed in 1927–1928. The Stalinist method embodied in the slogan "self-criticism" remained operative. But those problems were not the heart of the matter. When Yaroslavsky, the real head of the Central Control Commission, spoke to the Moscow party membership he made it clear that there was no need for them to work themselves up over drunkenness and "family matters." The focus of attention, he said, should be the fight against the "Trotskyists" and the "rightist capitulators." A new term, "double dealing" (dvurushnichestvo), circulated very widely in the party, referring to the alleged practice of expressing public support for party policy while secretly fighting against the leadership.[21] (This laid the basis for a frame of mind that played a terrible role in the mass purges of the 1930s.) The GPU, already involved directly in the purge campaign,[22] broadened its field of activity.

At this time, there were numerous arrests of Communist Party and Komsomol members who had come into conflict with official party policy. Nonparty members had often sought close acquaintance with Communist Party members as a safeguard against misfortunes that might otherwise fall upon a person. The situation began to change: being acquainted with party members was a risk—if a party member went to prison, it was possible that groups of friends and acquaintances would follow him there, depending on the whims of the GPU.

In terrorizing not only the broad masses of the population but his own party as well, Stalin obtained an instrument necessary for realization of his economic and political aims. Society began to take on striking new features: human life lost its value and the worst forms of social bondage reappeared.

Within the new year, the problem of food supplies came very sharply to the fore. Government procurement agencies continued to extract the last remnants of grain from ruined villages, especially in Siberia, the Urals, and Kazakhastan, but even the Stalinist wing of the leadership was aware that these methods could not make up for the huge grain deficit. Figures complied on Rykov's initiative were quite eloquent: the wheat harvest was 5.3 percent less than in the preceding year of crisis, and the rye harvest, 19.7 percent less, was even worse.[23]

The purchase of foreign grain seemed unavoidable. This threatened to use up the modest foreign currency reserves of the USSR* and minimized the chance of meeting the targets for the first year of the five-year plan. Therefore, Stalin pushed the leadership for a decision against the purchase of grain from abroad.[24] This decision was cruel in its content and consequences. The available grain could not last until the next harvest. In major Soviet cities, and in Moscow beginning in March 1929, "ration books" (*zabornye knizhki*)—special certificates for the purchase of bread within the state and cooperative trade networks—were introduced. Later, such certificates were required for the purchase of certain other goods as well.[25] This system of regulating food supplies and rationing consumption, which had existed in many parts of the USSR since the spring of 1928, became universal.

The full cruelty of Stalin's decision became evident in another connection. Because the government did not have enough food to meet the needs of the entire country, it concentrated on saving the cities (and the army, of course), its bases of support. Wide sections of the population, mainly the peasantry and "nonworking elements," were completely cut from the state's food provisioning system. Destitute villages were left to their fate. In some areas, the peasants had nowhere to turn. They ate whatever they found. Cattle were slaughtered, since no feed remained for them.[26] Reports of incipient famine came from a growing number of villages. Again, the rural poor were hardest hit. In the spring, rumors reached the foreign press of peasants starving to death in northeast Russia and the southern Ukraine. Similar rumors came even from the well-to-do farm communities of German settlers in the Volga region.[27] How things stood in other famine-struck regions is not known; no foreigners chanced to visit them. The fact remains that because of Stalin's policies, the Russian muzhik, the Ukrainian peasant, and the German colonist were all starving long before the tragic famine of 1932–1933.

The cities did not remain unaffected. That ration books would not mean reduced food quotas, that they were introduced solely to prevent food returning to rural regions from urban ones, was a promise that was not kept. The government treated the famished condition of the population with small doses in order to prevent the outbreak of open resistance. Consumption quotas were steadily reduced. Speculation and illicit trading in grain flourished; the GPU could not cope with them. According to Rykov, private market prices soared in the spring of 1929, with increases, depending on the region, of between 400 and 1,000 percent.[28] Prices

---

*Kalinin later spoke of the need to spend foreign currency reserves on a scale of 40–60 million rubles for grain. The Soviet Union's foreign trade balance improved slightly only in October 1928, after a long unfavorable period. The figure of 40–60 million rubles was given, of course, only to reassure public opinion. In 1928, a better year, the USSR spent 20–30 million rubles on grain from abroad. In 1929, as I have indicated, the deficit in grain supplies, compared to 1928, was 2.66 million tons. (See note 24.)

charged by illegal speculators were even higher. The Soviet population's standard of living, which had dropped sharply in 1928, plummeted.

Food was undoubtedly the most serious and important problem in 1929 and after. The logical consequence of Stalin's economic policy—famine—stood out most sharply in this area. Not as obvious, but no less vital were certain changes in the general pattern of social life. Pushing the country forward and imposing miserable conditions to realize or even exceed the optimum version of the plan immediately increased the scope and intensity of social pressure. No longer did such pressure come only from the traditional effort to obtain revenues for the government; it was expressed directly in altered social relations in the sphere of production.

In January 1929, the campaign to "tighten up labor discipline" was intensified. *Pravda* ran thundering articles on the subject. The "proletarian party" was no longer ashamed to publicly brand Soviet workers as loafers, drunkards, dawdling bums, and rowdies.[29] New letters of instruction were sent to local areas. In the name of the Politburo, Rykov informed local functionaries that the leadership was thoroughly determined to resort to draconian measures. The leaders of industry were threatened—for the umpteenth time—with dire punishment.[30]

Labor discipline was poor. The resistance of the workers had not been broken. (An influx of people from rural areas, unaccustomed to factory work, further complicated matters.) But labor discipline was not the root of the problem. Compared to the general living and working conditions, the internal regimen of the factories was relatively free. Some of the gains of the revolution survived here, buttressed by the fact that workers were the main social base of the government. It was difficult, in fact impossible, to "discipline" the workers without eradicating this freedom. The campaign for increased work productivity served exactly that purpose because it was quickly followed by a series of repressive measures: the principle of one-man management in the factories was institutionalized, and the unions were deprived of any voice in the appointment of personnel (February 2, 1929); management was given the right to impose punishments and dismiss workers unilaterally, without consulting with the unions (March 6, 1929); the Central Trade Union Council ordered local union bodies to make sure that the expanded rights of management were honored and to support all management efforts to tighten labor discipline (March 26,1929); the People's Commissariat of Justice prohibited the courts from accepting workers' complaints about improper punishments and firings—exceptions were strictly limited (March 17, 1929); the Central Trade Union Council decreed that it would refuse to defend workers in court (March 26, 1929), and so on. This attack against workers' rights was reinforced by threats of reprisal against management and union bodies in cases of leniency.[31]

The degree of exploitation of the workers rapidly intensified. This was reflected in the improved statistical indices for the quality of production (prime cost and labor productivity), while the plan's purely formal targets for wage increases and higher living standards were not met.[32] By the end of the fiscal year, the authorities resorted to a new measure. In addition to "broken shifts,"* which were already quite widely used, a "permanent work week" was introduced in industry. By virtually eliminating the workers' leisure time, the government obtained another sixty workdays per year.**

Serious changes continued to occur in the countryside. The famished condition of the peasants, the result of Stalin's grain procurement policies, meant lower productivity in agricultural labor. After the poor results of the autumn sowing season, there was a growing danger that the spring sowing would also fail. At the same time, because the goals of the autumn sowing were not met, the areas sowed in the spring had to be enlarged well beyond the originally projected 7 percent increase.[33] The reduced size of the cattle herd added to the problem.

The countryside lacked seed, traction power, machinery, and agricultural tools. As a special measure, the government hurriedly released funds to purchase the supplies essential to agricultural production; a special commissar for the spring sowing was appointed (People's Commissar of Agriculture N. A. Kubyak).†[34] These measures by themselves could not change the situation. The real reason for the difficulties lay with the condition of the peasantry, who had had to starve through the winter and spring. It was hardly possible to guarantee that the assigned resources would be used as intended. (In some regions there was a serious danger that seed grain would either be eaten or fed to the cattle.)[35] Moreover, to a large extent the funds that had been released had to be used for restoring the ruined basis of production.

The mechanisms of NEP in the village had been shattered, and the government saw no other solution than to further extend administrative control over the peasantry. The power apparatus was strengthened, and more and more urban activists arrived in the countryside to help ensure the fulfillment of various tasks. The enlarged areas that the peasants were to cultivate were prescribed for them by the village soviets.[36] The system of "contracting out" the next year's harvest (*kontraktatsia*) was greatly expanded, definitively harnessing the peasant to the chariot of the state. In official reports, the thesis of a positive change in the middle

*This means separated shifts. They were established so that machinery and equipment would continue operating during the three hours that were not used in the daily schedule of three seven-hour shifts. An employee working the "broken shift" system had to clock in twice to complete one shift.
**Sunday was abolished as a day of rest, and workers were assigned their day off at various times during the week, so that production would continue uninterrupted.
†This office was first created during the 1927–1928 sowing campaign.

peasant's attitude toward the collective farm was promoted ever more insistently.[37] The growth of collective farms exceeded the projections of the plan, and the authorities began to say that the five-year plan's targets for the socialization of agriculture would be exceeded significantly.[38] The system of supplying villages with machinery was revised. Expanded introduction of state-owned machinery and tractor stations (MTSs) was envisaged: a large part of the new traction power and equipment for agricultural tasks remained in the hands of the state; this equipment represented a means of influencing agricultural production. All this laid the basis for the future reconstruction of agriculture. However, a parallel and more rapid process was under way that cost the peasants their independence; their power to freely dispose of the product of their labor was infringed upon, as were many aspects of their productive activity and daily life. The extremely high degree of exploitation of the village that developed during 1928 was consolidated on a long-term basis. The power the new instruments of administrative control held over the peasants is best shown by the fact that the state was able—not without reviving extraordinary measures—to fully meet the grain procurement plan by January 1, 1930, that is, as early as the new fiscal year. In the second half of the fiscal year, of course, the giant repressive apparatus was hastily reassigned to the task of ensuring the success of the mass collectivization campaign.

The social tension in the country did not lessen. "Life has become intolerable," a contemporary wrote. "The man in the street is expecting a repetition of the year 1919; he hoards as much as he can. . . . At the market and in the waiting lines people curse the government; everything is blamed on the Jews. . . . The anti-Semitism is enormous."[39] The system of repression developed rapidly and included all the various elements of violence and social manipulation. Arrests became a mass phenomenon, affecting entire categories of persons.[40] The state acted increasingly on a preventive social principle: individuals were not persecuted because of political activity but because they belonged to a certain social group. This principle was also expressed in civil and social discrimination on an enormous scale.[41] Signs of any nationalist tendencies were brutally smothered; mass arrests took place, especially in the Ukraine.[42] Terror reigned in the village. Peasant resistance was answered with stepped-up persecution of "kulaks" and "kulak supporters," and an increasing number of peasant "terrorists" were executed. A new idea was in the air: mass dekulakization and resettlement of large groups of peasants to remote areas.[43] Violence was also directed more and more frequently against the workers. In early 1929, for example, a series of public trials were held involving "hooligan" workers. Workers were also blamed for anti-Semitism; several show trails were held, where charges of anti-Semitism were brought against groups of workers as well as a few industrial officials.

Intensified class-struggle attitudes were whipped up; the blame for all the difficulties was heaped on speculators and capitalist elements. The politicans were very reluctant to acknowledge the evident improvement in the Soviet Union's international situation. They preferred the tense atmosphere of a besieged fortress. Speeches and reports included the assertion that "the danger of imperialist war and a direct attack on the USSR is becoming more and more immediate."[44]

Skillful propaganda methods were used to incite the workers against the peasants. Yet the real situation in the villages was carefully concealed; knowledge of it reached the workers only in roundabout ways. At the same time, the peasants continued to be held responsible for the food crisis. They were said to have refused to sell grain and to be buying up large quantities of flour and bread on urban markets to feed their cattle.* They were even blamed for the lack of wage increases for workers: because of excessive procurement prices, it was said, the funds needed for wage increases had been drawn off into the pockets of the wealthier upper crust of village society.[45]

The hounding of specialists was intensified—somebody had to be made responsible for the difficult conditions faced by industrial workers. Official publications contained such comments as that the years 1928–1929 had "revealed to us all the main hiding places and nests of the wreckers in industry."**[46] The authorities also made the first modest attempts to "mobilize the moral factor," artificially initiating socialist competition among the workers on a mass basis.

Stalin moved quickly to consolidate the victory of his policy over that of the moderates. The joint plenum of the Central Committee and Central Control Commission, and the Sixteenth Party Conference—both held in April 1929—gave full approval to the optimum version of the five-year plan and even raised its targets in some respects. Bukharin and Tomsky lost their posts and a short time later were dropped from the party's Politburo as well. Rykov was demonstratively removed from his position as the chairman of the Sovnarkom of the RSFSR and replaced by a Stalin protégé, the Siberian party secretary S.I. Syrtsov. (After serving in this post for a year and a half, Syrtsov himself was made

---

*There could have been cases of such buying. The disproportionately low prices for grain and bread in urban areas tended to promote such things. But of course, that was not the heart of the problem.
**The most notorious case involved two transport specialists, M. K. Fon-Meck and A. F. Velichko, and a specialist in the gold and platinum industry, P. A. Palchinsky, a former minister of the Provisional Government. They were shot in May 1929 on the basis of a ruling by the GPU Collegium under charges equivalent to those brought in the Shakhty case. The authorities apparently could not bring themselves to hold a public trial; the consequences of the Shakhty affair, an experience that was still very fresh, prevented them.

out to be an "antiparty conspirator.")[47] Stalin could not bring himself to remove Rykov from his post as chairman of the Council of People's Commissars of the USSR; apparently the possibility of replacing him with Molotov or someone else still seemed absurd to Stalin—Rykov was removed in 1930.

Through concentrated measures and enormous pressure, the planning targets were met more successfully in the second half of 1929. If the official statistics can be believed, industry overfulfilled its yearly production plan, and the area sown to grain was said to have increased as well—although contemporaries familiar with the situation firmly maintained that the opposite was true. Contrary to all optimistic reassurances by officials, the difficult food-supply situation continued to build toward disaster. A few years later, the disaster struck with full fury, taking the lives of millions of peasants.

The essential structure of the Stalin regime was now in place. Rumors that Stalin was mentally ill, that he had simply gone out of his mind, circulated in Moscow—thirty years later similar rumors would inspire the official Soviet critics of Stalinism. Some of his contemporaries equated Stalin's rule with the cruelest periods of medieval times.[48] They were exaggerating, however. The USSR was merely entering the most tragic phase of its postrevolutionary history.

NINE

The Phenomenon of Stalinism

I have reviewed the process of the formation of Stalinism, of its central sociopolitical conception, and of important elements of the Stalinist regime and system in the critical years 1927 to 1929. Of course, the development of Stalinism was not completed at that time, but this book is limited to the period of its beginnings.

Observers have always been struck by the extreme cruelty of Stalinism, the monstrous extent and apparent irrationality of its methods of terror and mass extermination, and the absolute character of Stalinist totalitarianism and political dictatorship. This is apparently why one finds so many references in the literature to its arbitrariness or to aspects of Stalinism that cannot be accounted for in any precise way. These aspects include, for example, the peculiarities of Stalin's personality, his character, and his personal and political motives; but also certain specific aspects of socialism, of the socialist world outlook, theory, and ideology and their effects on society; and certain features of the Russian national character, Russian history, the Russian national political tradition, and so on. I cannot deny the importance of such factors, but they are not the heart of the problem; they simply fill out the picture with particular features and circumstances.

The key consideration in any attempt to understand Stalinism—as I have tried to demonstrate in detail in the preceding chapters,—is that it was not a product of positive social development or the positive development of a social doctrine or conception, but the result of a deep and all-embracing crisis; it evolved as a special kind of instrument or means of finding a way out of this crisis. Such situations generally do not lead to favorable changes in social relations or bring out the positive aspects of political and social systems. This has been proven a number of times in the last few decades of world history.

The tendency to view the problems of Russian and Soviet history as those of a country modernizing and industrializing at an accelerated rate holds a prominent place in Soviet studies literature, especially in the United States. Such literature has provided a wealth of material to explain not only various aspects of the Soviet system but also similar phenomena in other countries. It has also made important contributions to the analysis of the essential content of the economic and social crisis that led to the rise of Stalinism.

From a more general point of view, the problem of Stalinism must not be formulated simply as the problem of a society taking the road of accelerated development toward industrial civilization and therefore using the instruments of state power on a very large scale. It is far more the problem of a people's revolution and its consequences in a country that had already made a certain amount of progress on the road of accelerated development and was forced to continue along this road after the victory of the revolution.

The October revolution—or the revolution of 1917 as a whole—was essentially a plebeian revolution that, despite the powerful role still played by remnants of the traditional economic and social order, resulted in the implementation of a whole series of popular demands and aspirations such that the previous forms of industrial civilization were obliterated. This meant enormous material and cultural losses, although here again it is essential to recall the extremely destructive effect of the wars that took up six full years of Russian and Soviet history (1914–1920). For a period of between ten and fifteen years (from 1914–1917 to 1927), virtually no progress was made on the tasks of accelerated development. (What essentially occurred was the destruction of the economy, followed by its restoration to the prewar level.) The result was that the magnitude of unsatisfied needs grew enormously, becoming the main cause of the crisis and demanding an exceptionally intense mobilization of social forces and resources.

But these circumstances were complicated by another aspect of the consequences of October 1917. In carrying out a program of social change, the revolution not only destroyed the old mechanisms of industrial growth but, along with them, the social preconditions for those mechanisms. Without trying to enter into the complicated, yet extremely important, problems involved in the organization of the state-owned sector of the economy and the functioning of the mechanisms of the market, I must point to two pertinent problems. First, ties between the Russian and world economies, especially those of the leading industrial nations, were sharply curtailed because of the October revolution, as I have pointed out. This substantially reduced the resources available for financing industrial growth and the influx of modern industrial technology, equipment, and scientific know-how, factors that previously played a significant part in Russia's industrial development. Foreign resources had to be replaced from within the Soviet Union, which significantly increased the burden on an ailing society and economy.

A second factor was no less important: the entire structure of agrarian relations was reorganized after the revolution, which threw off the balance between industrial and agrarian production. Significant disparities arose between industry and agriculture in their methods of functioning and rates of growth, making cooperation and coordination between them difficult. I have shown the consequences this had. To restore the agricultural-industrial balance was not easy; the achievement of such a balance before the revolution had been difficult enough. The imbalance evidently would have persisted for many years, during which industry would have been forced in one way or another to "wait" for agriculture.

The crisis in the USSR exerted a powerful pressure to mobilize the forces and resources of Soviet society and also to reorganize existing economic structures and social relations (such as the introduction of collective and state farms, the new regimen for labor in industry, and so on). The general state of the productive forces and the conditions necessary for raising the productivity of social labor could not, however, guarantee that this reorganization would have the desired effect on production. The reorganization became secondary to the administrative mobilization of resources, intensified growth in purely administrative forms of economic management, contributing to the emergence of an all-embracing system of state control over society.

The content of the crisis determined its possible consequences: in order to surmount it, all possible forms of oppression were increased substantially, which undermined the essential gains of the October revolution, its very meaning and substance. There arose a growing danger of social counterrevolution in special forms that would remain within the framework of the regime. The crisis also accelerated the social evolution going on within the power structure, shaping the deepening conflict of interest between that structure and broad sections of the population.

Stalinism arose from the social background and historical context of the postrevolutionary crisis. The crisis was unfolding in a country emerging from a period of very severe social upheaval, and the new order was still clothed in tenuous forms that could easily be torn apart. All traditional standards of human communal existence, the entire previous scale of values, had been destroyed; new ones were just arising. The system of social relations was also unstable; it had not yet taken root.

I have said that crisis situations everywhere, not only in the USSR, create the danger of unfavorable changes in the social and political system. In the USSR, a rather harsh political dictatorship already existed at the end of the 1920s. During the period of the New Economic Policy, this dictatorship abandoned the worst extremes of revolutionary times, but those extremes had not faded into the distant past. There had not been time to erase them from the thoughts and actions of the social stratum that wielded power. From the very beginning, therefore, the development of the crisis inevitably entailed the danger of an extreme revival of all the violent methods of the first postrevolutionary years.

The rise of Stalinism was not the only possible result of these events. The accumulation of negative features in the social and political system of the USSR was hardly avoidable, but prompt political intervention could probably have reduced their severity. For a number of reasons—

most of which I have discussed above—official Soviet politics did not recognize in time the great danger of the crisis that was brewing. Instead, a number of actions helped deepen it.

Intensive efforts to solve the crisis were undertaken only when it had entered its most severe stage, bringing the country to the verge of economic, social, and political collapse. This created fertile soil in which the most radical and unhealthy solutions could thrive. Stalin's independent political conception was one result of the crisis, which influenced the direction and ultimate form that Stalin's thought would take. The crisis also brought together the forces that were to become the vehicles of extremist solutions. The social pressure exerted on the broadest sections of the population far exceeded all imaginable limits, bringing all the negative tendencies to a head and greatly increasing their number. Stalinism became a reality.

The aspects of the formation of the Stalinist system that I have reviewed are extremely important. In describing Stalinism, the literature has assigned a major role to political repression and terror. This is fully explicable: the phenomena of political terror were the most visible aspect of Stalinism and penetrated the consciousness of contemporaries on a wide scale. Additionally, the terror in daily life was generally explained politically, carried out on the basis of certain political articles in the penal code, and became an inseparable part of every political campaign. It was implied that the terror directed against society was political in nature, while the true nature of Stalinism remained concealed. While political terror played an important role, the real core of Stalinism—as Aleksandr Solzhenitsyn has demonstrated convincingly—was social terror, the most brutal and violent treatment of very wide sections of the population, the subjection of millions to exploitation and oppression of an absolutely exceptional magnitude and intensity.

The social function of terror and repression explains the apparent irrationality, senselessness, and obscure motivation of Stalin's penal system. As a social instrument, terror could not be aimed narrowly, at particular persons. It was an instrument of violent change, affecting the living and working conditions of millions, imposing the very worst forms of social oppression, up to and including the slave labor of millions of prisoners. Even when it took on the outward appearance of political terror, it continued as a social instrument. Indeed, political repression only supplemented social repression. Thus, it remained as inexplicable and senseless in individual (political) cases as in its main field of operations, social relations.*

I have not dealt with the character of the social stratum that served as

*Within this framework, political terror was aimed at individuals, opponents of the system in general as well as opponents of Stalin's regime or Stalin himself. Political terror continued to have significance as a social instrument even though the functions it fulfilled

the Stalinist system's vehicle. This problem, expecially of the bureaucracy's growth and function, has been the subject of many works,
from Trotsky to Djilas and others. This issue would have required a
different choice of subject matter, organization of material, and form of
presentation than I chose. Moreover, I could hardly have done justice to
a question of such magnitude on the basis of the brief historical period I
selected, covering only a few years.

Nevertheless, there can be no doubt that implementation of Stalin's
program required the existence of a ruling social stratum, separated
from the people and hostilely disposed toward it. In this regard, a
certain aspect of the political struggle within the Soviet Communist Party
necessarily deserves attention. Those groups removed from the leadership had spoken against the social tendencies of Stalinism. This pattern represented a fundamental principle of political selection: elements
within the ruling stratum that tried to represent or even consider the
interests of the people were suppressed. This can be seen clearly enough
in the positions of the left opposition and in the essential objections the
moderates raised against Stalin's conception of "building socialism" in
the USSR. From this point of view, then, Stalinism appears as a regime
with a sharply expressed social character based on inequality and priv-
ilege.

The picture that can be reconstructed on the basis of the available
material does not confirm the argument that Stalinism was accidental. In
this connection, I must comment on the interpretation of Stalinism that
reduces the problem of its origin to the peculiarities of Stalin's character,
his political mistakes, and certain external circumstances in the Soviet
Union's development during the 1920s and 1930s. This point of view is
represented primarily by official Soviet historiography—insofar as it
deals with the problems of Stalinism at all—but it also appears in a
number of "dissident" Communist writings, for example, Roy Medvedev's interesting work *Let History Judge*. Such an interpretation is
purely apologetic; it ignores the question of social background. Stalin is
sacrificed to save the reputation of the social and political system he
created. However, the Stalin of 1926 was not the Stalin of 1929, neither
in the general nature of his politics—above all, his conception of social
and economic relations—nor in the type of practical solutions he proposed. While I fully acknowledge the undeniable fact that Stalin left the
mark of his personality on the evolving pattern of Soviet life, at the same
time, I cannot fail to stress that the new crisis situation in the USSR and
the substance of the problems it posed strongly influenced Stalin; this is

differed from those of mass terror: it was used to reorganize the power structure, change
the composition of the ruling stratum as a whole, and break continuity with the revolutionary period. This corresponded to the change in the general character of the social and
economic structures that I have already discussed.

true of his personal role in the system as well as his individual personality traits.

A general characterization of Stalinism cannot be exhausted, of course, by an account of its initial phase. Once it came into existence, Stalinism acquired its own internal dynamic. The blocks laid in its foundation served as preconditions for its functioning and produced similar results for many years. The nature of the tasks performed by the Stalin regime changed with time. The external (foreign-policy) functions of the system (consolidating the USSR's position as one of the leading powers in the world) gained increasing importance, especially in the postwar period, and with that change the social content of the Stalinist system changed. But until Stalin's death in 1953, Stalinism remained a system with a unique and distinctive structure: an all-embracing totalitarianism which, in the political arena, turned into the despotic rule of a dictator whose power was absolute; a system of massive preventive terror and repression, derived from social relations whose character was defined by the mechanisms of the economy; a system of violent suppression of all contradictions in society, ruling out any expression of ideological or political disagreement or difference.

Stalinism should not be given too broad an interpretation as a historical phenomenon. It is wrong to apply it as a label to other forms of political dictatorship, totalitarianism, and repression that have developed on a different basis and in a different historical setting. In this regard, I must refer again to the interpretations of Stalinism as a general phenomenon, essentially rooted in the socialist movement and resulting from the attempt to apply principles of socialist theory, or simply from the general influence that socialist ideology and the socialist world outlook have had.

To be sure, Stalinism was not restricted to the USSR. After World War II, it spread to a number of other countries. But these are primarily cases of "exported Stalinism." Relying on certain international conditions, "exported Stalinism" has undoubtedly created an economic, social, and political base for itself. Nevertheless, this is hardly a convincing argument in a discussion of the theoretical roots of Stalinism.

The real key to the problem of the recurrence of Stalinism in other countries evidently lies—as I have said—in the circumstances and tasks faced by some countries developing their economies at an accelerated pace, a situation similar to that faced by the USSR. It is also important to consider the fact that while the Stalinist system and structure were taking shape, more than thirty years experience in accelerated industrial growth was accumulated. Leaving aside the serious social problems accompanying this growth, Soviet industrialization was, on the whole, quite dynamic. This bestowed a certain authority on a whole series of Stalinist decisions, providing a basis for attempts to reproduce them. One may, however, seriously question whether such a reproduction by itself could cause the replication of the Stalinist system.

THE PHENOMENON OF STALINISM

I do not mean to say that there is no substantial basis for questioning the role of socialist theory and ideology in the history of Stalinism. Socialist ideology, or what is understood in the Soviet Union as socialist ideology, has been the ruling ideology for nearly seventy years, the only permissible doctrine, supported by all the resources of the state. Socialist theory played a significant role in the development of the outward forms of the economic, social, and state system in the USSR. Present-day antisocialist and anti-Communist views, especially those coming from the East, reflect a concrete (institutionalized) experience of the negative sides of Soviet history, a desire to destroy the theoretical foundations of Stalinism, and a fear of the possible further spread of Stalinism in the world.

Yet the political and emotional reasons for the antisocialist reaction against Stalinism in Eastern Europe do not change the essence of the problem. Those who support the view that the roots of Stalinism are found in the extremely destructive consequences of the application of socialist theory, in the influence of socialist ideology, or in the socialist movement itself, must first prove the correctness of at least the following premises: (1) that the Soviet system, including Stalinism, developed on the basis of a socialist revolution; in other words, that the October revolution was a socialist revolution, that it was such in its objective preconditions, in the social composition of its driving forces, and in the degree of maturity of those forces, and not only in the nature of the ideology and ideas of the leading party; (2) that the ideology of Stalinism as well as the ideology of today's "existing socialism"* is in its content, its methods and methodology, and its social functions identical or close to the original content of socialism; and (3) that in the development of the Soviet Union, socialist theory had priority over pragmatism in regard to the aims and tasks pursued by those in power. It is my experience and my conviction that these three premises are not provable.

I am not seeking, under all circumstances, to shield socialist beliefs, theory, and ideology from reproach. In fact, in the 1980s it is difficult to speak of socialism as a uniform phenomenon. Socialism has been fragmented into an entire spectrum of factions and tendencies that perform the most varied functions. When I speak of socialism, I have in mind primarily Marxism in its original social meaning, as well as those tendencies that have carried on this tradition. In the 1980s, it is hard to deny that this variety of socialism, with its theoretical and ideological constructs, suffers from a number of weak points. Socialism's main weakness is that no matter how strong it might be in the realm of social criticism, it has, to a considerable extent, shown itself to be helpless and utopian in its positive programs, its plans for attaining its social ideals. This weakness, apparently, was one of the main reasons for the strong influence of

*The term "existing socialism" is often used in Soviet official jargon for the present-day system in the USSR and Eastern Europe.—Trans.

the October revolution, and, later, of Stalinism on the ideological and theoretical conceptions and politics of radical socialist, especially communist, tendencies outside the Soviet Union. This influence was later reinforced by political, organizational, and material relations with the USSR. However, the high point of such influence has passed and has been left well behind, at least in Europe.

Socialism, in its original meaning, should not be confused with Stalinism. These two systems of ideas are not only different; in many respects they are diametrically opposed. The irreplaceable, unique function of socialism is its role as the most fully developed, complete theory and ideology of social criticism in modern times. This has made socialism the natural basis for social movements among broad sections of the population in many countries. No other contemporary ideology has succeeded in performing this function without borrowing the essential content of socialism. This is one of the key reasons why socialists in the West and democratic antisocialists from the East experience great difficulty in finding a common language.

Present-day "dissident" thought in the East, especially in the USSR, has leaned more and more distinctly toward various forms of antisocialism. As I have said, this trend is, to a certain extent, understandable. The result is, however, that the social function of socialism has remained unfulfilled there. This situation has fatal consequences. One of the real and urgent tasks in the Eastern countries is the revival of social criticism as the essential content of socialist thought, and the consistent demarcation of this body of thought from Stalinism and "existing socialism." The rebirth of socialism in the East, the revival of the socialist movement and the social movement—which have been stifled and suppressed, shot down and broken apart—could only help to improve and democratize the conditions of life there and serve as an effective weapon against surviving Stalinist elements. This follows quite logically from everything I have said about the social basis of the Stalin regime.

APPENDIXES

APPENDIX I

Documents

LIST OF DOCUMENTS

1. Letter from J. V. Stalin to the Central Committee, November 11, 1927. Enclosure: Report of V. R. Menzhinsky, November 10, 1927.   123
2. Letter from J. V. Stalin to the Central Committee (undated, but apparently from November or December 1927).   126
3. Letter from J. V. Stalin to the Politburo and Central Committee, December 27, 1927.   128
4. Excerpts from the speeches of V. R. Menzhinsky and V. V. Kuibyshev at a Politburo session in late January 1928.   133
5. Letter from M. M. Litvinov, deputy people's commissar of foreign affairs, to diplomatic representatives of the USSR, February 9, 1928.   138
6. Resolution of the USSR Council of People's Commissars, March 2, 1928.   142
7. Letter from A. I. Rykov to V. R. Menzhinsky, March 12, 1928.   145
8. Letter from G. V. Chicherin to V. R. Menzhinsky, March 13, 1928.   147
9. Letter from N. A. Kubyak to A. I. Rykov and J. V. Stalin, March 19, 1928.   149
10. Letter of instructions (*direktivnoe pismo*) from G. K. Ordzhonikidze to local bodies of the Workers' and Peasants' Inspection, March 23, 1928.   150
11. Letter of instructions from M. I. Kalinin and A. I. Rykov, March 22, 1928.   151

AUTHOR'S NOTE:

The documents presented here have been taken from secret reports that were forwarded in late 1927 and early 1928 to Herbert von Dirksen, ministerial director at the German Foreign Ministry (Auswärtiges Amt). (In the fall of 1928 Dirksen became German ambassador to Moscow.) The complete German-language texts are preserved in the Political Archive of the Foreign Ministry (Politisches Archiv des Auswärtigen Amtes) of the Federal Republic of Germany, under the designation Geheimakten (Secret Documents), 1920–1936, Abteil IV Ru, Po 2, Adh. I: russische Geheimdokumente, vols. 1–4. I have not succeeded in finding the Russian originals of the documents. For this reason, the documents have been translated from the German versions and therefore may diverge in some ways from the original Russian texts.

I.

The General Secretary of the Communist Party
Moscow, the Kremlin. November 11, 1927
Secret.

To the Central Committee of the Bolshevik Party
Copy to the President of the Central Control Commission, Comrade
Ordzhonikidze

On the whole the celebrations went smoothly.[1] There were some isolated,
insignificant disturbances in Moscow and some more serious conflicts in
Leningrad. From Kharkov and Kiev have come reports of smaller demonstrations directed against the Central Committee. As we can now confirm on the
basis of incontestable evidence, an uprising was definitely planned by the opposition for the period from the 6th to the 8th [of November]—in order to seize
power. The farsighted and energetic measures taken by Comrades Voroshilov
and Menzhinsky are to be credited first of all for the fact that the opposition, in
view of these actions, suspended its plans at the last minute, since—as we were
told by a contact person in the opposition—a coup attempt had become hopeless
in the face of the measures that had been taken. On the other hand, we have
reports from many different sources, independent of one another, that even
though the plan was postponed, it was not abandoned altogether. Therefore, we
must take into account the possibility that at any time there might be an unexpected move by the opposition with the aim of seizing power. Although Comrade Menzhinsky has taken all necessary measures with [his] accustomed
thoroughness, we must remain at our posts nonetheless in order to crush from
the outset any possible blows unexpectedly directed against us.
    The interests of the party demand that now, after all the patience we have
shown, the opposition must be eliminated once and for all. The international
situation also makes decisive measures against the opposition necessary. Even
today, in London and Washington the view is held that our present government
is on the verge of collapse, that the opposition is about to take the helm, and that,
therefore, it is pointless to conclude any agreements with us. The seriousness of
the economic situation demands that we show the world that this view of the
opposition's strength is completely wrong and that the opposition leaders are
really nothing but generals without armies. The opposition's collaboration with
avowed counterrevolutionary organizations in other countries is a proven fact,
and if the opposition does not give up its fight as hopeless, we must not hesitate
to expel from the party all of their leading figures even before the party
congress.[2]
    In order to document and underline the seriousness of the situation, I enclose
a report by Comrade Menzhinsky.

                                                            signed: Stalin

Enclosure:
The President of the GPU
November 10, 1927

    Even though the anniversary celebrations seem, on the surface, to have gone
smoothly, we can by no means indulge in illusions or false hopes. The fact that an
elaborately planned insurrection was being considered, including numerous
assassination attempts, with the aim of overthrowing the workers' and peasants'
government, has been established beyond all question. The reports from our
numerous contact people about the preparations for the rising, of secret telephone installations in every city district, of street patrols that were to maintain
contact with these telephone communications centers, have by now been confirmed beyond question. I called attention to these facts at the appropriate time
although several leading figures in the party, with unjustified optimism, seriously
spoke of my statements as being exaggerated. Nevertheless, we have irrefutable

proof that the projected coup was called off only at the last minute, and only—it seems—on the advice of Trotsky himself because of the unlikelihood of success. Had we not taken extraordinarily wide-ranging countermeasures, the coup would have been attempted—whether with success or not will not be discussed here. At the same time, we have reliable information that from the very beginning Trotsky was against a coup attempt during the anniversary celebrations, and based his view on the argument that such timing would be extremely unfavorable, that one could not expect success at a moment when we were mobilizing all our forces. The same contact persons mentioned above, whose reports about an intended coup proved to be accurate, now say that while the combat organization[3] has postponed the coup, it has not abandoned the idea for good.

There are several reports from sources independent of one another, according to which the combat organization issued a secret order explicitly indicating that in view of the extensive countermeasures taken by us, the plans for insurrection were canceled as hopeless but only in order that they might be successful at a later time, when we would be unprepared, and the balance of forces more favorable. In this order, which referred to the insurrection as an action to take place during the anniversary celebrations, it was indicated that the first thing to be done was to occupy the Kremlin, the GPU building, the main telegraph office, and the radio stations. The rail lines to and from Moscow were to be destroyed at various points to make the transfer of reliable troops from the provinces more difficult or even impossible. Similar actions were to be undertaken in Leningrad and Kharkov at the same time as in Moscow.

In this secret report of the combat organization it is further stated that propaganda among the workers and in the Workers' and Peasants' Army should continue by all possible means until further orders. Especially in the army. The destructive effect of this propaganda in the army, I have already pointed out many times—though, unfortunately, not always with the desired results. The events in Leningrad on November 7 must be viewed as very serious from the point of view of the morale of the troops.[4] We must not delude ourselves at all about the fact that this was not an isolated occurrence, and that the state of affairs in the Ukraine, as comrades Balitsky and Yakir unanimously report, is not any better.

We must therefore expect, in the time immediately ahead, that opposition propaganda will be at least as vigorous as it has been until now. It will be directed first of all, judging from the present state of affairs, at subverting the army. Comrade Voroshilov has acknowledged to me without question the pernicious effect of the opposition slogans. The present difficult economic situation and the interruptions in food supply quite naturally encourage such propaganda.

If, in the future, we tolerate this propaganda at its present level, we will be committing an act of unforgivable lightmindedness, and I must again call special attention to the consequences of such action. The events in Leningrad quite obviously show that the seditious propaganda of the opposition has affected even the lower levels of the command staff and in the event of a decisive battle their reliability is very much in question. It makes me very sad to have to assert here, in this place, that the army today, unlike before, has already been partly contaminated and that the commanders now are often not reliable in the full sense of the word. Comrade Voroshilov is thoroughly aware of the seriousness of the situation and fully shares my pessimistic mood.

We must be completely clear about the fact that the interests of the workers' and peasants' government can continue to be protected only so long as we can continue to rely on the unconditional loyalty of the Workers' and Peasants' Army. If this is no longer the case, we face an entirely different situation.

In my various reports I have repeatedly pointed to the disagreements among opposition supporters. There is a widespread view—which I too uphold and am hereby representing—that the opposition movements on the whole would not be by any means so large and dangerous if we were to eliminate the leaders in question all together, at one stroke. I believe that I can say with certainty that in the case where we were to eliminate these leaders from one day to the next, the movement as such would disappear by itself. I understand completely the thinking expressed by the Central Committee, and in particular by comrades Stalin and Bukharin, against any premature move to render the opposition leaders harmless. I fully grant that the first impression in Western Europe, if we eliminated the opposition leaders at one blow, might be quite unfavorable. I grant that foreign Social Democracy would take advantage of these measures of ours to make propaganda against us on the largest scale. Once again, however, we must not forget that the Communist press abroad orients the masses along the same lines as the thinking of our party's Central Committee. Reluctance and softness must for these reasons be set aside, and also because of the fact that the opposition is arming itself for a decisive struggle.

Once again, in view of the seriousness of the situation, I raise my voice in warning: further hesitation and indecisiveness would, today, be criminal lightmindedness. We must steel ourselves for energetic action, even if we have to arrest them all overnight. For now we have the forces and resources to do that, but there is a question as to whether three or four months from now we will still be able to do that. From our indecisiveness, the opposition concludes that we are weak and afraid of it. They have very cleverly foisted this view of theirs onto the statesmen of the great powers, a fact that makes itself felt in an extremely unpleasant way in our attempts to reach agreements [with those powers].

I emphasize once again that in my opinion, in view of the highly varied political differentiation within the opposition, this danger is not nearly so great as one might think, presuming that the leaders themselves can be rendered harmless at one blow. It is my hope that in view of the very serious internal political situation and the incipient demoralization in the army, the Central Committee will decide, before it is to late, to take the resolute measures against the opposition leaders that I have proposed.

signed: V. Menzhinsky

2.

The General Secretary of the Bolshevik Party
Jr. A47. 27.
Secret. By messenger.

1. To the Central Committee of the Bolshevik Party
2. Copy to the President of the Central Control Commission, Comrade Ordzhonikidze

The expulsions from the party have not, in general, had the success we expected, as was unanimously agreed at the last meeting of the Politburo, although a number of leading figures in the opposition have capitulated. Therefore, we must not relax after these successes, because they did not lead to a definitive liquidation and we must not shelve this problem as though it had been solved. Even in the case of those who have capitulated publicly, there is still a very big question as to whether they will actually hold to their promises honestly. I cannot believe in the honesty of these assurances for the sole reason that the submission took place at a time when things seemed to be lost anyway.

Our past experience with capitulations has shown that we are not dealing with an honest submission to the leadership of the party, but with skillful tactical maneuvers, which we have fallen for again and again. I am afraid we will encounter the same thing this time. Although I cannot fully share the very pessimistic viewpoint of the GPU Collegium, I also consider the situation very serious, especially because the activity of the opposition has recently been focused on the strongest bastions of communism, the working class and the Workers' and Peasants' Army, with the aim of undermining and destroying them.

While the opposition's access to the Workers' and Peasants' Army was rendered much more difficult by the well-timed defensive measures we took, the opposition has a great many opportunities to continue its disruptive work, directed against the Central Committee, in industrial cities and factory districts.

Concerning new recruits to the Workers' and Peasants' Army, I cannot share the serious concerns of the GPU Collegium and I formulate my opinion on this point as follows: The peasants have not the slightest sympathy for the opposition; rather, they are even hostile toward it because of its program.

I fully concur with Comrade Menzhinsky's suggestions for taking more severe measures against opposition propagandists who are arrested. This may be the only way we can seriously combat this destructive propaganda, which is also discrediting the party's leadership. Persons who are convicted of such active propaganda, in oral or written form, should not be treated any differently than spies, because they actually are spies and accomplices of our internal and external enemies. I also agree that in such cases judgment should not be made by the common courts, but by the appropriate bodies of the GPU. A few such intimidating examples will not fail to produce results.

Concerning the apparatus of the party and government, I do not view it as pessimistically as does the GPU Collegium, but I also consider the situation intolerable. We cannot accept being spied upon in all areas and up to the highest levels. Hardly any secret order remains secret. Within less than eight days, multiple copies are being handed out in Berlin, Paris, and Warsaw. From the leftist radicals to the Mensheviks to the German Social Democrats they go, then to the capitalist governments, so that the latter are always informed about our most secret materials and our most secret decisions. The case of Beloborodov tells us enough.[1] I do not want to leave unmentioned the fact that such actions are considered high treason in the capitalist states and therefore punishable by death, and I see no reason why we should not protect the dictatorship of the proletariat with the strictest measures.

After much consideration, I can only approve the enclosed plan of the GPU Collegium. It has been worked out perfectly, in organizational as well as practical respects. I also hope for a significant improvement in surveillance over, and disclosure of, hostile elements inside the party, the party leadership, and the government apparatus by setting up the cells proposed [by the GPU]. In the party's Central Committee I will also support the immediate establishment of these cells, based on the rules Comrade Menzhinsky has worked out, because the present situation is impossible. The apparatus of party and state has to be purged of all unreliable elements immediately and the apparatus has to become again what it used to be.

I hope the leadership of the party will no longer remain deaf to these serious concerns of mine. Our gentleness, which is the result of our strength, is interpreted, contrariwise, as weakness by our enemies. Not without reason do some sections of the Comintern complain about the unfavorable impression produced in foreign countries by this situation. Although I personally used to be opposed to radical measures in the interest of the unity of the party, constantly hoping that the turncoats would come to their senses, I now have to admit that I made a mistake here. But our strength lies precisely in the recognition of mistakes and the open acknowledgment of them, in contrast to the bourgeois governments, which consider themselves infallible.

The fact that all sercret reports and original documents in all fields of internal and foreign policy, including military and economic questions, are being passed along to foreign governments by the opposition and its agents *has already done us tremendous harm.* There is no way we can further tolerate each of our steps being watched, not by our enemies, who can easily be caught, but by colleagues, who pretend to work with us and who are therefore especially dangerous. We have too many weak points, which are joyfully seized upon by the capitalists. The exploitation of these weaknesses constitutes a heavy blow to our reconstruction program. Without this we would be much farther along. The apparatus of the party and government *has to be purged as quickly as possible.* Not by half-hearted measures, but radically. Everybody has to be removed from the apparatus who is under even the slightest suspicion. Soft-headed "humanitarianism" *(Human-itatsduselei)* is inappropriate here, for if there should actually turn out to be some innocent persons among them, it would not be of any consequence in the interest of the overall cause.

For the above-mentioned reasons I support the immediate acceptance of the GPU Collegium's proposal. We cannot, under any circumstances, let the mood of the working class, which is already badly depressed because of the economic situation, become any worse. There simply cannot be any half-hearted measures, as the GPU Collegium very correctly warns.

signed: Stalin

3.

The General Secretary of the Communist Party
Moscow, the Kremlin, December 27, 1927
Top Secret.

1. To the Politburo
2. To the Central Committee of the Communist Party
3. Copy to the People's Commissar for Foreign Relations, Comrade G. T. Chicherin
4. To the Archives.

Re: The Monopoly on Foreign Trade

During the last meeting of the Politburo, held jointly with the Council of People's Commissars of the USSR, a memorandum written by Comrade Chicherin was submitted to the Presidium of the Central Executive Committee on which I must express my viewpoint as authorized by the Central Committee.[1] While declaring my agreement with Comrade Chicherin on all major points, I shall spell out my opinion on the question of a certain relaxation in regard to the inviolability of the foreign trade monopoly, making reference to my memorandum of December 1926,[2] in which, as is generally known, I was the first to urge reconsideration of this question, as follows:

The attacks on us in this connection by the Trotskyists and other oppositional groups are completely unjustified. There cannot be any question of a so-called betrayal of the socialist cause; the opposite is true. They are traitors to the cause of the proletariat who sabotage the construction of the socialist economy. We would surely not agree to a modification in the terms of the foreign trade monopoly if our economic situation were bright and rosy. But this, as we all know, is unfortunately not the case. Even our opponents in our party must know that we adhered to the inviolability of the foreign trade monopoly to the last moment, as long as was at all possible. But we would have to be fanatics to ignore logical reason. I have warned repeatedly and often enough that we should not, for purely dogmatic reasons, knock our heads against the wall and end up cracking our skulls.

When I raised this question, which now demands an immediate solution, at a certain meeting of the Politburo a year ago, only Comrade Chicherin was on my side, while all the other members of the Politburo and Central Committee thought the reconsideration of this question was not timely or urgent. Unfortunately, in the months that followed, the economic and financial situation of the Soviet Union deteriorated more and more, so that the question of modifying the regulations governing the foreign trade monopoly became, from month to month, more and more urgent. It is significant that after that meeting, although a couple of months later, Comrades Serebrovsky and Bryukhanov[3] were the first to follow my proposals.

Although we could not reach full agreement on several points concerning the question of modifying the regulations during the last joint meeting, I was able, nevertheless, to note with satisfaction that my previous proposals, now current once again, were generally accepted by the assembled members. I note in particular that it was Comrade Chicherin who most enthusiastically supported my proposals again. As in the cases of Comrades Serebrovsky and Bryukhanov, it was again an experienced expert who realized the need for my proposals.

That I was not wrong in my proposals is proven to me by Comrade Chicherin's support for my project. It can hardly be doubted that Comrade Chicherin is better informed about the mood in foreign economic circles than any of us. Because of that, the advice of Comrade Chicherin should probably have the greatest importance for such far-reaching decisions as must now be made.

Today, with the exception of certain incorrigible fanatics like Zinoviev and Radek, no reasonable party member any longer doubts that the heritage of the late Ilyich, the socialist construction of our state, would not be practicable without the help of foreign capital. I refer at this point to the latest report of the people's commissar of finance,[4] which shows anything but a pleasing picture of the financial situation of our Soviet state. I surely do not have to emphasize this to the members of the Politburo and the Central Committee to justify my opinion. This fact is clear to every reasonable thinking human being who has insight into the finances of our state.

When the Politburo, after long consideration and partly with strong doubts, decided to approve the treaties with Persia and Latvia, it surely took a step forward.[5]

As our diplomatic representatives in foreign countries report unanimously, and as Comrade Chicherin stresses in his review of this question, the signing of those two treaties provoked lively interest in all the Western European capitalist countries. Furthermore, even in the United States, which used to be so reserved toward us, the effect of these treaties could be felt.

Comrade Chicherin writes: "The effect of the treaties with Persia and Latvia was felt even inside such reserved governments as London and Washington. The possibility of investing money in the Soviet Union now has partly become the topic of the day in certain financial and trade circles in London and New York. The effect of the treaties goes so far that in recent weeks a relaxation can unquestionably be felt in the reserved attitude of official bodies in London and Washington, a change that should not be without effect on the position of capitalist circles in other countries on the so-called Russian question."

I can only agree in full with Comrade Chicherin's conclusions, and I would like to stress especially that I pointed most vigorously to these possibilities, that is, an improvement in the question of an understanding *(Verständigung)* with the capitalist states, as early as half a year ago. The experience of the last few years and months has shown that broader financial support for our economic construction by foreign countries was not possible under the existing regulations of the foreign trade monopoly. I also refer to Comrade Krestinsky,[6] who reported in October that, in spite of intensive contacts, the attraction of foreign capital would not be possible as long as we remained inflexible on these regulations. Comrade Krestinsky stressed that all the negotiations, which looked so promising at the start, failed because of the regulations of the foreign trade monopoly. I further refer to Comrade Rozengolts's report, which, shortly before his departure, he submitted to Comrade Chicherin[7] and in which he said, among other things: "In general, there is great interest in England, because of the economic problems there, in the economic market of the Soviet Union. Although horror stories are told in these circles, under the influence of anti-Bolshevik propaganda, about alleged anti-English and Communist propaganda, they are on the other hand still businessmen, and they are becoming increasingly aware that it would be more reasonable to come to terms with the Soviet government, because the loss of the so-called Russian market would in the long run put more and more pressure on their trade and industry. The English business world, at least part of it, would not at all be indisposed to helping us financially and economically, if certain regulations of the foreign trade monopoly were either abolished or at least modified, because English capital could not work successfully under the present regulations."

A confidant of a well-known English entrepreneur told Comrade Rozengolts the following: "As long as the Soviet system rigidly insists on the existing regulations in the foreign trade monopoly, English capital cannot take part in the economic construction of the Soviet Union despite all the interest that is evident. The foreign trade monopoly regulations are so restrictive and anticapitalist that the English business world cannot take any action right now except to wait until the Soviet government decides to moderate its laws for its own benefit."

I remind you that the late Comrade Krasin[8] reported similar things from London as well as Paris much earlier, and that even Comrade Rakovsky spoke repeatedly about these same difficulties in his reports about his negotiations with de Monzie.[9]

Comrade Chicherin has summarized his opinion in this matter in his report of October 27,[10] which is known to the members of the Politburo and Central Committee: "According to the results of the negotiations so far, agreements are possible only if certain clauses in the foreign trade monopoly are relaxed or dropped. Foreign capital is apparently not at all willing to give in on these points and it is not satisfied with the previous changes, because it considers them insufficient. Therefore, further modifications would have to be made if we want to reach an agreement, because foreign capital holds the position that successful work in the Soviet Union is not possible under present conditions. Therefore, further modifications must be made in order to achieve an agreement. I do not see any other solution in this situation."

It is, of course, nonsense to say that by this, that is, by a certain relaxation of these regulations, the gains of the October revolution would be betrayed. Such opinions can only be held by people who, in contrast to the legacy of the late Ilyich, want to return to war communism. The period of war communism is over. It was necessary in order to break the power of the capitalists and to replace it with the power and the dictatorship of the proletariat. This challenge was met brilliantly in the years 1917 to 1921 by the people themselves and the people's commissars they had elected. But after the dictatorship of the proletariat had won indisputable control over the whole union, this period, whose purpose was to destroy the old, was logically over. Our greatest leader, Ilyich himself, proclaimed the period of the New Economic Policy to be one of transition to state socialism, to the building of the economic dictatorship of the proletariat, after the political dictatorship of the proletariat had been firmly and unshakably established.

The enemies of our reconstruction program, which is under way, try to make it look as though we were giving up one achievement after another, year after year, as if we were moving more and more toward bourgeois Western European conditions. Such an idiotic opinion cannot withstand any reasonable criticism. It has its origin in the minds of crazy fanatics who want to dig a grave for the socialist economy with the slogan: "Back to war communism." That the development of the New Economic Policy as the transition to state socialism has nothing to do with a so-called turn to the right or betrayal need not be underlined here. The Central Committee, which has the responsibility of carrying out the legacy of the late Ilyich, is fully aware of the burden of this responsibility; but on the other hand it is also aware that it has to go the right way, the way that leads to the economic development of the country in order to establish the economic dictatorship of the people. The late Ilyich described measures such as Comrade Chicherin and I propose as a necessary breathing spell, in view of the fact that we, as the only socialist state, are surrounded on all sides by capitalist states.

I have no doubt that in a case like this the late Ilyich would also have favored a breathing spell in view of the extremely difficult situation of our country and the impossibility of achieving an agreement under other conditions. I remind you again that the late Ilyich, whenever the situation demanded, would, as he used to express it so magnificently, initiate a breathing spell.

Therefore, we are not at all deviating from the path Ilyich showed us if we create some breathing space now, that is, if we modify the so far inflexible system in order to carry through the program, the implementation of which was bequeathed to us by Ilyich.

We would be in poor shape if we followed the crazy advice given us by Zinoviev, Kamenev, and others.[11] I can clearly see the consequences of such a policy: the collapse of economic construction and the end of the economic dictatorship of the proletariat. Therefore, without listening to the destructive advice of those fanatics, who incline more and more in part toward the Anarchists and in part toward the Mensheviks, today, more than ever, we have to follow the path Ilyich showed us.

This path demands that we create some breathing space, that is, concede to the wishes of foreign capital to some extent. We are forced to do this anyway for the single reason that, as I already mentioned, the reconstruction program, which we want to complete, would become impossible without the help of foreign capital.

Therefore, we have only two possibilities: (1) to give in, to create modifications in questions of the foreign trade monopoly in order to get the money we need for reconstruction and the help of foreign industry for the expansion of the socialist state, that is, to carry through the legacy we inherited from Ilyich; or (2) to abide strictly by the inviolability of the foreign trade monopoly, that is, to give up the policy of seeking agreements that we have followed so far. This would mean to remain dependent on our own resources, to give up the reconstruction of our economic life and also the realization of the economic dictatorship of the proletariat, because the transition to state socialism is not possible without foreign financial help.

For all those who wish to carry through and realize the legacy of the late Ilyich in all its magnitude, it must be quite clear that we can only choose the first possibility, even if we have to make temporary concessions. Making concessions is unquestionably the lesser of two evils. Insisting stubbornly on the [existing] arrangements, knocking our heads against the wall, does not help us; it helps our enemies. Here we see that the opposition and their program do not serve the people, as they pretend, but play indirectly into the hands of the foreign cap- italists.

It is absolutely no sign of weakness if we admit openly among ourselves that our financial and economic situation is extremely serious and that we are suffer- ing from a chronic lack of money and a lack of intelligent economic forces so that we are unable to carry out our program with our own resources alone, to create the economic dictatorship of the proletariat as well as its political dictatorship. Therefore, to be able to realize our program, we have to make use of foreign help. The decision to create certain modifications does not in any way mean we want to give up the foreign trade monopoly, which is one of the strongest bastions of the proletariat. Nor are we thinking of giving up the foreign trade monopoly step by step, although certain opposition groups accuse us of that out of their crazy ignorance of these matters. Did the late Ilyich give up communism when he proclaimed the transition to the New Economic Policy? No, of course not. And exactly the same is true for the steps we are considering in view of the economic situation.

Let me briefly summarize: We can only take the first of the two roads I have mentioned. The second way leads to the abyss, to catastrophe, to the collapse of the economic dictatorship of the proletariat. Nothing remains for us to do, regardless of political factors, but to agree to such concessions in order to achieve the desired agreements, which the Politburo voted for a year ago. The minor modifications of the regulations that were put into the treaties with Persia and Latvia have already clearly shown how vast the interest is in the market of the Soviet Union among the leading capitalist states. This fact, and the competition among the various capitalist groups, has to be used to our benefit. As already mentioned, these two treaties have led to a considerable improvement in our foreign relations, as was intended and as one could have foreseen. Therefore, we can rightly be proud of our diplomatic success. I do not want to list here all the different and numerous reasons that have brought me, after long talks with Comrade Chicherin and after studying his memorandum, to present my pro- posals about certain modifications of the foreign trade monopoly to the Polit- buro.

Although opinions were divided and although these opinions were partly contradictory during the last meeting of the Politburo, I hope, at any rate, that in light of Comrade Chicherin's detailed memorandum, on which I have expressed my view, the party leadership, keeping in mind the seriousness of the situation and the path Ilyich showed us, will now also accept paragraphs 5, 8, 11, and 17.[12] By accepting these paragraphs, we will be taking a great step forward toward reconstruction. Standing in full agreement with Comrade Chicherin on these points, I have no doubt that such a decision by the Politburo will make future talks with the foreign capitalists much easier. The objections of foreign capitalists that they could not work successfully in the Soviet Union under the present conditions would become invalid. By agreeing upon Comrade Chicherin's pro- posals and by agreeing on my point of view on this subject, we would remove a major obstacle, as our diplomats in foreign countries have reported again and again during their negotiations. The prospects for coming to an agreement with the English and the Americans, that is, of obtaining the needed means for reconstruction, would become much more favorable.

Furthermore, if the Politburo accepts the aforementioned paragraphs, it would be necessary to implement the resolution as quickly as possible, in view of the deterioration of the economic situation during the last few months. In supporting the opinion presented in Comrade Chicherin's memorandum, which is under consideration here, I express the hope that the Politburo will not be deaf to these proposals, considering the tasks that lie ahead, and that it will follow the advice of such a competent expert as Comrade Chicherin.

It will not hurt us to sacrifice certain paragraphs temporarily, in view of the situation and considering the necessity for it, in order to achieve our goals. I would not know any other advice to give.

signed: Stalin

4.

Excerpts from Speeches by V. R. Menzhinsky and V. V. Kuibyshev at a Meeting of the Political Bureau of the Central Committee of the All-Union Communist Party (Bolshevik)—(probably a joint meeting with the Council of People's Commissars and the Presidium of the Central Executive Committee of the USSR— end of January 1928)

Comrade Menzhinsky: Before I take a position on Comrade Voroshilov's presentation,[1] I would like to give a short survey of the internal political situation as I personally see it.

On the basis of Article 58,[2] following the example of the capitalist states, we would be fully justified in taking the most severe measures against the opposition and they could not accuse us of using terror. On this point, I only remind you of the German law for the protection of the republic and the various treason trials in Leipzig, in which the death penalty was imposed.[3] Therefore, I think that the Central Committee's decision to remove all opposition elements from the cities and suspend them from their positions in the government and party was actually a very skillful solution.[4] What the opposition has done, if we apply the concepts used by the capitalist states, was obvious treason.[5] Treason is punishable in Germany, England, and France either by long prison sentences or by death. But we found a much more skillful solution. Without putting the opposition leaders in jail, which we could have done with full justification, we put an end to their further activity. In the places they are now, although they are free, they are as little able to do anything as if they were in prison. The connection between the opposition and its supporters has been broken. That is the main thing and our purpose has been achieved. (Loud applause.) Still, after our victory, which is generally acknowledged in foreign countries, it would be wrong to rest, as the saying goes, on our laurels. (Loud applause.) Now we have to mop up the opposition's supporters. (Loud applause.) The Central Committee has, in view of the situation, accepted all the points in my proposal as regards a purge operation. Working hand in hand with Comrade Ordzhonikidze,[6] all measures have been taken for purging the party apparatus of unreliable elements. I estimate as of now about 70 percent of these unreliable elements have already been expelled from the party. The work in regard to the administrative apparatus has been much more difficult; here, in my opinion, not even half of the oppositional elements have been disposed of. The establishment of surveillance cells, which I proposed a while ago, has shown good results.[7] Nevertheless, the work in this field has only begun, and it will take months to purge the administrative apparatus enough for us to be able to speak of total success. But at least a big step forward has been taken. On the whole, the opposition movement must be regarded as eliminated. What remains of it is in its death agony; but this agony must be brought to completion before the opposition has a chance to rise again and eventually renew the fight against us under new leadership.

I fully share Comrade Chicherin's opinion that the negotiations with foreign countries have been disrupted by the opposition movement, because the impression was created abroad with the support of the Social Democratic press, which is in the pay of the capitalists, that the worker's and peasant's government has been destabilized and that the Soviet Union was facing another revolution. It is quite understandable that the capitalist financial groups have been reserved toward us since this point of view was put over on them in a very skillful manner. The experience of the party congress and the condemnation of the opposition by the people has not been without consequences. As Comrade Chicherin correctly reports, an obvious change in the assessment of the internal political situation in the Soviet Union is noticeable in foreign countries. In the interest of reconstruction, we have to take even stronger measures in order to eliminate the opposition forever and to prove to the other countries that there cannot be any talk of destabilization of the workers' and peasants' government in the Soviet Union and that an opposition movement no longer even exists in the Soviet Union today. I have instructed all sections of the GPU under me along these lines. On my part at least, all the necessary instructions have been given to purge the party and administrative apparatus of all unreliable elements as energetically and quickly as possible. The results so far have been good and we have no reason to doubt that the operation can be carried through completely, and thus we will remove all Menshevik and counterrevolutionary elements from the party and government apparatus once and for all. (Loud applause.) . . .[8]

To conclude my report, I would like to tell you something about another aspect of opposition activity. After the failure of the opposition movement in the Soviet Union, and after the defection of some of their leaders, the opposition seems to want to try another method of fighting, that is, splitting the various Communist parties in other countries by inciting them against the Central Committee of the Bolshevik Party. This activity has made itself felt first of all in Germany, secondly in Austria, but also in France.[9] The left-Communist efforts in these countries, but also in others, are apparently financed and supported by [those with] greater resources.[10] They appeal to the raw instincts of the ignorant masses by accusing the Bolshevik Party of betrayal, while promising things that cannot be delivered. This left-Communist movement has been growing substantially of late, in particular in Germany, so that even the German section of the Comintern has called attention to the seriousness of the situation that has arisen. Comrade Bukharin, who is here, will confirm that almost all the sections of the Comintern complain about a growth of the left-Communist movements in their parties.

Comrade Bukharin (calling out from the floor): Quite right!

Comrade Menzhinsky (continuing): This propaganda, orchestrated undoubtedly by the Trotskyists, or even more likely by Zinoviev,[11] involves a very great danger for the unity of the Communist parties in other countries, where the fight against the opposition is naturally much more difficult than here.

According to confidential reports, the number of opposition supporters in the Comintern is growing. Comrade Bukharin himself complained to me about this day before yesterday. Together, we discussed what measures should be taken. We did not come to full agreement in our discussion. Comrade Bukharin is going to send me a short memorandum, on which I will express my view, based on my information, and then present it as a joint memorandum to the party's Central Committee. In any case it is certain that this left-Communist movement within the other Communist parties represents a great threat to the unity not only of those parties but also of the entire Comintern and that, on our part, measures must be taken immediately to eliminate the opposition abroad the same way we have eliminated it inside the Soviet Union.

In view of the seriousness of these developments I suggest that the Central

Committee deal thoroughly with this question, which has become so urgent, in a special meeting as soon as possible.[12] (Prolonged stormy applause.)

[Excerpts from Kuibyshev's speech]
Kuibyshev:[13] I return now to my original topic, the state of the economy, in connection with Comrade Chicherin's proposals,[14] which were sent to the Central Committee and the acceptance of which depends mainly on the conclusions of the experts. I have not yet finished putting together a final compilation of all the comments by our most experienced experts and advisers, but, after having studied all of them thoroughly, I can give you an overall impression, which is the main thing anyway. You will receive the final compilation within the next few days and you will find that it confirms what I am presenting to you now. In regard to the grain procurements I had, as you will recall, some strong doubts about their practicality when we first started to plan the (current?) budget: not, because the assumed quantity [of grain] is not there; the quantity is there. (Expressions of agreement.)[15]
Menzhinsky (calling out): It is there in abundance. Because the harvest was above average, in some places even good.
Kuibyshev (continuing): The mistake is that the peasants, prompted by the goods famine in nearly all fields—I would almost say in all fields—are holding their grain back, because they do not want to exchange it for money. But in exchange for manufactured goods they would undoubtedly surrender their surpluses. Unfortunately, the opinion is still very common in the countryside that our money is not safe, and the opposition as well as other reactionary groups do everything to strengthen the peasants in this belief. They whisper in the peasant's ear: "Don't take money, because it's worthless; soon there'll be another round of inflation and you'll have lost everything." The peasant, who is on an even lower cultural level than the city dweller, listens and becomes suspicious. He holds back as much as he can. Not out of hostility toward the system, not at all; he has rejected the anti-Bolshevik movement once and for all. He knows that any other government would be against his interests and that the first thing a bourgeois government would do would be to take away his privileges. That's how the peasant thinks!
Shout from the floor by Comrade Kalinin: Quite right!
Kuibyshev (continuing): Our propaganda and education on this question leaves much to be desired. (General agreement is voiced.) The peasant is an *unconditional* supporter of our system, but he indirectly becomes our enemy when, lacking in consciousness and left to the propaganda of our enemies, he openly sabotages our economic program by holding back his grain stocks.
Menzhinsky (from the floor): I think the word "unconditional" is at least a little exaggerated. The peasant has his peculiarities and I doubt that he is really such a good friend of the workers.[16]
Kuibyshev (continuing): There are only two ways to realize the program on which so much depends for us: increased production in industry, to overcome the goods famine, so that the peasant *is able to* buy; and a fight against the propaganda in the countryside and against the rumors circulated by hostile elements that our money is no good. The latter requires fewer resources, unlike the former, which is unfortunately closely connected to the grain procurements. Industrial production depends on an increase in the export of grain and raw materials. So we must *first* have the grain procurements and the production of raw materials because we do not have any other sources we can use to purchase imports. There is no other way without foreign financial help. In the long run, we cannot allow our foreign trade balance to become more and more unfavorable. The new fiscal year started very poorly and, as far as we can forecast

conditions for the period ahead, is likely to be affected by the severe downturn. The statements I have seen by all our experts tend to agree that there cannot be any talk of an improvement in the grain and raw materials markets as long as we cannot overcome the goods famine. But in order to overcome the goods famine, our industry needs not only money but also a considerable improvement in machinery and inventory, which means increased imports. But how are we to achieve that, since the goods famine is not only dependent on industry itself but mainly on the fact that imports, which are necessary to overcome the goods famine, are in turn dependent on a more favorable balance of trade, that is, increased exports of grain and raw materials? Unfortunately, we are confronted with the opposite situation. The trade balance, which is decisive for reconstruction, has become increasingly unfavorable from month to month and in December it reached such a low point that the present situation causes us profound concern. (Commotion in the hall.) January will not bring any improvement; on the contrary, we must expect a further deterioration because it is winter. The situation on the raw materials market is particularly serious, as the experts report unanimously. This fact accounts for 80 percent of the goods famine.

Industry obviously needs help; it cries out for help. It lacks not only certain materials that we import from foreign countries; it also lacks domestic raw materials and urgently needed new and improved equipment. Consider the fact that many factories have worked for twenty or thirty years and often even longer using the same machines, which have by now become worn out and obsolete. Every machine, even the best, has to be replaced some day. (Expressions of agreement.) I had experts put together a production list corresponding to the condition of machinery and equipment and divided this list into three parts: *Class I,* recently imported new machinery; *Class II,* factories with machinery that is not too old, that is, still usable to some extent; and *Class III,* factories with very old machinery and equipment. It is extremely interesting and enlightening, this example. The difference in quantity of production between Class I and III is as high as 40 percent. That is an incredible amount. (Expressions of agreement.) Just think how much we could produce if we had only factories of classes I and II, as we should. What a position we'd be in if that were so. There certainly wouldn't be a goods famine! (Applause.)

But there is no point in complaining here about how things are or how they could be. Things are the way they are and we have to try to find a solution. Although I *personally* do not see a realistic solution, I do not want to say that the situation is hopeless and that we should throw in the towel. The situation was more difficult in 1921 and we overcame it anyway.[17] (Loud applause.) On the other hand, I don't want to hide the fact that the economic situation is extremely serious and that at the moment and under the given circumstances, we cannot talk of construction but must deal with the fact of an economic downturn which, in connection with the grain and raw materials crisis and the decrease in industrial production, is making itself felt very severely in all areas of economic life. I wish only to present some figures to you, worked out by experienced statisticians, to make you aware of how much the situation has recently deteriorated. There was an increase of 8.4 percent in the *unfavorable balance of trade* in November, compared to October. *Raw materials production* declined by as much as 9.2 percent. *Grain procurements* also showed a substantial loss, while *production in heavy and light industry,* taken together, was 21.5 percent below the expected amount. These are terrible figures. (Agreement.)

I am sorry that I have the thankless task of giving nothing but bad news, unlike those who have preceded me, but with the best will in the world, I am unable to report any good news on this subject. Even the naphtha industry shows a decline, although not to such a serious degree, and in the industrial part of the Ukrainian

Soviet Republic the outcry for new machinery and equipment has become louder and louder. The same is true of the Urals industrial area and a regressive trend is also reported from the coal mines of Siberia. As a logical consequence of these events, *the cost of living index* rose by 4 percent during November and December, and the *shortage of money* has become more and more serious, as [people's commissar of finance] Comrade Bryukhanov has reported. Everywhere there are delays in matters of revenue. *Tax revenues* show a deficit of about 16.5 percent, which must be regarded as extremely serious. Back taxes owed by heavy industry increased 3.1 percent in November and 5.8 percent in December. There is no chance that the situation will improve in January in any of the fields mentioned. I do not want to arouse useless and unjustified hopes, and therefore I say that the situation will almost certainly deteriorate further in January and February.

Generous and long-term credits would be the only way to improve the situation. I do not know any other way. All of you realize yourselves that this downturn is, in the long run, intolerable. Our aim is reconstruction, but from month to month we are going backwards. So what we have is not reconstruction, but—to put it harshly—a *slow death*. (Commotion.) Therefore, we have to undertake an energetic surgical operation, just as an energetic doctor would in order not to let the patient, in this case our economic life, die. Because we do not want to die, we want to live! (Lively expressions of agreement.) . . .[18]

. . . I know that some comrades from other areas of work have objections, partly of a very serious kind, regarding further concessions in the matter of the foreign trade monopoly. A relaxation of the monopoly is certainly anything but ideal for us. (Applause.) But we must not forget that we, as the only proletarian state, *must* allow for the *necessity* of temporary compromises. I remind you that Ilyich signed the peace of Brest-Litovsk, which was very unfavorable for us, in the interest of the maintenance of the dictatorship of the proletariat and by this he destroyed the possibility of the restoration of a monarchy with the help of the German military. (Loud applause.) . . .[19]

We are in a similar situation today . . .[20] Ilyich played off one group against the other. Today it is exactly the same . . .[21] We must, as Comrade Stalin so correctly proposed, incite the entire capitalist herd against each other; England against the United States, Germany against France, Japan against the United States, England against France and so on. Friendship [among the capitalists] breaks down as soon as the matter of competition comes up. On a smaller scale, that is precisely our experience in the case of the Urquhart concession.*

We must stir the fire. Let them butt their heads against each other, while we stand by laughing. Because of all the considerations I have mentioned and because of the terribly difficult economic situation, I set aside my concerns and agree fully with Comrade Chicherin's position. In any case, it is definitely better to compromise than to break down. In the next few days you will receive, as I said, the final compilation of assessments by economic experts and from that you will gather the extreme seriousness of the situation as well as the fact that this is the only choice we have.

Any further backward tendency in our economic life is intolerable. The figures I

*Leslie T. Urquhart was an English entrepreneur whose company had worked a large mining area in Russia before the revolution. In the early 1920s negotiations were held with him about the possibility of allowing him to operate those mines again as concessions. (They had been nationalized during the revolution.) In the end, at Lenin's insistence, no agreement was reached with Urquhart, because in his view the British government had not made sufficient diplomatic concessions to the USSR; instead economic concessions were given to German companies in an attempt to play Germany off against the Western powers. Cf. E. H. Carr, *The Bolshevik Revolution*, vol. 3, pp. 354, 427–430.

have presented tell enough. Or do we want to break down for the sake of abstract principles? That would be a betrayal of Ilyich's legacy! In any case, things cannot go on the way they are now. You will all have to admit that after thoughtful consideration. (Loud applause.)

5.

The People's Commissar of Foreign Affairs of the USSR
Personal Journal I. February 9, 1928

To the diplomatic representatives of the USSR

In the last few days the economic situation, contrary to earlier expectations, has deteriorated sharply.

Serious breakdowns in supply have already occurred on the food market, which will probably force the workers' and peasants' government to start rationing the most important food items within the next few days.

In order to avoid a further escalation of the situation, the Council of People's Commissars adopted extraordinary measures at yesterday's meeting.[1] Instructions in this regard will be sent out today to particular people's commissariats and appropriate government agencies. How far this will succeed in improving the situation is still a question at the moment. The workers' and peasants' government has authorized me to instruct you right away about this change in the seriousness of the situation. These instructions are, of course, to be regarded as strictly confidential and are intended for your personal orientation and the orientation of your closest co-workers.

All day yesterday, telegrams were arriving from various parts of the Soviet Union about serious interruptions in the food supply system. These reports, in some places, gave real cause for concern. Parallel to this, the grain procurements have been declining from one ten-day period to the next, so that our calculations have been seriously endangered.

We can expect with certainty that the opposition as well as ultraleft groups in foreign countries will use this serious distress of the workers' and peasants' government not only to stir up discontent among the population in the Soviet Union itself but also to sabotage economic negotiations in foreign countries by every possible means.

There is no way to avoid the fact that if there is a further deepening of the food crisis, foreign journalists in the Soviet Union will write about this for their newspapers. I certainly do not need to emphasize that such reports will be anything but pleasant for us at this time.

The downturn in numerous areas of economic life during the last several months has not passed without influencing the position of foreign governments toward us. While in October, and also at the beginning of November, a change in our favor had taken place in the capitals of the Western European powers, an increasingly reserved attitude has been evident since around the beginning of the year. Certain diplomatic representatives have pointed out that not only sabotage by the opposition but also reports in our own press about economic matters have made negotiations more difficult. After presenting this information to the Central Committee, the People's Commissariat of Foreign Affairs has advised the Council of Labor and Defense and the press department of the Commissariat of Foreign Affairs as to what is desirable.

Since the beginning of January, a changed attitude toward us has become evident all over Western Europe; it is marked by a more reserved attitude on the part of certain financial groups.

The relatively lively negotiations with various American companies have also cooled off noticeably. An increasing lack of interest in our market is also reported from Germany.

A campaign to sabotage the negotiations that were just beginning is unquestionably coming from London again, and this is putting pressure on the other European countries along the same lines.[2] Even in France, where matters were quite favorable, negotiations have come to a standstill in the last few days. The above-mentioned campaign emanating from London is intended to influence the world of trade and finance to hold off [from any agreements] for the time being, in view of the deterioration of our economic situation. Unfortunately, this effort has not been without results. Our diplomatic representatives unanimously report increased reservations on the part of financial groups that until now, had shown a lively interest.

Under the impression of a backward movement in our economic life, negotiations that had started have come to a stop everywhere and, as I said, London's pressure can be felt more and more strongly. As we have learned from very reliable sources, the English government, in contrast to numerous statements in the press, has once again come out with an intensified fight against us. Hand in hand with avowed anti-Bolshevik financial groups, they are pushing the following line of argument:

"The economic crisis in the Soviet Union is getting worse from month to month. Therefore, it seems urgently advisable to await the further outcome of events. It is necessary to warn insistently against the conclusion of any major deals in view of the instability of the economic situation in the Soviet Union. The concessions that the workers' and peasants' government has made so far are not sufficient for successful trade with the Soviet Union. If we hold off a little longer, the workers' and peasants' government will be forced in a short time to capitulate on a broader scale in regard to the foreign trade monopoly. In other words, the longer we wait, the more advantageous for us. Therefore the slogan for the time immediately ahead must be: maximum restraint. Only in this way can we force the Bolsheviks, who are in a terribly difficult economic and financial situation, to their knees."

Unfortunately, this English slogan, as we have mentioned, has not failed to have an effect. The situation is therefore to be regarded as *exceedingly serious.*

The Council of People's Commissars of the USSR addressed the seriousness of the situation at yesterday's meeting in the form of a unanimous resolution. The workers' and peasants' government is well aware that, because of the deepening of the crisis, the situation is now more serious than it has been for a long time.

The downturn in all fields of economic life seriously endangers not only the budget but also our foreign currency reserves *(valuta).* The Council of People's Commissars also passed a resolution that noted that at the moment the workers' and peasants' government does not have the resources at its disposal to overcome this crisis on its own. The chairman of the Council of People's Commissars,[3] after hearing various reports by experts on the seriousness of the situation, authorized me to inform you confidentially along the present lines, so that you will be fully oriented on the situation in any ongoing negotiations. It is absolutely essential that you not remain ignorant of these events, so that, wherever possible, you can intervene more energetically than ever.

From the events here described you can see for yourself how urgently necessary it would be, wherever possible, to speed up the negotiations. Of course it goes without saying that in spite of the seriousness of the situation any open display of haste or insistence is to be avoided at all costs. On the other hand, no matter what, the English slogan calling on others to hold back in order to bring us to our knees must be countered by all possible means.

Other than giving unofficial hints as to a modification of the foreign trad' monopoly, this subject must not be discussed publicly along such lines. The Executive Committee of the Comintern has announced once again through the Communist press in various foreign countries that there can be no talk of abandoning the monopoly on foreign trade. Publicly, our diplomatic representatives, of course, have the task as before of denouncing any reports of coming modifications in the foreign trade monopoly. This necessity arises first of all because we must fight the propaganda of the ultra-leftists, who have recently threatened the continued unified existence of the foreign Communist parties in a serious way. I enclose an assessment of the situation in this regard made by the Executive Committee of the Comintern. You will see from this assessment that the Comintern also views these developments within the foreign Communist parties as very serious. This is reason enough to avoid anything that may give our opposition and the foreign ultra-left groups the opportunity to bring up anything concrete against us.

In any such case you should immediately make contact with the press through the channels known to you. But I would like to remark at this point that we must refrain from any direct communication with the foreign Communist press and foreign Communist organizations. Therefore, it should only be by way of an exception that you answer the propaganda of the ultra-lefts and bourgeois anti-Bolshevik organizations in any official statements. The rest is not up to you. [In general] the struggle against the ultra-left propaganda will be carried out through the joint efforts of the Central Committee and the Comintern.

Because the deterioration of the economic situation is already bringing grist to the mill of the bourgeois circles hostile to us, you will have to be more careful than ever not to let yourselves be compromised. Bourgeois capitalism is only waiting for a chance to accuse you of such things so as to proclaim loudly in its press: "Don't give them money; they are promoting world revolution."

In connection with the new situation that has arisen, which is regarded as extremely serious by the workers' and peasants' government, the Central Committee of the party and the Politburo will convene an extraordinary meeting, under the chairmanship [sic] of the Central Executive Committee of the Soviet Union,* within the next few days to take further necessary measures to stabilize the situation.[4] I am authorized to inform you that the Central Committee and the Politburo will again deliberate on the question of modifications of the foreign trade monopoly. I wish to inform you unofficially and on a preliminary basis that at the meeting in all likelihood new decisions along these lines will be made. In view of the fact that the economic crisis has deepened in recent days, it is to be expected that the Central Committee will accept Comrade Chicherin's proposals. In any case you can indicate, although in a confidential and noncommittal way, that the Soviet government will issue new directives on this question in the next few days.[5]

As for the rest, I call to your attention the fact that the workers' and peasants' government places a very high value on reaching agreements with the capitalist groups. The present situation is, in the long run, intolerable. When interruptions in the area of food supply occur, as is happening right now, the vital nerves of the state itself are very seriously threatened. Although the experts pointed to this danger a while ago, we did not want to believe it. The danger the experts predicted has now, unfortunately, become fact. The people's commissar of finance[6] has no resources with which to combat the situation. The goods famine

*This is apparently an error in the translation from Russian to German. Probably what was meant was a joint session of the Politburo, the Sovnarkom, and the Presidium of the Central Executive Committee.

renders every accumulation of raw materials and grain illusory. As long as industrial production is declining from month to month, there cannot, of course, be any question of an increase in grain procurements. The peasant does not want money but goods, and these goods are not available. The workers' and peasants' government is not able to intervene in a helpful way here with its own financial resources.

From the standpoint of the capitalists, who see the Soviet Union as an arena for earning profits, it is understandable that they should take a reserved attitude if they are presented with the news that our economic crisis is deepening more and more. Although the foreign capitalists have long stopped believing in the scare stories of the anti-Bolshevik news agencies and news sources, they become at least puzzled when these sources bring them news translated from our own newspapers. In this case they tell themselves: "Well, it must be true." And naturally they close their wallets. It was certainly politically wrong not to instruct our press in this sense. But nevertheless there is still time to correct this mistake. I leave it to the diplomatic skills of our representatives in foreign countries to respond in an adroit and tactful manner to this new campaign against us. I think it unnecessary for me to point out once again the extraordinary value of an agreement with the capitalist groups. In view of the extremely difficult situation the workers' and peasants' government is in, the diplomatic representatives of the USSR must, of course, strive more energetically than ever to take advantage of the possibilities, not overlook any opportunity, and speak out vigorously in favor of agreements.

It is particularly regrettable that the campaign directed against us finds its most fruitful soil precisely in the two financially strongest countries, and that London's slogans have also affected the United States.

If we make concessions because of our poverty, which puts us in serious distress, in order to get financial help and credits, that does not mean at all that we will surrender all our gains. Although the impossibility of reconstruction without foreign help has been an obvious fact for months, that situation has become more evident now than ever. Without wanting to deliberately paint things as worse than they are, I cannot hide the fact that our economy has been very gravely shaken by the events of the last few months and that at the moment, under the given circumstances, there can, of course, not be any talk of [further] construction.

Under the existing circumstances, we shall have to be content if we manage to prevent a further downturn. I look to the future with great concern, and I agree with Comrade Chicherin in being very worried about the course of events. The serious irregularities and disruptions in the food supply system could, if the propaganda of the opposition continues, even lead to internal political difficulties, which definitely must be avoided at the moment. I need only remind you what setbacks we suffered in negotiations toward agreements during the weeks before the party congress,[7] when the opinion was widely held in foreign countries that the internal political situation was so insecure that, in view of that, it would be better to refrain from major business deals for the time being.

Let me briefly summarize the instructions I have been asked to give you, as follows:

In view of the fundamental deterioration in the economic situation and, unfortunately, even in the food supply system, the workers' and peasants' government finds itself in an extremely difficult situation. At this point we should not leave unmentioned something that was stated by the Central Committee, that we were wrong in our assessment of the crisis. It has widened much faster than we expected. One of the few among us who predicted the present extent of the crisis, back at the turn of the year, was Comrade Chicherin.[8] Therefore in our negotiations with capitalist countries we must leave aside considerations of prestige. Prestige is at any rate a word that does not belong in the Marxist vocabulary. Today more than ever we must hold to the viewpoint that every means is justified in order to achieve the intended purpose. But the purpose of a workers' and peasants' government is not only the maintenance of the power of the proletariat but also the consolidation of the same. The goal we have set for years is the realization of socialism also in the economic field. But this goal can only be achieved by reconstruction of the country. Therefore we have to set aside all dogmatic considerations at the moment and take our stand on the ground of practical needs. We need money and/or credits. But we must not forget that we need this money or credit at an extremely unfavorable moment. The workers' and peasants' government is fully aware of this fact. It is in the interest of the proletariat—and not against its interest—that the government is willing to make further concessions. Today more than ever, therefore, you must exert all your strength to persuade the forces that are interested in our market that it would be quite profitable for them to help in the reconstruction of our country, that the workers' and peasants' government is willing to make further concessions on the question of the foreign trade monopoly in the interest of the reconstruction of the country. It is particularly important that you not overlook any means whatsoever to combat the economic propaganda against us. I advise you, for this reason, to establish contact with the press agencies subordinate to you and to issue new instructions concerning this matter. Two copies of such instructions are to be sent here. Furthermore, you must notify us in a lengthier report, in triplicate, before February 26, how the economic situation in the USSR is seen in important financial and trade circles in the country you are accredited to and how you personally judge the chances for achieving an agreement.[9]

I repeat once again that the workers' and peasants' government is seriously concerned about the future course of events and has ordered me to urge you not to overlook any measures to counteract the campaign aimed at paralyzing our policy of seeking agreements.

If there is not a significant improvement in our foreign relations in the period ahead, it will be absolutely impossible to carry out the program we have projected. . . .[10]

For:
signed: Litvinov

Top Secret.
Personal.

6.

The All-Union Council of People's Commissars has issued the following decree at the recommendation of the people's commissar of agriculture[1] and the chief of the GPU:[2]

Chairman of the Council of People's Commissars of the USSR.
1. b. 137.
Moscow, the Kremlin. March 2, 1928.
Secret. Personal. To be destroyed after reading.
Resolution.

According to reports by Comrade Menzhinsky, intensive propaganda is being carried out among the rural population with the purpose of sabotaging and seriously endangering the entire economic program of the workers' and peasants' government. That the kulaks eagerly seize upon such propaganda needs no particular mention here. Much more critical is the fact that this propaganda, which so seriously endangers our economic life, is winning strong support among the middle peasants and even the poor peasants.

Comrade Menzhinsky has quite correctly expressed the opinion that the party organizations in question here have, for the most part, completely failed to do their work, for that is the only explanation of how this counterrevolutionary propaganda could have set in on such a large scale.

As the GPU units report unanimously, the peasantry's mood is extremely bad and is already taking an outspoken petty-bourgeois counterrevolutionary form.

Local party activists are, for the most part, completely unaware of what their duty is and how far the scope of their authority extends. They think, for the most part, that it is up to the GPU to do the educational work, so that they themselves do not have to do this work. It is hard to believe that after ten years of rule by a proletarian government, party activists would not know that educational work comes first of all within their range of duties.

The GPU units do not have an active function; their role is strictly one of surveillance. They have nothing to do with propaganda or any similar work.

In connection with the decision of the party's Central Committee, the Central Control Commission will organize an investigation to determine which responsible agencies or party officials have failed to measure up to the tasks before them. The Central Control Commission in collaboration with the Council of People's Commissars of the USSR has ordered ruthless action to be taken against those elements that were not aware of the importance of their tasks and that neglected their duties. The Central Committee of the party has, in this regard, granted the Central Control Commission unlimited authority in carrying out its decisions.

A sad indication of the low level of party activists[3] is the fact that the GPU has for the past several months reported, with full justification, that some local party activists and/or responsible party bodies have very obviously sabotaged the work of the GPU and want to see it as an enemy that keeps an eye on them instead of as their ever-present ally. We have to fight with fire and sword against this. The GPU and its units are the coercive force that implements the will of the proletariat and of the workers' and peasants' government as well.

It is their duty to maintain surveillance everywhere, so that the will of the people is executed everywhere, even in the most remote areas.

The units of the GPU are there, as we have said, to observe whether the will of the people is being carried out everywhere as ordered by the workers' and peasants' government.

The workers' and peasants' government, in agreement with the Central Committee of the party, has asked Comrade Menzhinsky to report to the Central Control Commission every single case, without exception, in which unfriendly behavior toward the GPU is demonstrated as an object for further investigation by the Central Control Commission and for the punishment of offenders. At the same time I have ordered that, until such investigations are completed, local party officials be suspended from their posts immediately. In no case will the workers' and peasants' government permit agencies of the proletarian dictatorship itself to support the sabotage policy of counterrevolutionary elements in the countryside by passive behavior.

As in all such cases of counterrevolutionary activity, the GPU is the most valuable co-worker in the struggle for the maintenance of the dictatorship of the proletariat. As such an agency, it has to monitor all events throughout the Soviet Union, no matter whether they are political, economic, or military in nature.

After the workers' and peasants' government, backed by the overwhelming mass of the proletariat and the people, suppressed the internal political, counter-revolutionary action of opposition elements, it has shown that it represents the will of the working masses. The people have unanimously condemned the counterrevolutionary action of the opposition, which sought to split Lenin's united party. When the opposition leadership had to realize that it could not achieve anything with its slander and distorted slogans, it gave up its hopeless attempts in the political field. Yet they did not intend, even though the government condemned them most rigorously, to give up their criminal fight. After their defeat on the political front, they shifted their activity to that of subverting the Workers' and Peasants' Army.

Although appropriate and extremely skillfully prepared proclamations were circulated in vast numbers in the Workers' and Peasants' Army, they had no success.

The responsible military units of the party proved to be completely up to their tasks. Assessing the situation with complete accuracy, they began educational work even before this propaganda material appeared, so that our enemy's counterrevolutionary propaganda had no effect. The decline of our enemies' propaganda activities is the best proof that the oppositionists realized that they cannot achieve any more on the political front.

Although no immediate danger of contamination of the Workers' and Peasants' Army ever existed, still another convincing victory was won by the Central Committee over the counterrevolutionary elements, this time in the military field.

But even after this defeat, the opposition was not satisfied. When they realized that they could never win the Workers' and Peasants' Army for their goals, they shifted their activity to the economic field, a field in which, in view of our obvious encirclement by the capitalist powers, we are extremely vulnerable.

The goals of our enemies were very obvious: to take advantage of the difficult economic situation of the workers' and peasants' government to sabotage the ongoing [economic] negotiations with foreign countries. While our enemies suffered a defeat on the internal political as well as on the military front, they have dealt us many blows in the economic sphere.[4]

Since the end of December, the effect of this propaganda against us has made itself felt more and more noticeably in our negotiations with foreign capitalist groups. The propaganda of our enemies against us in foreign countries was still not enough for them to achieve their goals. The workers' and peasants' government was to be hit inside the country so hard that the foreign governments would lose all confidence in the strength of our economy and our reconstruction [program].

While up until now the work of our enemies was focused on the urban population, since about mid-January the main activity has been shifted to counterrevolutionary work in the countryside.

In support of counterrevolutionary activity they used the difficult situation of our industry. By this I mean primarily the decline in industrial production and the increase of the goods famine. Everywhere rumors were spread about war supposedly about to come, about a new round of inflation in the immediate future, about a general blockade supposedly to be imposed against us. The agents of our enemies whispered in every ear: "Hold back your grain and food; the *chervonets* will soon be worthless; this way at least you'll have something of solid value."

It is highly regrettable that in the eleventh year of the proletarian dictatorship such propaganda, in most cases, falls on fertile ground. While the grain procurements had already declined considerably in January, compared to December, the decline reached a catastrophic extent in February. According to the statistics just completed for the month of February, only 40 percent of the expected amount was procured. This fact is catastrophic and it sabotages in the full sense of the word every constructive activity of the proletarian government. Things are hardly any different in the area of raw materials production, which in February went down 23 percent compared to January.

Such a regressive movement in all fields is, in the long run, intolerable. In addition, serious regression in the supply of food was noted.

If this crisis were to continue to the same extent, an economic collapse would be unavoidable.

In the interest of the maintenance of the dictatorship of the proletariat, the Council of People's Commissars has decided, in full agreement with the Central Committee of the party, to use the most rigorous means against those who wish to overthrow the dictatorship of the proletariat by passive or active resistance in the economic field.

In agreement with the party's Central Committee, the Council of People's Commissars of the USSR has given extraordinary authority in these matters to Comrade Menzhinsky. The previous energy and success demonstrated by Comrade Menzhinsky guarantee that he will also succeed in defeating our enemies in this last field, the economic one, and in forcing them to capitulate. It is, of course, necessary in this matter that the units of the party support the work of the GPU everywhere and with all their strength and in no case offer passive resistance, as has unfortunately happened frequently in the recent past.

I repeat once more that the Council of People's Commissars of the USSR, in full agreement with the Central Committee, is determined not to shrink from any necessary measures in order to maintain the dictatorship of the proletariat.

We will proceed relentlessly and most severely against every party worker and every party body that has been proven to have sabotaged the instructions of the workers' and peasants' government by passive or active resistance.

I emphasize explicitly that Comrade Menzhinsky has been given extraordinary powers to monitor the work of party bodies that, unfortunately, have shown themselves absolutely not to be up to their tasks.

Every single case of direct or indirect sabotage in the delivery of grain or in the delivery of food must be reported to the competent judicial authorities, with a copy for the local section of the GPU. Every omission of such a report will be punished as support of counterrevolutionary activity. It is regrettable that, in the eleventh year of its existence, the workers' and peasants' government must take measures of a kind that are usually taken only in the capitalist states. Nevertheless the workers' and peasants' government is determined to be victorious on this final front too, even if that means it must not shrink from any necessary measures. We will defeat the counterrevolution! We will maintain the dictatorship of the proletariat, even though our enemies make the strongest efforts to overthrow the dictatorship of the proletariat. With the mass of the people united behind us, we are also sure of victory in this last part of the battle.

signed: Rykov

[at bottom of document:]

I. A. [signature illegible], office manager [*zaveduyushchii delami*] for the Council of People's Commissars of the USSR

7.

Chairman of the Council of People's Commissars of the USSR
Journal: Office Manager [*zav.del.*] of the Council of People's
Commissars of the USSR II/42. Personal.
March 12, 1928. Moscow, the Kremlin.

To the President of the GPU, Comrade Menzhinsky
Personal. By messenger. Top Secret. (Refers to March 10, 1928.)

On the basis of the prosecutor general's reports, which I have just received, I cannot, for my part at least, share the opinion of the GPU units in Kharkov[1] concerning the engineers Goldstein and Wagner.[2] The charges against Goldstein are not even legally definable.

Since these matters will now pass from the jurisdiction of the prosecutor general to the Council of People's Commissars this very day, the Central Committee of the party will deal with this question immediately and will make a concrete decision. But even today I can say that in such a case, where it is a question of the help of foreign experts in the reconstruction of our industry, the local GPU units at least have to investigate reasons and factors for suspicion thoroughly before they take a step that is likely to sabotage not only our foreign policy position but also our entire economic life. The Central Committee, and I along with it as chairman of the Council of People's Commissars, unanimously passed a resolution that Comrade Balitsky did not take the necessary precautionary measures *and that he tolerated independence on the part of the local units that they do not have under Soviet law.*[3]

Such independence on the part of the GPU's lower-level units, as in this case, is likely to disrupt the workers' and peasants' government's policy toward foreign countries most severely.

As Comrade Chicherin reports, because of this incident we have to take into account the possibility of major complications, which is directly contrary to the interest of the proletariat, especially at this moment.

Of equal importance is the fact that the whole affair was at first presented to the workers' and peasants' government in a light that cannot now be justified.

The workers' and peasants' government was presented with documents that in these proportions did not correspond at all to reality. It was, therefore, misled into making decisions it cannot maintain anymore. According to a phone conversation just held with the prosecutor general, numerous claims and so-called proofs, which were presented by the GPU of the Ukrainian Soviet Republic in this matter, are completely invalid.

By such reports, the workers' and peasants' government was led to make decisions that are incompatible with its sense of responsibility toward the proletariat.

I assume that the Central Committee's resolution of February 26, 1928[4] was passed on to the various government and party agencies in a form that did not correspond to the spirit of this resolution.

In the name of, and by the authority of, the Central Committee of the party, I will therefore reformulate the resolution of February 26, 1928—and I will have the corresponding decree sent out to all appropriate government agencies today—because the resolution seems to have been frequently misunderstood.

Although at the moment it is of the greatest importance to maintain party unity, which is most seriously endangered by the actions of oppositional and ultra-left elements—the latter in foreign countries—the program of new construction remains one of our *prime tasks. The Central Committee has declared that the reconstruction of the socialist economy is not possible without the help of foreign capital and foreign experts.*

Our political position toward the bourgeoisie is not supposed to play a role here. I only remind you that Ilyich in his time already pointed to this necessity in the interest of our proletariat.

The resolution of the party's Central Committee concerning the most important tasks was apparently passed on to the lower-level bodies in such an incorrect way that we have already received complaints about a wrong interpretation of these instructions from numerous agencies, first of all from the People's Commissariat of Foreign Affairs.

Not infrequently, certain agencies have even reported that the policy of the workers' and peasants' government was directly sabotaged by this misunderstanding.

The party's Central Committee will not tolerate such sabotage, even though it be indirect and certainly not deliberate, and it will take actions against the persons responsible with the full severity of the proletarian law.

The workers' and peasants' government, in full agreement with the opinions and resolutions of the Central Committee, will never tolerate a situation in which lower-level units of the party or government sabotage the implementation of our decisions, because this would ultimately become just what the opposition is doing.

The GPU Collegium itself forwarded the instructions it received in quite the correct way, but the lower bodies, for their part, perhaps overly anxious to do their duty and not even aware of the consequences, passed these instructions on in an unquestionably incorrect sense, because the actions of the GPU units in the Ukrainian Soviet Republic would otherwise be totally incomprehensible. At a moment when we are particularly in need of the help of foreign capital and foreign experts in order at least to halt the continuing regression in our economic life, the workers' and peasants' government's own agencies stab us in the back.

In full agreement with the opinion of the party's Central Committee, I concur with Comrade Chicherin's opinion that such actions endanger our construction program most gravely.[5] I would not waste words over this if I knew that all the accusations that have been raised were based on indisputable facts. Obviously, it is the prime duty of the GPU to safeguard the workers' and peasants' state against the hostile plans of the capitalists. But in this case, as far as I can now judge from information received from the prosecutor general himself, it seems that the necessary limits were far exceeded. Such measures, especially since a foreign country is concerned here, do not at all serve the workers' and peasants' government.

To the contrary, because it cannot present sound arguments, it is forced to acknowledge the mistakes that have been made, and this is interpreted by our enemies in foreign countries as a sign of the constantly growing weakness of the workers' and peasants' government, which, particularly now, is not at all in the interest of the proletariat of the [Soviet] Union.

Today more than ever, the proletarian agencies must be mindful of impressing people in other countries with the thought that the situation here is not as difficult as is generally assumed.

The Central Committee's resolution concerning the arrested engineers, which will probably be decided on tomorrow or the day after, will be forwarded to the GPU Collegium immediately.[6]

Furthermore, I would like to point out that the party's Central Committee intends to carry out a detailed investigation, probably [to be headed] by Comrade Bubnov, in order to definitively prevent repetition of such incidents, which not only sabotage our economic life but also undermine the prestige of the Soviet government most seriously.

signed: Rykov

8.

The People's Commissar of Foreign Affairs of the USSR
Personal Journal. No. A 57/28
Moscow, the Kremlin. March 13, 1928

To the President of the GPU Collegium, Comrade Menzhinsky

In reference to our earlier telephone conversation and the information from Comrade Krestinsky,[1] which we discussed, it would be very desirable to receive clarification as soon as possible as to exactly what happened with the arrested German engineers.[2]

Far be it from me to interfere in the internal affairs of the GPU; nevertheless, I would not want to leave unmentioned the fact that hostile bourgeois forces in foreign countries, who for weeks have been working quite openly to try to win Germany definitively to a Western orientation and include it in the English front,[3] will not only blow up this incident but will also use it to "convince" the German government and German business along these lines.

Even though the unity of the party and the protection of the proletarian power is our prime task at the moment, we should not forget how extremely serious our economic situation is. Any aggravation of our foreign relations—let alone the arrest of German engineers—is, as the Central Committee decided on March 11, *very undesirable* at the moment.[4] Our economic negotiations in Berlin are taking an extremely slow course as it is. The effect on other countries will, without any question, be very unfavorable if the Germans, *using as a pretext* the arrest of the engineers, decide to discontinue the negotiations. It must be known there as well how unfavorably the negotiations with France are going.[5]

As the responsible leader of the foreign policy of the workers' and peasants' government, I have the duty, without wishing to criticize the measures that have been taken, to point out the possibility of major disadvantages not only for our foreign policy position but also, and to the same extent, for our economic life.

I enclose a copy of a letter, which I just received from Comrade Krestinsky, and ask that it be treated as top secret. He expects, with full certainty, a discontinuation of the economic negotiations[6] and emphasizes that the propaganda for a change to a so-called Western orientation is apparently growing not inconsiderably in important circles in Germany.

Obviously, I am far from demanding that the GPU Collegium, because of foreign policy considerations, should tacitly tolerate counterrevolutionary activities by foreign specialists—activities directed against the interests of the USSR. When I inquired at the GPU Collegium yesterday, they still had not received any positive information, although by this time—and according to the terms of the agreement with Germany—it should have been presented [to the German authorities]. From our phone conversation, I was convinced to my own satisfaction that the GPU Collegium fully shares the opinion of the People's Commissariat of Foreign Affairs on this point. Without wishing to subject the activities of the GPU organs to any criticism, I fear that at least the local units of the GPU have not reacted quickly enough regarding the transmission of reports and have thereby placed the workers' and peasants' government in a difficult situation in regard to foreign relations.

I certainly do not have to emphasize that the German ambassador,[7] who has always shown honest sympathy for us during his five years of service here, deeply regrets the incident and is honestly endeavoring to resolve the matter in the interest of both parties as quickly as possible. But his work on this matter is greatly complicated by the fact that I am not in a position—entirely lacking any documented information myself—to aid him in his efforts, in spite of my earnest desire.

The German ambassador, who, as I said, is honestly seeking to resolve the conflict and to do so in a way that would not be embarrassing to either party, informed me confidentially that his policy toward the Soviet Union, which he has maintained through all these years, would be very gravely endangered if the arrest turned out to be a blunder by the local units. Besides other things, he told me his purely personal opinion, that he strongly doubts the justice of the charges against the arrested Germans.

I, therefore, think that the affair would have to be most thoroughly investigated from the center before we were to decide to bring the arrested men to trial. Should it turn out that the local units, convinced they were doing their duty, for some reason acted incorrectly, there is still time *now* to solve the problem in a relatively favorable way.

After hearing the views of the German ambassador, which were very convincing and clarifying to me, I would like to recommend the solution indicated [above], in view of the foreign and economic situation and in the interests of the workers' and peasants' government.

I do not want to hide the fact that these events, as the German ambassador *particularly stressed,* have made an extremely unfavorable impression in Germany, even in circles that favor close economic cooperation with us and that the events are being used against us by the press in other European countries as a so-called object lesson against economic dealings with the Soviet Union—in short, to sabotage us.

I hope that the GPU Collegium will ignore neither the opinions stated here nor the possibility of disposing of this matter in a way that is advantageous for both parties.

signed: Chicherin

9.

The People's Commissar of Agriculture of the USSR.
III/127
Moscow, the Kremlin. March 19, 1928
Personal.

1. To the President of the USSR Council of People's Commissars, Comrade Rykov
2. To the Central Committee of the Bolshevik Party, attention: General Secretary Comrade Stalin

The rough estimates and statistics as of March 15 show that about 30 percent of the grain procurements may have been secured during the first half of March, and since an improvement in the situation is not likely during the second half of March, this month of March would also bring a deficit of 40 percent of the expected amount.

Even though this unquestionably means an improvement in the situation compared to February, things still remain as serious as they were before, if 40 percent less grain is to be brought in.

I do not doubt that first of all the GPU's expert and farsighted measures contributed to the fact that the grain procurements rose not insignificantly in March compared to February. The regressive tendency of the grain procurements could hardly have been halted by any other measures. But in spite of these measures by the GPU and in spite of Comrade Menzhinsky's energetic and farsighted actions, our organizations were not able to bring in an amount even close to what we had expected. I also see no change in the situation for the second half of March, as I said.

While undeniable progress was made in procuring grain, the measures for reviving raw materials production, unfortunately, did not have any success at all. The existing rough estimates and statistics of March 15 even show a decline in raw materials production of about 8 or 9 percent compared to the already catastrophic second half of February.

Our experts on industry are generally of the opinion that this further decline in raw materials production will affect industry most seriously and that such a decline will paralyze our economic program completely. As far as the People's Commissariat under me is concerned, I personally see no way to counter this regressive trend. On the other hand, I fully share the above-mentioned experts' point of view and see these incidents as a grave danger to our industry and to the reconstruction program. We have to reckon with the possibility that the decline in raw materials production will continue at the same rate during the second half of March.

This means, without any question, a catastrophic threat to our entire economic life, further closings of factories, and increasing unemployment. In view of the extreme seriousness of the situation, I therefore suggest that an extraordinary conference be called on this issue as soon as possible and that experts, whom I would recommend, be invited.

signed: Kubyak

10.

The Workers' and Peasants' Inspection of the USSR.
II. 127. Secret.
Moscow, March 23, 1928

For several weeks a sabotage action, which is working hand in hand with the counterrevolutionary efforts of our enemies, has made itself felt more strongly in the industrial areas.

Surveillance of bourgeois elements in our socialist economic life by units of the Workers' and Peasants' Inspection has proved to be insufficient. The frequently poor collaboration with the GPU units has encouraged the hostile elements once again. They believe their time has now come. The GPU correctly points out that the local units of the Workers' and Peasants' Inspection have often not been equal to their tasks.

The GPU units report a renewed flare-up of counterrevolutionary activity in all industrial areas. The difficult economic situation is used by our internal enemies to discredit the Soviet government in the eyes of the proletariat.

I fully share the opinion of Comrade Menzhinsky, who has proven himself repeatedly in difficult times and who judges the counterrevolutionary movement in the industrial areas to be extremely serious, demanding an urgent and energetic manner of action against this counterrevolution. It is extremely regrettable that the inactivity of the local agencies has led to a considerable deterioration of the workers' mood. The monitoring of bourgeois co-workers has become so loose that the latter interpret this apathetic behavior as a sign of weakness on our part.

We must not, under any circumstances, allow these bourgeois specialists to win more influence over the workers and play them off against us by taking advantage of the difficult situation.

Every sign of political unreliability among the bourgeois specialists has to be reported immediately to the highest bodies as well as to the competent GPU units. We have use for only those bourgeois co-workers who maintain the closest contact with the Workers' and Peasants' Inspection and the GPU and who support these agencies in every way.

Ultimately, we must not forget that these bourgeois co-workers were inwardly, in spite of their outward loyalty, our enemies and will always be our enemies; that they yearn passionately for the restoration of a capitalist economic system and secretly support such efforts.

On the other hand, I have repeatedly been informed of cases in which specialists whom we regarded as entirely proletarian were suspected of sabotage because of the unserviceability of some machinery. Such treatment of specialists is self-evidently crazy. When they deserve punishment they should be struck with sure and relentless blows. But it would be wrong to brand them as scapegoats for mistakes that are not their responsibility.

The party's Central Committee and the Presidium of the Central Executive Committee of the USSR hereby order the strictest surveillance over the bourgeois specialists at their work places as well as in their private lives.

In case of discovery of counterrevolutionary activity, they are to be suspended from their positions immediately, while at work. This is the only way to save industry from further acts of sabotage. By April 5, it must be reported to me what measures have been taken in this regard.

signed: Ordzhonikidze

11.

The Chairman of the Presidium of the Executive Committee of the Russian Republic (RSFSR)
I. 323.7
Moscow, the Kremlin, March 22, 1928

(For distribution according to plan)

The measures aimed at increasing grain procurements and accelerating the production of raw materials, unfortunately, have had hardly any success. The first half of March, in comparison with the second half of February, shows such a slight increase in grain procurements that there can be no talk of any improvement in the extremely serious situation.

Our enemies continue, as before, to use propaganda to sabotage our economic policy and in particular the prestige of the workers' and peasants' government in the countryside as well as in the industrial centers.

After a brief period when food prices stopped rising, a new upward movement in prices for the most important food items has made itself felt in the last few days.

It is quite understandable that the proletariat should display mounting dissatisfaction because of this continuing deterioration in the economic situation and in food supply. In connection with the inflationary surge that is starting again, the question of an increase in wages becomes urgent. The workers' and peasants' government, in view of the difficult situation in regard to finances in general and the difficult financial situation in industry in particular, is not in a position even to discuss a rise in wages.

The Presidium of the Executive Committee of the Russian Republic on the basis of absolutely reliable information from the GPU has the impression that the local administrative bodies of the Workers' and Peasants' Inspection have not measured up at all in the struggle against this sabotage. Comrade Menzhinsky complains that the local party and administrative bodies often work directly against the GPU's agents. In this way they are indirectly sabotaging the policies of the workers' and peasants' government.

The situation as it exists today can by no means be tolerated any longer. A decline in production from one month to the next, as has been the case for the last half year, most severely disrupts the economic life of the Union. Since the beginning of the new fiscal year, the raw materials crisis has made itself felt more and more strongly. And during the first half of March, it has intensified further. This way, the closing of some factories will be unavoidable. The specter of unemployment is staring us in the face. Already the work force at a considerable number of factories is abnormally large relative to production.

The responsible bodies must be instructed immediately and most explicitly that sabotage on the part of the rural population and the lack of initiative and inactivity of the local party and administrative units there not only threaten economic life most severely but also endanger the existence of the proletarian government in the most serious way. Now as never before, energetic action is indispensable. Lack of energy in today's difficult situation is a crime against the proletarian cause. Those in positions of responsibility who do not fulfill their duties, or who lend tacit support to sabotage through their inaction, will be immediately removed from their posts and reported to the proper authorities to have judgment passed upon them.

Chairman of the Presidium of the Central Executive Committee

[of the RSFSR?]

signed: M. Kalinin

Chairman of the Council of People's Commissars of the RSFSR

signed: A. Rykov

Secretary of the Central Executive Committee of the RSFSR

for

[signature illegible]

APPENDIX II

Composition of the Highest State and Party Institutions of the USSR, 1927–1929

GOVERNMENT OF THE USSR

COUNCIL OF PEOPLE'S COMMISSARS (Sovet narodnykh komissarov—Sovnarkom, or SNK)

Chairman:	A. I. Rykov
Deputy Chairmen:	J. E. Rudzutak, G. K. Ordzhonikidze, V. V. Shmidt (from August 11, 1928)

ALL-UNION PEOPLE'S COMMISSARIATS

Foreign Affairs	G. V. Chicherin
Army and Navy	K. E. Voroshilov
Foreign and Domestic Trade	A. I. Mikoyan
Communications	J. E. Rudzutak
Post and Telegraph	A. M. Lyubovich (from November 12, 1927), N. K. Antipov (from January 16, 1928)

UNION-REPUBLIC PEOPLE'S COMMISSARIATS

Supreme Economic Council (Sovnarkhoz, VSNKh, or Vesenkha)	V. V. Kuibyshev (chairman)
Labor	V. V. Schmidt, N. A. Uglanov (from November 29, 1928)
Workers' and Peasants' Inspection	G. K. Ordzhonikidze
Agriculture (for the RSFSR)	A. P. Smirnov, N. A. Kubyak (from February 1928)
Central Statistical Agency (TsSU)	N. Osinsky, V. P. Milyutin (from March 3, 1928)
State Planning Commission (Gosplan)	G. M. Krzhizhanovsky
Council for Labor and Defense (STO)	A. I. Ruykov (chairman)
State Bank of the USSR (Gosbank)	A. L. Sheinman, Yu. L. Pyatakov (from the fall of 1928?)
Unified State Political Administration (OGPU, or more commonly, GPU)	V. R. Menzhinsky (chairman)

LEADING ORGANS OF THE CPSU

BEFORE THE FIFTEENTH PARTY CONGRESS

Members of the Politburo (Political Bureau of the Central Committee)—up to the Fifteenth Party Congress, December 12, 1927: Bukharin, Kalinin, Molotov, Rudzutak, Rykov, Stalin, Tomsky, Voroshilov

Candidate Members: Petrovsky, Uglanov, Andreyev, Kirov, Mikoyan, Kaganovich, Chubar

Secretariat of the Central Committee: Stalin, Molotov, Uglanov, S. Kosior, Shvernik

Central Control Commission (CCC): G. K. Ordzhonikidze (chairman)

AFTER THE FIFTEENTH PARTY CONGRESS

Members of the Politburo after the Fifteenth Congress: Bukharin (until November 11, 1929), Kalinin, Kuibyshev, Molotov, Rudzutak, Rykov, Stalin, Tomsky, Voroshilov

Candidate Members: Petrovsky, Uglanov (until April 29, 1929), Andreyev, Kirov, Mikoyan, Kaganovich, Chubar, S. Kosior, Bauman (until April 29, 1929)

Secretariat of the Central Committee: Stalin, Molotov, Uglanov (until April 29, 1929), S. Kosior (until July 11, 1928), Kubyak, Kaganovich (until July 11, 1928), Bauman (until April 29, 1929)

Central Control Commission (CCC): G. K. Ordzhonikidze (chairman), Y. M. Yaroslavsky (secretary)

NOTES

PREFACE

1. M. Reiman, *Ruská revoluce: 23 února–25 října 1917; Russian edition: Russkai revoliutsiia, 23 fevralia–25 oktiabria 1917.* 2 vols. (Prague, 1968).

2. Moshe Lewin, *Russian Peasants and Soviet Power* (London, 1968).

1. ON THE THRESHOLD OF CRISIS

1. According to data given by Stalin at the Fifteenth Party Congress in December 1927, industry reached 100.9 percent of the prewar level during the fiscal year 1926–1927, and agriculture reached 108.3 percent (Stalin, *Sochineniia* [hereafter cited as *Soch.*], vol. 10, Moscow, 1950, p. 293). Other figures are often given in the literature of that time as well as later. Cf. the methodologically interesting article by V. Bazarov, "O metodologii kontrol'nykh tsifr," *Ekonomicheskoe obozrenie*, January 1927, pp. 13–24.

2. At the Fifteenth Party Congress, Stalin claimed that Soviet foreign trade during the fiscal year 1926–1927 was only 35.6 percent of the prewar level (*Soch.*, vol. 10, p. 294).

3. See, for example, Rykov's concluding remarks under the report on the five-year plan directives at the Fifteenth Party Congress, *Piatnadtsatyi s"ezd VKP(b), dekabr' 1927 g. Stenograficheskii otchet* (hereafter cited as *Piatnadtsatyi s"ezd*), pt. 2, Moscow, 1962, pp. 1163–1172. This problem is referred to in a whole series of other sources of the time.

4. See, for example, the above-cited remarks by Rykov, as well as the speech by Anastas Mikoyan at the Fifteenth Party Congress, ibid, pp. 1163–1172, 1091–1108.

5. Cf., for example, Stalin, *Soch.*, vol. 11, Moscow, 1952, p. 85. Stalin cites data prepared by Vasily Nemchinov, a member of the Collegium of the Central Statistical Bureau. A whole series of differing estimates exists as to the marketable portion of agricultural output, but they do not change the overall picture of Soviet agriculture's extreme backwardness.

6. The official figures of that time give the number of workers at large state-owned industrial enterprises as 1,223,000 in the fiscal year 1927–1928 and the number of unemployed as 1,596,000, as of April 1, 1928; according to the trade unions, there were as many as 1.8 million unemployed in the spring and summer of 1928. See L. S. Rogachevskaia, "Reshaiushchii etap likvidatsii bezrabotitsy v. SSSR", *Istoriia SSSR*, 1968, no. 3, p. 47. Because of the peculiarities of Soviet statistics, which counted only part of the unemployed, most specialists of that time enlarged their estimates to two and a half million or more.

7. A. I. Rykov, "Doklad ob Ob"edinennom plenume TsK i TsKK VKP(6) na aktive moskovskoi organizatsii, 11.8.1927 g.," *Izvestia*, August 14, 1927 (hereafter cited as A. I. Rykov, "Doklad ob Ob"edinennom plenume").

8. Cf. K. E. Voroshilov, "Voprosy oborony i piatiletka," in *Piatnadtsatyi s"ezd*, pt. 2, pp. 973–994. The state of preparedness of Red Army personnel was discussed in detail at a joint session of the Politburo and the Presidium of the Central Control Commission, presumably in late January or early February 1928; a record of this session is in the "Political Archive" of the German Foreign Ministry: Politisches Archiv des Auswärtigen Amtes, Abt. IV Ru, Po 2, Adh. 1, Bd. 2. (Materials from this archive will be cited hereafter according to the following pattern—PA, IV Ru, 2–I, 2).

9. According to the Commissariat of Finance, the balance of income over expenditure in favor of industry was 77.3 million rubles in 1925–1926, 313.4

million in 1926–1927; and 477.3 million in 1927–1928. See A. I. Rykov, "Itogi noiabr'skogo plenuma TsK," *Pravda*, December 4, 1928.

10. A. A. Barsov indicates, for example, that in 1928 surplus product was alienated from agriculture through "nonequivalent exchange" *(v poriadke bezek-vivalentnogo otchuzhdeniia)* and transferred to other sectors of the economy on a scale of 1.6–1.8 billion rubles, depending on various different estimates. This accounted for 65 percent of the funds accumulated by the nonagricultural sector, which amounted to approximately 40 percent of its surplus product and 16 percent of its share of the national income. See A. A. Barsov, "Sel'skoe khoziaistvo i istochniki sotsialisticheskogo nakopleniia v gody pervoi piatiletki (1928–1932)," *Istoriia SSSR*, 1968, no. 3, pp. 64–82; and A. A. Barsov, "NEP i vyravnivanie ekonomicheskikh otnoshenii mezhdu gorodom i derevnei," in *Novaia ekonomicheskaia politika: Voprosy teorii i istorii*, ed. M. P. Kim (Moscow, 1974), pp. 93–105.

11. According to figures of that time, the USSR covered as much as 75 percent of the budget of foreign Communist parties as well, of course, as the activities of the Comintern and the international organizations allied with it (PA IV Ru, 2–I, 3).

These figures were given by an informed Soviet official who arrived in Riga in early February 1928. They are corroborated by other documents in the German Foreign Ministry archive. Soviet support for the Kuomintang revolution and for a number of other revolutionary actions required huge sums that cannot be estimated exactly.

12. A detailed account of the Soviet economic discussions may be found in Alexander Erlich, *The Soviet Industrialization Debate, 1924–1928*, Harvard University Press, 1960. Much attention is devoted to them by other authors as well, in particular the following: Moshe Lewin, *Russian Peasants and Soviet Power* (London, 1968); Robert V. Daniels, *The Conscience of the Revolution* (New York, 1960); Isaac Deutscher, *The Prophet Unarmed, Trotsky 1921–1929* (London, 1959); E. H. Carr, *Socialism in One Country, 1924–1926*, 3 vols. (London, 1958–1959); Robert C. Tucker, *Stalin as Revolutionary, 1879–1929* (New York, 1973); R. Lorenz, *Sozialgeschichte der Sowjetunion*, vol. 1, 1917–1945 (Frankfurt, 1976); Alec Nove, *An Economic History of the USSR* (London, 1969).

13. Stalin, "Politicheskii otchet Tsentral'nogo komiteta s"ezdu VKP(b)," in *Soch.*, vol. 10, pp. 271–276.

14. See, for example, E. H. Carr and R. W. Davies, *Foundations of a Planned Economy 1926–1929*, vol. 1, pt. 1 (London, 1969), pp. 284–292 (hereafter cited as Carr and Davies).

15. This may be deduced from an undated speech by Chicherin (apparently given on June 19, 1927) at a joint session of the Politburo and Council of People's Commissars (Sovnarkom) and from a memorandum produced by him immediately after that session. Both are found in PA IV Ru, 2–I, 4. Chicherin's proposals were not accepted at that time by the Politburo.

16. Stalin's letter of December 27, 1927, to the members of the Politburo and to Chicherin, in PA IV Ru, 2–I, 2. From this letter, it appears that Stalin was supported by Chicherin and had been since mid-1927 by Commissar of Finance Bryukhanov and several other economic functionaries. Stalin's proposals were not adopted.

17. A memorandum by Chicherin, written apparently on October 27, 1927, in PA IV Ru, 2–I, 1.

18. See *Kommunisticheskaia partiia Sovetskogo Soiuza v rezoliutsiiakh i resheniiakh s"ezdov, konferentsii i plenumov TsK* (hereafter cited as *KPSS v rezoliutsiiakh*), vol. 3, 1924–1927, Moscow, 1970, pp. 431–432.

19. K. E. Voroshilov, "Voprosy oborony i piatiletka," in *Piatnadtsatyi s"ezd*, pt. 2, p. 980.

2. THE BREAK WITH BRITAIN: CONFLICTS IN THE SOVIET LEADERSHIP

1. See *Dokumenty vneshnei politiki SSSR* (hereafter cited as *DVP*). vol. 10, Moscow, 1965, pp. 245–247 and 280–288 (an exchange of diplomatic notes between the USSR and Britain, May 27–28, 1927); *Documents on British Foreign Policy, 1919–1930* (hereafter cited as *DBFP*), ser. Ia, vol. 3, London, 1970, pp. 338–340 and 370–378 (Chamberlain's note of May 26, 1927 and a record of the Geneva conference of foreign ministers of Britain, France, Germany, Italy, Japan, and Belgium on June 14, 1927); *Akten zur deutschen auswärtigen Politik, 1918–1945: Aus dem Archiv des Auswärtigen Amtes* (hereafter cited as *ADAP*), ser. B, 1925–1933, vol. 5, pp. 405–406 (letter from Sthamer, the German ambassador in London, to the German Foreign Ministry, May 25, 1927). For an assessment of the substance of Soviet policy, see Chicherin's June 1927 memorandum cited above (PA, IV Ru, 2–I, 4).

2. See, for example, *DVP*, vol. 10, pp. 300–306 (record of a conversation between Chicherin and Stresemann of June 7, 1927); and *DBFP*, ser. Ia, vol. 3, pp. 370–378 (the above-cited record of the June 14 foreign ministers' conference).

3. *DVP*, vol. 10, pp. 300–306 and 306–308 (records of Chicherin's talks with Stresemann on June 7 and 9, 1927); also, *ADAP*, ser. B, vol. 5, pp. 465–473.

4. See, for example, the June 20, 1927 memorandum by H. Gordon in *DBFP*, Ser. Ia. vol. 3, pp. 396–398.

5. See, for example, *DBFP*, ser. Ia, vol. 3, pp. 370–376 (the foreign ministers' conference); and *ADAP*, ser. B, Vol. 5, pp. 536–540.

6. *ADAP*, ser. B, vol. 5, pp. 536–540 (record of the foreign ministers' conference).

7. *DBFP*, ser. Ia, vol. 3, pp. 354–356 (diplomatic information of June 13, 1927); also, PA, IV Ru, 5, Ukraine, 3 (information from the German consulate in Kiev, May 26, 1927). The question of industrial workers leaving the party became one of the hottest issues in the dispute between the party leadership and the opposition.

8. *Piatnadtsatyi s"ezd*, pt. 2, pp. 1091–1108 (the speech by Mikoyan, commissar of trade).

9. "Die internationale Lage von SSSR (March 15, 1927)," in PA, Handakten Direktoren: Dirksen, Pol. Aufzeichnungen, vol. 1.

10. See, for example, A. I. Rykov, "Doklad ob Ob"edinennom plenume," *Izvestia*, August 14, 1927; "Vystuplenie K. E. Voroshilova na kreisere 'Marat,' 22.7.1927 g.," *Izvestia*, July 26, 1927. These speeches were given after the danger of war had been reassessed more correctly. For the earlier period, see, for example, the memorandum by von Dirksen of June 3, 1927, in *ADAP*, ser. B, vol. 5, pp. 454–458.

11. See also *ADAP*, ser. B, vol. 5, pp. 465–473 (the record of the conversation between Chicherin and Stresemann of June 7, 1927).

12. See, for example, the records of the foreign ministers' conference of June 14, 1927, in *DBFP*, ser. Ia, vol. 3, pp. 370–378, and in *ADAP*, ser. B, vol. 5, pp. 536–540.

13. See, for example, the statement by the Central Committee of the Communist Party (Bolshevik) of the Ukraine to the Executive Committee of the Communist International in *Izvestia*, July 5, 1927. The reference is to a group of Ukrainian party and government officials (Shumsky, Maksimovich, Hvylovyi) who were supported by a number of party cadres of Ukrainian nationality and by the Central Committee of the Communist Party of the Western Ukraine.

14. See, for example, *ADAP*, ser. B, vol. 5, pp. 418–421 (an excerpt from the record of the foreign ministers' conference: the report by Foreign Minister Stresemann).

15. See the above-cited speech by Chicherin, apparently on June 19, 1927, at the joint session of the Politburo and Sovnarkom.

16. "Kak proizoshlo ubiistvo Voikova," *Pravda,* June 8, 1927. The results of the investigation into the explosion in Leningrad were published in a report "From the GPU Collegium" in *Izvestia,* September 2, 1927. In these two attacks a number of circumstances remained unclarified. As for the Leningrad explosion, a direct connection was made soon after the event between the explosion and an organization called "Trest" (the Trust), which was active in White Russian emigre circles but was actually controlled by the GPU. In particular, the explosion was linked with a man called Operput (whose real name, according to some sources, was A. O. Upenlis), one of the GPU's chief agents at that time, who had earlier betrayed Boris Savinkov to the Soviet authorities.

17. Remark made by Menzhinsky during Chicherin's speech at the joint session of the Politburo and Sovnarkom, cited above.

18. I have not been able to establish the exact date the GPU was granted these special powers. At the above-mentioned joint session of the Politburo and Sovnarkom, apparently June 19, 1927, they were extended for an additional six weeks. *Tägliche Rundschau,* June 14, 1927, reported that they had been extended to September 1 of that year.

19. According to figures in the German press in mid-1927, the number of prisoners was approximately 15,000 (*Vossische Zeitung,* August 16, 1927). This number should be regarded as greatly minimized. There are no figures for the number executed. We can assume that at least several hundred were shot.

20. *ADAP,* ser. B, vol. 5., pp. 513–518 (record of a conversation between Stresemann and Briand in Geneva, June 14, 1927).

21. *ADAP,* ser. B, vol. 5, pp. 466–473 (record of a conversation between Stresemann and Chicherin in Baden-Baden, June 7, 1927). Here, Chicherin indicates quite definitely the existence of two groupings in the leadership.

22. From the above-cited materials on the joint session of the Politburo and Sovnarkom, apparently June 19, 1927, and Chicherin's memorandum after that session, in PA, IV Ru, 2–I, 4.

23. See, for example, Boris Bazhanov, "Pobeg iz nochi: Iz vospominanii byvshego sekretaria Stalina (Flight from the Night: Memoirs of a Former Secretary of Stalin's), ch. 9: "Stalin," in *Kontinent,* 1976, no. 9, pp. 379–393. (Bazhanov was technical secretary for the Politburo in the 1920s.) For a characterization of the leading personalities in the Soviet Communist Party, see, for example, Stephen F. Cohen, *Bukharin and the Bolshevik Revolution: A Political Biography, 1888–1938* (New York, 1973), ch. 7.

24. "Pis'mo V. iz Moskvy," *Sotsialisticheskii vestnik* (hereafter *Sots. vestnik*), no. 9 (151), May 9, 1927.

25. They defended their China policy with extreme cynicism. The blame for the Comintern's failure in China was laid on the Chinese Communist Party (CCP). Cf. "Postanovlenie IKKI o tekushchem momente kitaiskoi revoliutsii" (Resolution of the ECCI on the Present Phase of the Chinese Revolution), *Izvestia,* July 14, 1927.

26. "Pis'mo iz Moskvy, 29.6.1927 g.," *Sots. vestnik,* no. 14 (156), July 8, 1927; Stalin, "Mezhdunarodnoe polozhenie i oborona SSSR. Rech' na ob"edinennom plenume TsK i TsKK VKP(b), 1.8.1927 g.," in *Soch.,* vol. 10, pp. 3–84. This speech contains direct attacks on Chicherin without naming him.

27. *Berliner Börsen Zeitung,* June 30, 1928. (A report from an informed source in Riga, dated June 29.)

28. PA, IV Ru, 5, 19 (telegrams from the German embassy in Moscow, dated July 10 and 23, 1927).

29. *DVP,* vol. 10, p. 372 (Narkomindel report of August 31, 1927).

30. The reference is to plans for replacing Stalin with Tomsky in the post of general secretary. See below.

3. THE OPPOSITION REVIVED

1. *Mitteilungsblatt. Linke Opposition der KPD* (Hugo Urbahns ed., Berlin), no. 10, May 15, 1927. ("Aus dem letzten Plenum des ZK der WKP.")

2. The account of the proceedings of the ECCI plenum is based on the following sources: "Izveshchenie o rabotakh Plenuma IKKI," *Pravda*, May 31, 1927; PA, IV Ru, 5, 3 (a typed informational report, with the date July 18, 1927, written in pencil); "Das Plenum des EKKI," *Fahne des Kommunismus: Zeitschrift der orthodoxen Marxisten-Leninisten* (hereafter cited as FdK), no. 15, June 24, 1927; "Diktatura na rasput'e: Pis'mo iz Moskvy, 24.6.1927," *Sots. vestnik*, no. 13 (155), July 2, 1927 (hereafter cited as "Diktatura na rasput'e"); *Die linke Opposition in der Sowjetunion, 1923–1927*, 5 vols. (hereafter cited as *Die linke Opposition*), Bd.V, 1926–1927 (West Berlin, 1977), pp. 96–113; Ruth Fischer, *Stalin and German Communism* (London, 1948); Avina Di Biagio, "L'ultima bataglia dell' opposizione (1926–1927)," in Bertolissi, Di Biagio, Benvenuti, and Sestan, *Studi di storia sovietica* (Rome, 1978), pp. 139–145 (hereafter cited as Di Biagio).

3. *Die linke Opposition*, pp. 84–95.

4. PA, IV Ru, 5, 3 (informational report of July 18, 1927).

5. PA, IV Ru, 2-I, 4 (information of April 18, 1928). A different acount may be found in Deutscher, *Prophet Unarmed* p. 333, based on Trotsky's letter to Krupskaya of May 7, 1927, the draft of which is in the Trotsky Archive at Harvard.

6. PA, IV Ru, 5, 3, (information of August 18, 1927; and Yagoda's speech at the Sovnarkom session of July 7, 1927).

7. "Pis'mo iz Moskvy ot 29.6.1927 g.," *Sots. vestnnik*, no. 14 (156), July 18, 1927.

8. PA, IV Ru, 5, 3 (information of August 18, 1927; and Yagoda's speech at the Sovnarkom session of July 7, 1927); also, "Diktatura na rasput'e."

9. Ibid. For a different version, see "La Session du Comité Central: Avant, Pendant, Après," *Bulletin Communiste*, no. 20–21, 1927 (hereafter cited as "La Session du CC").

10. See "O narushenii partiinoi distsipliny tt. Zinov'evym i Trotskim (Rezol. plenuma TsK i TsKK VKP [b], 29.7.–9.8.1927 g.)," in *KPSS v rezoliutsiiakh*, vol. 3: 1924–1927 (Moscow, 1970), pp. 492–499; also, "Diktatura na rasput'e."

11. PA, IV Ru, 5, 3 (informaton of July 18, 1927); also, "Diktatura na rasput'e." For a detailed account, drawing on the Trotsky Archives, see Carr and Davies, vol. 2, pp. 26–29.

12. L. D. Trotsky, "Dve rechi na zasedanii TsKK, iiun' 1927 g.," in *Stalinskaia shkola fal'sifikatsii* (Berlin, 1932), pp. 132–164; also Stalin, "Mezhdunarodnoe polozhenie i oborona SSSR: Rech' 1 avgusta 1927 g.," in *Soch.*, vol. 10, pp. 3–59 (which includes a quotation from Trotsky's letter to Ordzhonikidze of July 11, 1927).

13. *Pravda*, June 26, 1927; also, "La Session du CC"; cf. Di Biagio, pp. 161–162.

14. See FdK, no. 18, July 15, 1927, and no. 27, September 16, 1927. The Soviet version of this correspondence, with all the rough edges removed, was published in *Pravda* July 1, 1927, and in *Izvestia* September 3, 1927.

15. "Doklad tov. A. I. Rykova ob Ob"edinennom plenume TsK i TsKK VKP(b) na aktive moskovskoi organizatsii 11.8.1927 g.," *Izvestia*, August 14 and 17, 1927 (hereafter cited as A. I. Rykov, "Doklad ob Ob"edinennom plenume");

"Doklad tov. A. I. Rykova na X vseukrainskom parts"ezde 20 noiabria s.g.," *Izvestia*, November 25, 1927.

16. Ibid.; see also "Partei und Opposition in Russland," *Stuttgarter Neues Tageblatt*, July 9, 1927.

17. See, for example, PA, IV Ru, 5, 3 (information of July 18, 1927).

18. See Stalin, "Po povodu 'zaiavleniia' oppozitsii ot 8.8.1927 g.: Rech na Ob"edinennom plenume TsK i TsKK VKP(b) 9.8.1927 g."; and "Trotskistskai oppozitsiia prezhde i teper': Rech' na zasedanii ob"edinennogo plenuma TsK i TsKK VKP(b) 23.11.1927 g.," in *Soch.*, vol. 10, pp. 85–91, 172–205; *FdK*, no. 23, August 19, 1927; *Sots. vestnik*, no. 18(160), September 22, 1927, esp. the letter from "S" in Moscow dated September 4, 1927; see also "La Session du CC"; and compare Deutscher, *Prophet Unarmed*, p. 350, in reference to a statement by high-ranking Red Army commanders Muralov, Putna, Yakir, and others in favor of the opposition.

19. "Rezoliutsiia plenuma 'O mezhdunarodnom polozhenii,'" in *KPSS v rezoliutsiiakh*, vol. 3, pp. 463–476.

20. Stalin, "Rech' 5 avgusta," in *Soch.*, vol. 10, pp. 82–83.

21. A. I. Rykov, "Doklad ob Ob"edinennom plenume," *Izvestia*, August 17, 1927.

22. "Erklärung der Opposition auf dem Vereinigten Plenum des ZK und der ZKK der KPSU," in *Die linke Opposition*, pp. 282–283.

23. "O narushenii partiinoi distsipliny tt. Zinov'evym i Trotskim," in *KPSS v rezoliutsiiakh*, vol. 3, pp. 492–499.

24. A. I. Rykov, "Doklad ob Ob"edinennom plenume," *Izvestia*, August 17, 1927.

25. "Pis'mo iz Moskvy ot 6.8.1927 g.," *Sots. vestnik*, nos. 16–17 (158–159), August 20, 1927.

26. Chicherin's memorandum to the Politburo, apparently of October 27, 1927, and his weekly information report to Soviet diplomatic representatives, dated November 23, 1927, in PA, IV Ru, 2–I, 1.

27. "Mezhdunarodnoe polozhenie SSSR v 1926–27 gg. Razdel: Frantsiia," in *DVP*, vol. 10, pp. 575–577; several other documents in vol. 10 are also pertinent. See also "Pis'mo Chicherina Erbettu ot 4.10.1927 g. i otvet Erbetta Chicherinu ot 7.10.1927 g.," *Izvestia*, October 13, 1927. (Herbette's letter presented the French position.) Further, see "Nota Narkomindela SSSR G.V. Chicherina frantsuzskomu poslu v SSSR Zh. Erbettu ot 12.10.1927 g.," *Izvestia*, October 14, 1927.

28. "Russlands Selbstauschhaltung und deren Folgewirkungen für Deutschland, 26.11.1927," in PA, Handakten Direktoren: Dirksen, Politischen Aufzeichnungen, Bd. I.

29. A. I. Rykov, "Doklad ob Ob"edinennom plenume," *Izvestia*, August 14 and 17, 1927; "Ob itogakh Ob"edinennogo plenuma TsK i TsKK: Doklad tov. Bukharina na sobranii partaktiva leningradskoi organizatsii VKP(b), 11.8.1927 g.," *Izvestia*, August 18, 1927.

30. Cf., for example, "Pis'mo iz Moskvy ot 6.8.1927 g.," *Sots. vestnik*, nos. 16–17 (158–159), August 20, 1927.

31. These places were mentioned in Soviet documents and foreign diplomatic documents, in reports reaching the outside world from various sources in the USSR, in GPU correspondence and other GPU documents that found their way into foreign archives, the press, and so on. Also compare the article signed "Tovarishch" and entitled "Iz provintsial'nykh nestroenii i nastroenii," *Revoliutsionnaia Rossiia*, no. 63, November 1, 1927, with a reference to a report on the situation in the USSR that was prepared for the Central Executive Committee of the Soviets.

32. Trotsky, *My Life* (New York, 1970), pp. 531–532.

33. See, for example, the dispatches of the German consulate in Kiev dated September 5 and 30, 1927, in PA, IV Ru, 5 (Ukr.), 4.

34. PA, IV Ru, 5, 22 (information of October 17, 1927).

35. PA, IV Ru, 2–I, 1 (two information reports on the situation inside the Soviet party leadership, dated November and mid-December 1927); *FdK*, no. 7, February 17, 1928; and compare Carr and Davies, vol. 2, p. 34.

36. "Die Plattform der Vereinigten Opposition (Die wirkliche Lage in Russland)," in *Die linke Opposition*, pp. 328–466.

37. *Die linke Opposition*, p. 328; Carr and Davies, vol. 2, p. 35.

38. "Die Lage in Sowjet-Russland, 17.10.1927 g."; PA, Abt. IV Ru, Pol. 5, Sbd. 23; Deutscher, *Prophet Unarmed*, p. 357, with reference to the banning of the platform of the opposition mainly as the result of Stalin's insistence.

39. PA, IV Ru, 2–I, 1 (from the records of speeches at an undated Politburo session or the October Central Committee plenum—the speech by Trotsky).

40. "Postanovlenie Prezidiuma TsKK ot 29.9.1927 g.," *Pravda*, September 30, 1927; "Postanovlenie Prezidiuma TsKK ot 13.10.1927 g.," *Pravda*, October 13, 1927; *FdK*, no. 31, October 14, 1927.

41. See, for example, *FdK*, no. 29, September 30, 1927.

42. "Izveshchenie ob iskliuchenii tt. Trotskogo i Vuiovicha iz IKKI. Vsem sektsiiam Internatsionala," *Pravda*, September 30, 1927; Stalin, *Soch.*, vol. 10, pp. 152–167; cf. Carr and Davies, vol. 2, p. 36.

43. PA, IV Ru, 2–I, 1 (from records of speeches at an undated Politburo or Central Committee session around the time of the October plenum).

44. Stalin, "Trotskistskaia oppozitsiia prezhde i teper'," in *Soch.*, vol. 10, pp. 172–205; for more detail, see Di Biagio, pp. 200–205.

45. For the fullest account, see Trotsky, *My Life*, pp. 532–533.

46. Menzhinsky's letter of November 9, 1927, addressed to Kalinin, Rykov, Voroshilov, Stalin, and Ordzhonikidze, in PA, IV Ru, 2–I, 1.

47. For details, see "XVI Moskovskaia gub. konferentsiia VKP(b): Doklad t. E. Iaroslavskogo o rabote TsKK VKP(b)," *Izvestia*, November 27, 1927; and "Dokumenty mezhduusobitsy, I: Nastoiashchii 'podarochek' k prazdniku," *Sots. vestnik*, no. 1 (167), January 12, 1928.

48. See Menzhinsky's letter of November 9, 1927, cited above; also his informational letter for the party leadership of November 10 and Stalin's covering letter of November 11 (both reprinted in the appendix); and Red Army Chief of Staff Pugachev's order to heads of military districts, dated November 9, 1927, all in PA, IV Ru, 2–I, 1.

49. See *Rote Fahne*, November 10, 1927; Yaroslavsky's report in *Izvestia*, November 27, 1927; and "Pis'mo V. A. iz Moskvy ot 30.12.1927 g." and "Demonstratsii oppozitsii: Iz pis'ma ochevidtsa," *Sots. vestnik*, no. 1 (167), January 12, 1928.

50. Menzhinsky's letters, cited above, of November 9 and 10, 1927, in PA, IV Ru, 2–I, 1.

51. For an account of the leadership conflict over these issues see PA, IV Ru, 2–I, 1 (information from Moscow, December 1927).

52. "XVI Moskovskaia gub. konferentsiia: Doklad N. I. Bukharina, 20.11.1927 g.," *Izvestia*, November 23, 1927; "Doklad tov. A. I. Rykova na X Vseukrainskom parts"ezde, 20.11.1927 g.," *Izvestia*, November 25, 1927.

53. See Ordzhonikidze's letter of the second half of November 1927, addressed to Stalin, the Central Committee, and Menzhinsky; also the above-cited informational document from Moscow, December 1927 (both in PA, IV Ru, 2–I, 1).

54. "Ko vsem organizatsiiam VKP(b): ob antipartiinykh vystupleniiakh liderov oppozitsii," in *KPSS v rezoliutsiiakh*, vol. 3, pp. 544–547.

55. Trotsky, *My Life*, p. 532.

56. "Doklad tov. Tomskogo o rabote TsK VKP(b) na 1–i leningradskoi oblastnoi partkonferentsii, 15.11.1927 g.," *Izvestia*, November 19, 1927; "Doklad tov. A. I. Rykova na X Vseukrainskom parts"ezde, 20.11.1927 g.," *Izvestia*, November 25, 1927.

57. *Piatnadtsatyi s"ezd*, pt. 2, pp. 1417–1418 (the statement of Ordzhonikidze to the Presidium of the congress.)

58. An undated letter of Stalin's, numbered A 47–27, apparently dating from the end of November 1927, addressed to the Central Committee (Politburo) and CCC (Ordzhonikidze), in PA, IV Ru, 2–I, 1.

59. PA, IV Ru, 2–I, 1 (informational document of November 26, 1927, based on sources from the French embassy in Moscow).

60. Ibid.

61, See, for example, the above-cited letter by Chief of Staff Pugachev, dated November 9, 1927; a letter from Stalin to all central institutions of the union republics, to the CCC, the GPU, and the Commissariat of the Navy, dated November 11, 1927; and an order by the Central Executive Committee and the Sovnarkom, dated November 13, 1927, referring to an earlier order of November 4, 1927, all in PA, IV Ru, 2–I, 1. Later on, such measures were applied with increasing frequency and on the most diverse pretexts.

62. PA, IV Ru, 2–I, 1 (informational document form Moscow, December 1927).

4. ECONOMIC CRISIS AND POWER POLITICS

1. "O kapital'nom stroitel'stve v promyshlennosti," in *KPSS v rezoliutsiiakh*, vol. 3, pp. 431–432.

2. A. I. Rykov, "Doklad ob Ob"edinennom plenume," *Izvestia*, August 14, 1927.

3. A. Jugow, *Die Volkswirtschaft der Sowjetunion und ihre Probleme* (Dresden, 1929), pp. 240–245; see also O. Domanevskaia, "V porochnom krugu," *Sots. vestnik*, no. 1 (167), January 12, 1928. Both based on official Soviet data.

4. See, for example, A. Mikoyan, "Na perelome (khlebozagotovki v ianvare)," *Pravda*, February 8, 1928.

5. See, for example, *Berliner Tageblatt*, September 3, 1927; and the above-cited speech by Trotsky at a session of the Politburo or Central Committee in October 1927, in PA, IV Ru, 2–I, 1.

6. See Litvinov's entry in the personal journal of the Commissar of Foreign Affairs, February 9, 1928, in PA, IV Ru, 2–I, 3; also A. I. Rykov, "Tekushchii moment i zadachi partii: Doklad na aktive moskovskoi organizatsii, 13.7.1928 g." *Pravda*, July 15, 1928.

7. A. I. Rykov, "Doklad ob Ob"edinennom plenume," *Izvestia*, August 14, 1927; "Doklad tov. N. I. Bukharina na sobranii aktiva leningradskoi organizatsii VKP(b), 26.10.1927 g.," *Izvestia*, November 4, 1927; Carr and Davies, vol. 1, pt. 1, pp. 271–312.

8. A memorandum by Chicherin to the members of the Politburo, in PA, IV Ru, 2–I, 2. Stalin, in a note of December 27, 1927, to members of the Politburo (PA, IV Ru, 2–I, 2), gives the date of October 27, 1927, for a memorandum by Chicherin and links it with the joint session of the Politburo, Sovnarkom, and CEC at that time. However, Stalin's quotations from Chicherin do not correspond to the text of the Chicherin memorandum at my disposal. This leads me to suppose that Chicherin returned to this question in two or more separate memoranda.

9. Stalin's note of December 12, 1927, cited above, in PA, IV Ru, 2–I, 2.

10. "Izveshchenie ob iskliuchenii tt. Trotskogo i Vuiovicha iz IKKI," *Izvestia*, October 1, 1927. Cf. "Kontr-tezisy trotskistskoi oppozitsii o piatiletnem plane

narodnogo khoziaistva," in the Discussion Bulletin supplement to *Pravda*, November 17, 1927, Diskussionnyi listok, no. 5 (hereafter cited as "Kontr-tezisy oppozitsii o plane").

11. Information from Chicherin to Soviet diplomatic representatives, dating presumably from the first half of January 1928, in PA, IV Ru, 2–I, 2.

12. Information from Litvinov to Soviet diplomatic representatives: an entry in the personal journal of the commissar of foreign affairs, February 9, 1928, in PA, IV Ru, 2–I, 3.

13. Dispatch from Chicherin to Soviet diplomatic representatives (information of February 9, 1928), in PA, IV Ru, 2–I, 2.

14. Cf., for example, "Zapis' obmena mneniiami mezhdu predstaviteliami pravitel'stv SSSR i Germanii, 6.2.1928 g.," in *DVP*, vol. 11, pp. 59–66, and other documents in this volume.

15. Above-cited information from Litvinov to Soviet diplomatic representatives, February 9, 1928 in PA, IV Ru, 2–I, 3.

16. "K desiatiletiiu Oktiabria: Doklad N.I. Bukharina na VII Moskovskom gub. s"ezde profsoiuzov, 12.10.1927 g.," *Izvestia*, October 18, 1927 g.; "Rede Zinov'evs auf der Sitzung der komm. Fraktion des CIK, 15.10.1927," *FdK*, no. 36, November 18, 1927; and Kalinin's speech in *Piatnadtsatyi s"ezd VKP(b)*, vol. 2, p. 1230.. For more detail, see Carr and Davies, vol. 1, pt. 1, pp. 32–37.

17. See the speeches of Rykov and Mikoyan at the Fifteenth Party Congress, in *Piatnadtsatyi s"ezd VKP(b)*, vol. 2, pp. 855–880, 1091–1108. Cf. "Kontr-tezisy oppozitsii o plane," and Z. Goldenberg, "Iskhodnoe polozhenie," in the Discussion Bulletin supplement to *Pravda*, November 17, 1927.

18. *Piatnadtsatyi s"ezd VKP(b)*, vol. 2, pp. 43–91; "Es ist aus mit der Opposition," *FdK*, March 9, 1928.

19. *Istoriia Kommunisticheskoi partii Sovetskogo Soiuza* (hereafter cited as *Istoriia KPSS*), vol, 4, pt. 1 (1921–1929), (Moscow, 1970), pp. 524–525.

20. See, for example, *Istoriia KPSS*, vol. 4, pt. 1, pp. 543–544; S. P. Trapeznikov, *Leninizm i agrarno-krest'ianskii vopros*, vol. 2: Istoricheskii opyt KPSS v osushchestvlenii leninskogo kooperativnogo plana (Moscow, 1967), pp. 53–62. In recent years, however, it has been typical for literature of this kind to point to the broader economic causes of the difficulties in grain procurement.

21. Of the extensive Western literature on this question, see in particular Lewin, *Russian Peasants;* also Carr and Davies, vol. 1, pt. 1, pp. 3–66, which has a detailed account of the procurement campaigns in 1927 and 1928. In this connection one must also mention one of the first studies, an especially important one, by S. N. Prokopovich, *Russlands Volkswirtschaft unter Sowjets* (Zurich, 1944), pp. 110–144. Of the Soviet literature on the subject, see Roy Medvedev's critical work *Let History Judge*, Russian-language edition: *K sudu istorii: Genezis i posledstviia stalinizma* (New York, 1974), pp. 172–180, which still contains strong traces of the traditional notion of "a kulaks' strike."

22. See, for example, A. I. Rykov, "Direktivy po sostavleniiu piatiletnego plana razvitiia narodnogo khoziaistva, 12.12.1927 g.," in *Piatnadtsatyi s"ezd*, vol. 2, pp. 855–880.

23. See Mikoyan, "Na perelome (khlebozagotovki v ianvare)," *Pravda*, February 8, 1928; "Rech' A. I. Rykova na plenume Mossoveta, 9.3.1928 g.," *Pravda*, March 11, 1928 (hereafter cited as A. I. Rykov, "Rech' na plenume Mossoveta").

24. A. I. Rykov, "Doklad ob Ob"edinennom plenume," *Izvestia*, August 14, 1927; "Doklad tov. N. I. Bukharina na sobranii aktiva leningradskoi organizatsii VKP(b), 26.10.1927 g.," *Izvestia*, November 4, 1927.

25. See, for example, *Berliner Börsen Zeitung*, March 24, 1928; "Fabrikfriedhöfe in Sowjetrussland," *Vorwärts*, June 25, 1928 (a compilation of data from *Pravda*).

26. *Piatnadtsatyi s"ezd*, vol. 2, pp. 855–880, 1091–1108.

27. Ibid.

28. Ibid., pp. 855–880.

29. The distortion, falsification, and suppression of important economic data occurred not only out of considerations of a general political nature, in particular, the fight against the opposition. An additional factor, from early 1928 on, was the expressed needs of Soviet diplomats, who stated categorically that publication of such data would disrupt international economic negotiations. See the intercepted dispatch from Krestinsky (in information for Dirksen, February 18, 1928), in PA, IV Ru, 2–I, 2.

30. For data on the situation in the Soviet economy during this period, see, for example: Fischer to Dirksen, January 4, 1928 (general information, drawing on Rykov's speech at a Politburo session), in PA, IV Ru, 2–I, 2; information from Chicherin to Soviet diplomatic representatives, dating presumably from the first half of January 1928, in PA, IV Ru, 2–I, 2; Kuibyshev's speech, in the record of speeches at a Politburo session, presumably of late January 1928, in ibid.; information from Litvinov to Soviet diplomatic representatives, February 9, 1928, in PA, IV Ru, 2–I, 3; Fischer to Dirksen, apparently February 1928 ("Allgemeine Information"), in PA, IV Ru, 2–I, 2; and information for Dirksen (based on data from French intelligence in Moscow), February 20, 1928, in ibid. See also the numerous reports in the German press and in *Sots. vestnik.*

31. A. I. Rykov, "Rech' na plenume Mossoveta"; M. I. Kalinin, "O edinom sel'skokhoziaistvennom naloge na 1928–29 khoz. god," *Pravda*, April 20, 1928; Stalin, "O rabotakh aprel'skogo ob"edinennogo plenuma TsK i TsKK VKP(b), Doklad 13.4.1928 g.," "Na khlebnom fronte, beseda ot 13.4.1928 g.," and "Chlenam Politbiuro: Otvet Frumkinu," in *Soch.*, vol. 11, pp. 27–64, 81–97, 116–127.

32. Stalin, "Pervye itogi zagotovitel'noi kampanii i dal'neishie zadachi partii: Ko vsem organizatsiiam VKP(b), 13.2.1928 g.," in *Soch.*, vol. 11, pp. 10–19. (Hereafter cited as "Pervye itogi . . .")

33. Stalin, "O khlebozagotovkakh i perspektivakh razvitiia sel'skogo khoziaistva," in *Soch.*, vol. 11, pp. 1–9.

34. Ibid.

35. "Pis'mo X iz Moskvy ot 25.6.1927 g.," *Sots. vestnik*, no. 14 (180), July 23, 1928.

36. F. M. Vaganov, *Pravyi uklon v VKP(b) i ego razgrom (1928–1920 gg.)* (Moscow, 1970), p. 114 (with a reference to the Central Party Archives).

37. Stalin, "Pervye itogi . . .," in *Soch.*, vol. 11, pp. 10–19; also the telegrams from the German embassy in Moscow dated February 18 and 23, 1928 in PA, IV Ru, 5, Bd. 23.

38. Intercepted letter from a Narkomindel functionary to the Soviet diplomatic representation in Berlin (information of January 14, 1928), in PA, IV Ru, 2–I,2.

39. Memorandum by Stalin, apparently of late December 1927 or early January 1928 (information of January 14, 1928), in PA, IV Ru, 2–I, 2.

40. See, for example, Menzhinsky's (undated) report at a session of the Politburo (apparently held December 30, 1927) and the opinions of Politburo members (information of January 14, 1928), in PA, IV Ru, 2–I, 2).

41. Information from a Soviet specialist who arrived in Riga in early February 1928, in PA, IV Ru, 2–I, 2.

42. Menzhinsky's (undated) report cited above (information of January 14, 1928); Menzhinsky's letter of January 6, 1928, to the Central Committee and CCC; and letter from the German department of the Comintern to the Communist Party of Germany (information of February 20, 1928)—all in PA, IV Ru, 2–I, 2; also, Menzhinsky's letter to Voroshilov of March 4, 1928; and to Bubnov (of February 4 or 5, 1928), in PA, IV Ru, 2–I, 3.

43. Records of speeches by Stalin and Bukharin at the ninth plenum of the ECCI in February 1928 (the contents are not consistent with the published texts), in information of February 14, 1928, PA, IV Ru, 2–I, 2; speech of Menzhinsky from a record of a Politburo session, apparently in late January, in ibid; information from Chicherin, and a dispatch of Krestinsky's, mid-February—both in information of February 11, 1928, in ibid.

44. Speech by Bukharin at the ninth plenum of the ECCI, cited above (information of February 14, 1928); and letter from the German department of the Comintern to the Communist Party of Germany, cited above. The letter contains statements not only about a sum of money that had previously been released but also about rewards given by the Comintern and GPU for the ascertainment of border crossings into the USSR and discovery of the headquarters of the "combat organization of the opposition," allegedly located in Berlin.

45. Record of Kuibyshev's speech to the Politburo, presumably of late January, in ibid.; information on the views of a highly placed official in the Narkomindel (information of February 14, 1928), in ibid.; Litvinov's entry in the journal of the commissar of foreign affairs, February 9, 1928, in ibid.

46. Litvinov's entry in the journal of the commissar of foreign affairs, cited above.

47. Ibid.

48. Ibid. See also the above-cited information on the views of a highly placed official in the Narkomindel (information of February 14, 1928); information of February 10, 1928, based on reports from French sources in Berlin, in ibid.; information on the views of the British Foreign Office on questions of Soviet politics (information of February 10, 1928), in ibid.; and information on the attitudes of leading American circles on the development of relations with the USSR, in ibid.

49. Menzhinsky's speech (cited above) from the record of speeches at the Politburo, presumably late January 1928; the above-cited information on the views of a highly placed official in the Narkomindel; and the letter from a Moscow friend to a highly placed Soviet functionary in Berlin (information of March 14, 1928); also N. I. Bukharin, "Uroki khlebozagotovok, Shakhtinskogo dela i zadachi partii: Doklad na sobranii leningradskoi organizatsii 13.4.1928 g.," *Pravda*, April 19, 1928.

50. The above-cited letter from a Moscow friend to a highly placed Soviet functionary in Berlin; also, on Stalin's position, see "Pis'mo K. iz Moskvy ot May 10, 1928," *Sots. vestnik*, no. 10 (176), May 18, 1928.

51. Resolution of February 26, 1928, quoted from Rykov's letter to Menzhinsky of March 12, 1928, in PA, IV Ru, 2–I, 3.

52. Rykov's confidential letter of March 2, 1928, in ibid.

5. SOCIAL CRISIS AND SOCIAL REPRESSION

1. British information from Moscow, dating apparently from March 1928 (information of April 11, 1928), in PA, IV Ru, 2–I, 4.

2. "Pis'mo iz Moskvy ot 22.6.1928 g.," *Sots. vestnik*, no. 13 (179), July 8, 1928.

3. "Pis'mo iz Moskvy ot 10.2.1928 g.," *Sots. vestnik*, no. 4 (170), February 21, 1928.

4. Cf., for example, *Düsseldorfer Nachrichten*, February 28, 1928.

5. N. I. Bukharin, "Uroki khlebozagotovok, Shakhtinskogo dela i zadachi partii: Doklad na sobranii leningradskoi organizatsii 13.4.1928 g.," *Pravda*, April 19, 1928.

6. Letter of February 27, 1928, from I. S. Unshlikht to military leaders and commanders of military districts, as well as to Menzhinsky and Ordzhonikidze (information of March 10, 1928), in PA, IV Ru, 2–I, 3.

7. For data on the initial phase of the collectivization campaign, see Lewin, *Russian Peasants,* pp. 270–271.

8. M. I. Kalinin, "Doklad na Uchreditel'nom s"ezde Sovetov Ivanovskoi prom. oblasti," *Pravda,* July 19, 1928. Rykov's letter of March 2, 1928, for example, spoke of a mere 40 percent fulfillment of the grain procurement plan (PA, IV Ru, 2–I, 2); Kubyak's letter of March 19, 1928, to Rykov and Stalin, referred to a deficit in March of 40 percent (information of March 27, 1928, in ibid.).

9. A. I. Rykov, "Tekushchii moment i zadachi partii: Doklad na aktive moskovskoi organizatsii VKP(b), 13.7.1928 g.," *Pravda,* July 15, 1928.

10. Kubyak's letter of August 12, 1928, in PA, IV RU, 2–I, 6; on the slaughter of cattle, see information of August 21, 1928, in ibid.

11. For the text of the conversation between Bukharin and Kamenev, see "Zamechatel'nyi razgovor, I," *Sots. vestnik,* no. 6 (196), March 22, 1928. (For a complete English translation, see Leon Trotsky, *Challenge of the Left Opposition, 1927–1928* [New York, 1981], pp. 377–388).

12. See *Istoriia KPSS,* vol. 4, pt. 1, p. 544.

13. Compare the letters from Moscow dated February 9 and 10, 1928, in *Sots. vestnik,* no. 4 (170), February 21, 1928. This view of the situation is also confirmed by numerous statements by prominent officials dissociating themselves from the perspective of a return to "war communism."

14. V. V. Kuibyshev, "O khoziaistvennom polozhenii SSSR: Doklad na sobranii leningradskogo partaktiva, 19.9.1928 g.," *Pravda,* September 21, 1928.

15. *Trud,* October 30, 1927.

16. Menzhinsky's letter of November 27, 1927, to the Central Committee and Kuibyshev's letter of December 22, 1927, in PA, IV Ru 2–I, 1.

17. "Pis'mo iz Moskvy ot 23.1.1928 g.," *Sots. vestnik,* no. 2–3 (168–169), February 6, 1928; "Pis'mo V. iz Moskvy ot 10.2.1928 g.," *Sots. vestnik,* no. 4 (170), February 21, 1928; "Pis'mo iz Moskvy ot 17.4.1928 g.," *Sots. vestnik,* nos. 8–9 (174–175).

18. *Reutlinger Bote,* February 20, 1928 (a report based on Soviet data).

19. Information from a prominent Russian democratic politician (information of March 30, 1928), in PA, IV Ru, 2–I, 4.

20. British information from Moscow, dated June 14, 1928 (information of June 25, 1928), in PA, IV Ru, 2–I, 4.

21. See, for example, information of August 14, 1928, in ibid.

22. "Pis'mo iz Moskvy ot 23.1.1928 g.," *Sots. vestnik,* no. 2–3 (168–169), February 6, 1928; information from "a good friend," in close touch with members of the Politburo and sections of the Comintern (information of February 11, 1928), in PA, IV Ru, 2–I, 2); and Russian monarchists' information, intercepted by GPU agents in Berlin (information of August 22, 1928), in PA, IV Ru, 2–I, 5.

23. Stalin's letter (dating apparently from the second half of August 1928) to Menzhinsky, Ordzhonikidze, and Voroshilov, with copies to the Politburo and Rykov, in PA, IV Ru, 2–I, 4.

24. Information reports of February 10 and February 20, 1928, in PA, IV Ru, 2–I, 2; information of March 13, 1928, in PA, IV Ru, 2–I, 3; British information from Moscow, in "Information fur Dirksen, 11.4.1928," PA, IV Ru, 2–I, 4; and elsewhere.

25. British information from Moscow (information of April 11, 1928), in PA, IV Ru, 2–I, 4.

26. See, for example, the above-cited record of a Politburo session (dating apparently from the end of January 1928), in ibid. Similar assessments may be found in several documents of Soviet origin from that period.

27. See the well-informed report from the USSR, "Der Deutschenprozess in Moskau," *Stuttgarter Neues Tageblatt,* April 19, 1928; also A. Avtorkhanov,

Tekhnologiia vlasti (Frankfurt, 1976), pp. 68–70. Avtorkhanov's account must be read with great caution, for the author is inclined to treat facts rather arbitrarily.

28. V. V. Kuibyshev, "Shakhtinskoe delo i problema spetsialistov," *Pravda*, March 30, 1928; information of April 18, 1928, with reference to a Narkomindel official in a responsible position, in PA, IV Ru, 2–I, 4.

29. *Deutsche Zeitung*, April! 5, 1928, and *Reutlinger Bote*, February 20, 1928 (both with reference to official Soviet sources).

30. "Pis'mo V. A. iz Moskvy ot 30.12.1927 g.," *Sots. vestnik*, no. 1 (167), January 12, 1928; "Pis'mo Zh.V. iz Moskvy ot 23.2.1928 g.," *Sots. vestnik*, no. 5 (171), March 6, 1928; "Verhaftung deutschen Ingenieure im Donezgebiet," *Berliner Börsen Zeitung*, March 11, 1928; Al. Petrovskii, "Shakhty," *Pravda*, September 5, 1928.

31. See the excerpts from Bubnov's report in *Pravda*, March 21, 1928. This state of affairs was also confirmed, for example, by a Central Committee commission consisting of Yaroslavsky, Molotov, and Tomsky; see the above-cited speech by Bukharin in Leningrad, *Pravda*, April 19, 1928.

32. This point was made by Krylenko at the Shakhty trial during the cross-examination of the defendant Belenko, *Pravda*, May 31, 1928.

33. Ibid.

34. Avtorkhanov, *Tekhnologiia vlasti*, pp. 69–70; also compare Alexander Orlov, *The Secret History of Stalin's Crimes* (London, 1954), p. 28.

35. Information from the French embassy in Moscow (information of March 20, 1928), in PA, IV Ru, R–I, 3; information of March 27, 1928, PA, IV Ru, R–I, 4; Chicherin's letter of March 13, 1928, to Menzhinsky, in PA, IV Ru, R–I, 3.

36. Vaganov, *Pravyi uklon*, p. 102 (with a reference to the Central Party Archives); also Avtorkhanov, *Tekhnologiia vlasti*, p. 70.

37. Avtorkhanov, *Tekhnologiia vlasti* p. 70; the record of Kalinin's speech at a session of the Politburo and Sovnarkom (dating apparently from the end of August 1928), in information of October 24, 1928, PA, IV Ru. 2–I, 5; some judgments about the substance of the documentation presented to the Politburo can be made on the basis of Rykov's speech of March 9, 1928 (see below).

38. "Der Deutschenprozess in Moskau," *Stuttgarter Neues Tageblatt*, April 19, 1928.

39. Rykov's letter of March 12, 1928, to Menzhinsky (reprinted in the appendix of this book as document no. 7), in PA, IV Ru, 2–I, 3.

40. Chicherin's letter of March 13, 1928, to Menzhinsky (reprinted in the appendix as document no. 8), in PA, IV Ru, 2–I, 3.

41. Information of March 23, 1928, with reference to the Soviet trade mission, in ibid.

42. Rykov's letter of March 12, 1928, to Menzhinsky refers to Bubnov's mission. At the time the German press spoke of the mission of Commissar of Labor Schmidt as well as of Bubnov.

43. *ADAP*, ser. B. vol. 8, pp. 338–339.

44. *Stuttgarter Neues Zeitung*, March 16, 1928; *Berliner Tageblatt*, March 19, 1928.; intercepted information from the French embassy in Moscow (information of March 20, 1928), in PA, IV Ru, 2–I, 3; information on the opinion held in British parliamentary circles, in PA, IV Ru, 2–I, 4; and elsewhere.

45. See the record of conversations of March 13 and 21, 1928, between Soviet Ambassador Dovgalevsky and Berthelot, general secretary of the French Foreign Ministry, in *DVP*, vol. 11, pp. 156–159, 184–186; notes of March 23 and April 13, 1928, from the Soviet government to the French Foreign Ministry, in ibid., pp. 230–231, 266–268; and elsewhere.

46. See "Runderlass des Auswärtiges Amtes, 19.4.1928," in *ADAP*, ser. B, vol. 8, pp. 514–515; the dispatch of May 12, 1928, from Brockdorf, German ambassador in Moscow, in ibid., pp. 29–30; Brockdorf's dispatch of May 22, 1928, in

ibid., pp. 58–60; Külenthal's dispatch (the Defense Ministry, July 6, 1928), in ibid., pp. 282–284; and information about the April plenum from a highly placed Narkomindel official (information of April 18, 1928), in PA, IV Ru, 2–I, 4.

47. Stalin, "O rabotakh Ob"edinennogo aprel'skogo plenuma TsK i TsKK: Doklad na sobranii aktiva Moskovskoi organizatsii VKP(6) 13.4.1928 g.," in *Soch.*, vol. 11, pp. 27–64; see also *Dni* (Paris) March 6, 1928 (citing the press agency Havas).

48. Stalin, *Soch.*, vol. 11, pp. 27–64.

49. Information from the Soviet embassy in Riga (information report of March 23, 1928), in PA, IV Ru, 2–I, 4; opposition information intercepted by the GPU in Berlin and forwarded to Menzhinsky (information report of March 30, 1928), in ibid

50. Ordzhonikidze's letter of March 23, 1928 (reprinted in the appendix as document no. 10), in PA, IV Ru, 2–I, 4.

51. Yaroslavksy's commission, on which Molotov and Tomsky also served, was formed in the last third of March 1928.

52. My account of the plenum proceedings is based on the following sources: "Ob"edinennyi plenum TsK i TsKK VKP(b), Moskva, 6–11.4.1928 g.," in *KPSS v rezoliutsiiakh*, vol. 4, pp. 75–93; the previously cited reports on the plenum given by Stalin and Bukharin on April 13, 1928; Vaganov, *Pravyi uklon*, pp. 102, 125, 140 (with reference to the Central Party Archives); information from a highly placed Narkomindel official, based on the minutes of the plenum (information of April 18, 1928), in PA, IV Ru, 2–I, 4; "Pis'mo K. iz Moskvy ot 10.5.1928 g.," *Sots. vestnik*, no. 10 (176), May 18, 1928.

53. Stalin, "O rabotakh Ob"edinennogo aprel'skogo plenuma TsK i TsKK," in *Soch.*, vol. 11, p. 55.

54. *Pravda*, May 12, 1928.

55. Medvedev, *K sudu istorii*, pp. 237–238; "V tiur'makh GPU, iz rasskazov ochevidtsa," *Sots. vestnik*, nos. 22–23 (188–189), December 5, 1928.

56. See, for example, the testimony of Chemyshev, a director and Communist Party member, in the case of the defendant Kuzma (*Pravda*, June 8, 1928) and that of professors Skachinsky and Terpigorev in the cases of Kuzma and Rabinovich (*Pravda*, June 26, 1928).

57. *Pravda*, June 2, 1928.

58. *Pravda*, June 30, 1928.

59. See "Zamechatel'nyi razgovor, I: Zapis' besedy mezhdu N. I. Bukharinym, L. B. Kamenevym i. G. Ia. Sokol'nikovym 11.7.1928 g.," *Sots. vestnik*, no. 6 (196), March 22, 1929; "Dopolneniia k rasskazu Bukharina" and "Razgovor s Sokol'nikovym, 11.7.1928 g.," *Sots. vestnik*, no. 9 (199), May 4, 1929. The dating of the Politburo sessions is based on Vaganov, *Pravyi uklon*, pp. 144–145.

60. *Pravda*, July 6, 1928.

61. "Pis'mo K. iz Moskvy, 8.7.1928 g.," *Sots. vestnik*, no. 14 (180), July 23, 1928.

62. Ibid.; and "Pis'mo A. iz Moskvy ot 25.7.1928 g.," *Sots. vestnik*, no. 15 (181), August 3, 1928; see also Russian monarchists' information on the USSR, intercepted by the Berlin GPU (information of August 22, 1928), in PA, IV Ru, 2–I, 5.

63. "Pis'mo A. iz Moskvy ot 25.7.1928 g.," *Sots. vestnik*, no. 15 (181), August 3, 1928.

64. *KPSS v rezoliutsiiakh*, vol. 4, pp. 94–98.

6. INTERMEZZO AT THE TOP: THE CRISIS CONTINUES

1. "Zamechatel'nyi razgovor, I," *Sots. vestnik*, no. 6 (196), March 22, 1929.

2. Compare, for example, Stalin, "Ob industrializatsii i khlebnoi probleme: Rech' 9.7.1928 g.," *Soch.*, vol. 11, pp. 157–187.

3. See the dispatch from the German embassy in Moscow, March 6, 1928, in PA, IV Ru, 2, Bd. 23; also Em.Yaroslavsky, "Nikakikh kompromissov," *Pravda*, June 8, 1928.

4. "Pis'mo L. Sosnovskogo L. Trotskomu, Barnaul, 22.7.–22.8.1928 g.," *Biulleten' oppozitsii*, no. 3–4, September 1929.

5. "Pis'mo V. iz Moskvy ot 17.4.1928 g.," *Sots. vestnik*, no. 8–9 (174–175), May 3, 1928; *Dni*, March 8, 1928 (with a reference to a correspondent of the London *Times* in Riga).

6. A. I. Rykov, "Rech' na plenume Mossoveta, 9.3.1928 g.," *Pravda*, March 11, 1928; also N. I. Bukharin, "Uroki khlebozagotovok, Shakhtinskogo dela i zadachi partii, 13.4.1928 g.," *Pravda*, April 19, 1928 (hereafter cited as "Uroki khlebozagotovok").

7. Stalin, "O rabotakh aprel'skogo ob"edinennogo plenuma TsK i TsKK: Doklad na sobranii aktiva moskovskoi organizatsii VKP(b), 13.4.1928 g.," in *Soch.*, vol. 11, pp. 27–64.

8. Stalin, "Na khlebnom fronte: Iz besedy so studentami Instituta krasnoi professury, Komakademii i Sverdlovskogo universiteta, 23.5.1928 g.," in ibid., pp. 81–97.

9. "Ob"edinennyi plenum TsK i TsKK VKP(b), Moskva, 6–11.4.1928 g.: O khlebozagotovkakh tekushchego goda i ob organizatsii khlebozagotovitel'noi kampanii na 1928–29 gg.," in *KPSS v rezoliutsiiakh*, vol. 4, pp. 75–83.

10. British intelligence information from Moscow, June 14, 1928 (information of June 25, 1928), in PA, IV Ru, 2–I, 4; "Pis'mo A. iz Moskvy ot 14.6.1928 g.," *Sots. vestnik*, no. 13 (179), July 8, 1928; also Kalinin at the Politburo in September (information of September 24, 1928), in PA, IV Ru, 2–I, 5.

11. Vaganov, *Pravyi uklon*, pp. 155–156 (with a reference to the Central Party Archives).

12. Bukharin, "Uroki khlebozagotovok," *Pravda*, April 19, 1928.

13. "Dopolneniia k rasskazu Bukharina," *Sots. vestnik*, no. 9 (199), May 4, 1928; also Stalin, "Na khlebnom fronte," in *Soch.*, vol. 11, pp. 81–97.

14. "Zamechatel'nyi razgovor, I," *Sots vestnik*, no. 6 (196), March 22, 1929.

15. Ibid.; also opposition information intercepted by the GPU (information of March 30, 1928), in PA, IV Ru, 2–I, 4; and with great inaccuracies, Avtorkhanov, *Tekhnologiia vlasti*, pp. 73–74.

16. "Zur Charakter der Russischen Partei," *FdK*, October 5, 1928.

17. For details on the internal situation in the Soviet Communist Party, see "Stalins Position in der WKP," *FdK*, October 19, 1928; also, "Zamechatel'nyi razgovor, I," *Sots. vestnik*, no. 6 (196), March 22, 1929.

18. Vaganov, *Pravyi uklon*, pp. 98–99 and 141–142; Stalin, "Chlenam Politbiuro TsK: Otvet Frumkinu, 20.6.1928 g.," in *Soch.*, vol. 11, pp. 116–126; and with inaccuracies, Avtorkhanov, *Tekhnologiia vlasti*, pp. 79–81.

19. "Zamachatel'nyi razgovor, I," *Sots. vestnik*, no. 6 (196), March 22, 1929; also, "Dopolneniia k rasskazu Bukharina," *Sots. vestnik*, no. 9 (199), May 4, 1929; Vaganov, *Pravyi uklon*, p. 112 (with a reference to the Central Party Archives); Avtorkhanov, *Tekhnologiia vlasti*, pp. 80–81.

20. Vaganov, *Pravyi Uklon*, p. 112 (with a reference to the Central Party Archives).

21. Ibid., pp. 144–145 (with no indication of source); also "Dopolneniia k rasskazu Bukharina," *Sots. vestnik*, no. 9 (199), May 4, 1929.

22. Ibid., "Dopolneniia k rasskazu Bukharina" and "Razgovor s Sokol'-nikovym."

23. Ibid.

24. D. Maretskii, "Fal'shivaia nota," *Pravda*, June 30, 1928; V. Astrov, "K tekushchemu momentu," *Pravda*, July 1, 1928; V. Astrov, "Na dva fronta," *Pravda*, July 3, 1928; S. F. Cohen, pp. 286–291.

25. Daniels, *Conscience of the Revolution*, pp. 329–333 (with reference to the Trotsky archives at Harvard); Cohen, pp. 286–291; on the course of the plenum, cf. "Stalins Position in der WKP," *FdK*, October 19, 1928, and "Der Vorstoss der Rechten in der Russischen Partei," *FdK*, November 23, 1928.

26. Vaganov, *Pravyi uklon*, p. 125 (with a reference to the Central Party Archives).

27. Stalin, "Ob industrializatsii i khlebnoi probleme: Rech' 9.7.1928 g.," and "O smychke rabochikh i krest'ian i o sovkhozakh: Iz rechi 11.7.1928 g.," in *Soch.*, vol. 11, pp. 157–187 and 188–196.

28. Vaganov, *Pravyi ukklon*, p. 147 (with a reference to the Central Party Archives).

29. Daniels, *Conscience of the Revolution*, pp. 329–333 (with a reference to the Trotsky archives).

30. "Dopolneniia k rasskazu Bukharina" and "Razgovor s Sokol'nikovym," *Sots. vestnik*, no. 9 (199), May 4, 1929; "Der Charakter der russischen Partei," *FdK*, October 5, 1928.

31. Such rumors filled the information reports reaching the German Foreign Ministry throughout the year 1928, until late in the autumn, with references to reliable sources in Moscow. They also got into the press. For some details, see Deutscher, *Prophet Unarmed*, pp. 443–446, and "Der Charakter der russischen Partei," *FdK*, October 5, 1928.

32. "Zamechatel'nyi razgovor I," *Sots. vestnik*, no. 6 (196), March 22, 1929; "Razgovor s Sokol'nikovym" and "Dopolneniia k rasskazu Bukharina," *Sots. vestnik*, no. 9 (199), May 4, 1929.

33. Daniels, *Conscience of the Revolution*, pp. 332–333.

34. A. I. Rykov, "Tekushchii moment i zadachi partii, 13.7.1928 g.," *Pravda*, July 15, 1928: Stalin, "Ob itogakh iiul'skogo plenuma TsK VKP(b), 7.13.1928 g.," in *Soch.*, vol. 11, pp. 197–218.

35. "Stalins Position in der WKP," *FdK*, October 19, 1928; Daniels, *Conscience of the Revolution*, p. 33?.

36. "Postanovlenie SNK SSSR o provedenii khlebozagotovok novogo urozhaia ot 19.7.1928 g.," *Pravda*, July 20, 1928.

37. See, for example, M. I. Kalinin, "Nasha politika v derevne i sel'skokhoziaistvennyi nalog: Rech' na plenume Mossoveta, 18.9.1928 g.," *Pravda*, September 23, 1928.

38. See the editorial "K zadacham khoziaistvennogo rukovodstva v sviazi s povysheniem tsen," *Pravda*, July 21, 1928.

39. See, for example, *Hamburger Correspondent*, September 26, 1928; *Germania*, November 4, 1928: also "Otchet pravitel'stva na IX Moskovskom gub. s"ezde Sovetov: Sokrashch. stenogramma doklada tov. Rykova," *Pravda*, April 13, 1929.

40. A set of proposals for military modernization were prepared in the summer of 1928 under the direction of S. S. Kamenev, deputy people's commissar of war. See French information (information of August 8, 1928), in PA, IV Ru, 2–I, 4, and excerpts from British informational material on the Red Army (information of August 21, 1928), in PA, IV Ru, 2–I, 4.

41. Dispatch from L. M. Karakhan to Soviet diplomatic representatives (information of August 8, 1928), in PA, IV Ru, 2–I, 4.

42. Ibid.; also "Tov. Chicherin o pakte Kelloga: Interv'iu t. Chicherina," *Pravda*, August 5, 1928.

43. *Pravda*, September 16, 1928. Two hundred plants in twenty-five different sectors of the economy were mentioned.

44. Information from a secret source in the USSR and information from Moscow (both in information of August 14, 1928), PA, IV Ru, 2–I, 4.

45. Information of August 14, 1928, PA, IV Ru, 2–I, 4.

46. Stalin, "O pravoi opasnosti v VKP(b):Rech' na plenume MK i MKK VKP(b) 19.10.1928 g.," in *Soch.*, vol. 11, pp. 222–238.

47. "Deklaratsiia o prisoedinenii SSSR k Dogovoru ob otkaze ot voiny (6.9.1928 g.)," *DVP*, vol. 11, pp. 503–506.

48. Information on the new situation in Soviet concessionary policy (information of October 3, 1928), in PA, IV Ru, 2–I, 5; also A.Iugov, "Politika kontsessii," *Sots. vestnik*, no. 20 (186), October 28, 1928.

49. *ADAP*, vol. 11, pp. 318–322, 489–491 (documents no. 135, 199).

50. See "Otchet pravitel'stva na IX moskovskom gub. s"ezde Sovetov: Doklad A. I. Rykova," *Pravda*, April 13, 1929.

51. V. Molotov, "K tekushchemu momentu," *Pravda*, August 5, 1928.

52. Text of a letter by Menzhinsky (information of August 15, 1928), in PA, IV Ru, 2–I, 5.

53. See the editorial "Khlebozagotovki v tsentre vnimaniia," *Pravda*, September 5, 1928; also "Izvrashcheniiam v khlebozagotovitel'noi rabote dolzhen byt' polozhen konets (Beseda s Zam. Predsedatelia SNK i STO SSSR Ia.E. Rudzutakom)," *Pravda*, September 6, 1928.

54. V. Miliutin, "Ob urozhae," *Pravda*, July 21, 1928; G. Krumin, "Burzhuaznye mechty i sovetskaia deistvitel'nost'," *Pravda*, September 14, 1928.

55. Letter of Kalinin to the Politburo (information of November 23, 1928), in PA, IV Ru, 2–I, 6; also A. I. Rykov, "Itogi noiabr'skogo plenuma TsK: Doklad na sobranii aktiva leningradskoi partogranizatsii, 30.11.1928 g.," *Pravda*, December 4, 1928. For a more precise description of the grain procurement campaign of 1928–1929, see Carr and Davies, vol. 1, pt. 1, pp. 67–105, and Lewin, *Russian Peasants*.

56. *Pravda*, December 12, 1928. Throughout these months, grain procurements were considerably lower than those of fiscal year 1927–1928.

57. M. I. Kalinin, "Nasha politika v derevne i sel'skokhoziaistvennyi nalog, 18.9.1928 g.," *Pravda*, September 23, 1928; A. I. Rykov, "Itogi noiabr'skogo plenuma TsK, 30.11.1928 g.," *Pravda*, December 4, 1928.

58. A. Yugov, "Kolkhozy i sovkhozy," *Sots. vestnik*, no. 22–23 (188–189), December 5, 1928 (with a reference to *Ekonomicheskaia zhizn'*).

59. V. M. Molotov, "K itogam noiabr'skogo plenuma TsK VKP(b): Doklad na partaktive moskovskoi organizatsii, 30.11.1928 g.," *Pravda*, December 4, 1928.

60. Letter of Kalinin to the Politburo (information of November 23, 1928), in PA, IV Ru, 2–I, 6).

61. A. I. Rykov, "Itogi noiabr'skogo plenuma TsK, 30.11.1928 g.," *Pravda*, December 4, 1928; "Otchet pravitel'stva na IX moskovskom gub. s"ezde Sovetov," *Pravda*, April 13, 1928.

62. "Pis'mo B. iz Moskvy," *Sots. vestnik*, no. 6 (196), March 22, 1929.

63. Kalinin's letter to chairmen of the Central Executive Committees of the Ukraine and Byelorussia (information of November 23, 1928), in PA, IV Ru, 2–I, 6.

64. Ibid.

65. Kalinin's letter to chairmen of the Central Executive Committees of the union republics, in ibid.

66. See, for example, *Rote Fahne*, February 23, 1929.

67. This according to Kurbatov in the journal *Na agrarnom fronte*, no. 5, 1929, quoted in Lewin, *Russian Peasants*, p. 403.

68. See the editorial "Vnimanie khlebozagotovkam dolzhno byt' usileno," *Pravda*, January 5, 1929.

69. O. Domanevskaia, "Ot khlebnoi monopolii k meshochnichestvu," *Sots. vestnik*, no. 10–11 (200–201), May 25, 1929; for further details see Lewin, *Russian Peasants*, p. 386.

70. See the letter by R., "Iz derevni, 16.3 1929 g.," *Sots. vestnik*, no. 7–8 (197–198), April 12, 1929.

71. Kalinin's letter of November 7, 1928, in PA, IV Ru, 2–I, 7; and Kalinin's letter of October 22, 1928, in PA, IV Ru, 2–I, 6.

72. Kalinin's letter of February 13, 1929, to the Central Executive Committees of the union republics and autonomous republics, in PA, IV Ru, 2–I, 7.

73. "Vnimanie khlebozagotovkam dolzhno byt' usileno," *Pravda*, January 5, 1929.

74. See the letter by N. O-va, "Mertvaia zyb'," 8.11.1928 g.," *Sots. vestnik*, 21 (187), November 14, 1928.

75. *Vorwärts*, December 18, 1928; *Dresdener Anzeiger*, December 18, 1928.

76. Information of August 22, 1928, in PA, IV Ru, 2–I, 5.

77. Menzhinsky's circular letter of August 11, 1928 (information of September 1, 1928), in PA, IV Ru, 2–I, 5. Later on, even *Pravda* was forced to admit these facts (see note 78).

78. Information of August 29, 1928, referring also to articles in the Soviet press by Lomov (Donugol') and Birman (Yugostal'), in PA, IV Ru, 2–I, 5; also "Postanovlenie TsK VKP(b) o zadachakh ugol'noi promyshlennosti Donbassa, 17.1.1929 g.," in *KPSS v rezoliutsiiakh*, vol. 4, pp. 158–161.

79. See the speech by Kalinin in information of September 24, 1928, on the Politburo session dealing with Chicherin's proposals, in PA, IV Ru, 2–I, 5.

80. Text of a letter (information of September 1, 1928), in ibid.

81. Menzhinsky's letter to chiefs of the GPU in the union republics, September 1, 1928, in ibid.

82. Information of September 14, 1928, in ibid.

83. Text of a letter (information of October 24, 1928), in PA, IV Ru, 2–I, 6.

84. *Germania*, October 23, 1928 (with a reference to Rykov's speech at a session of the Ukrainian Council of People's Commissars in September 1928); also *Berliner Tageblatt*, October 31, 1928.

7. THE DEFEAT OF THE MODERATES

1. *KPSS v rezoliutsiiakh*, vol. 2, pp. 558–559.

2. See, for example, "Pis'mo A.: Vokrug plenuma TsK VKP(b), 27.11.1928," *Sots. vestnik*, nos. 22–23 (188–189), February 5, 1928.

3. Stalin, "Ob industrializatsii strany i o pravom uklone v VKP(b): Rech' na plenume TsK VKP(b), 19.11.1928 g.," in *Soch.*, vol. 11, pp. 245–290.

4. See, for example, Ia. Iakovlev, "K voprosu o khoziaistvennykh zadachakh predstoiashchego goda (Iz bloknota RKI)," *Pravda*, October 28, 1928.

5. Information of October 3, 1928, in PA, IV Ru, 2–I, 5; Lewin, *Russian Peasants*, pp. 278–279. For more on the drafting of the plans, see Carr and Davies, vol. 1, pt. 1, pp. 312–332.

6. Daniels, *Conscience of the Revolution*, pp. 350–357.

7. Ibid.

8. V. V. Kuibyshev, "Piatiletnii plan razvitiia promyshlennosti: doklad na VIII s"ezde profsoiuzov," *Pravda*, December 25, 1928.

9. V. V. Kuibyshev, "Zadachi promyshlennosti v 1928–29 g.," *Pravda*, November 27, 1928. Figures on the deficits were given without exception in all reports by directors of the Soviet economy in the fall of 1928.

10. V. M. Molotov, "K itogam noiabr'skogo plenuma, 30.11.1928 g.," *Pravda*, December 4, 1928.

11. R. D., "Die Kontrollziffern der Volkswirtschaft der UdSSR 1928/29," in *Die Volkswirtschaft der UdSSR*, no. 23, (Berlin, 1928). Various other figures were cited later on, primarily around 22 or 23 percent.

12. *Kontrol'nye tsifry narodnogo khoziaistva SSSR na 1929–30 god* (Moscow, 1930), p. 5; V. V. Kuibyshev, "Piatiletnii plan razvitiia promyshlennosti," *Pravda*, December 25, 1928.

13. "Promyshlennost' SSSR v 1928–29 g.: Prezidium VSNKh SSSR o Kontrol'nykh tsifrakh (Doklad Kossiora)," *Pravda*, September 14, 1928.

14. V. V. Kuibyshev, "O khoziaistvennom polozhenii SSSR, 19.9.1928 g.," *Pravda*, September 21, 1928.

15. A. I. Rykov, "Itogi noiabr'skogo plenuma, 30.11.1928 g.," *Pravda*, December 4, 1928.

16. See, for example, O. Domanevskaia, "Biudzhet i infliatsiia," *Sots. vestnik*, no. 2 (192), January 24, 1929.

17. Gr. Grin'ko, "Pod znamenem velikikh zadach (O kontrol'nykh tsifrakh na 1928–29 g.)," *Pravda*, October 30 and November 1, 1928; V. V. Kuibyshev, "O khoziaistvennom polozhenii SSSR, 19.9.1928 g.," *Pravda*, September 21, 1928; "Plenum TsK VKP(b), Moskva, 16–24.11.1928: O kontrol'nykh tsifrakh narodnogo khoziaistva na 1928–29 g.," in *KPSS v rezoliutsiiakh*, vol. 4, pp. 122–138.

18. Gr. Grin'ko, "Pod znamenem velikikh zadach," *Pravda*, October 30 and November 1, 1928; see also the resolution "O kontrol'nykh tsifrakh narodnogo khoziaistva na 1928–29 g.," in *KPSS v rezoliutsiiakh*, vol. 4, pp. 122–138.

19. "Za Kulisami VKP(b)," *Sots. vestnik*, no. 9 (199), May 4, 1929; "Vnutri pravo-tsentristskogo bloka (Pis'mo iz Moskvy, 20.3.1928 g.)," *Biulleten' oppozitsii*, no. 1–2, July 1929; see also, for example, L. Kamenev, "Po-novomu, po-delovomu," *Pravda*, November 16, 1928; and G. Zinov'ev, "Znamenatel'naia godovshchina," *Pravda*, November 20, 1928.

20. Deutscher, *Prophet Unarmed*, pp. 446–451.

21. *Pravda*, September 30, 1928.

22. *Pravda*, November 10, 1928 (speeches by Bukharin and Rykov at a plenum of the Moscow Soviet commemorating the October revolution); also Vaganov, *Pravyi uklon*, pp. 178–179 (with a reference to the Central Party Archives).

23. V. Molotov, "K tekushchemu momentu," *Pravda*, August 5, 1928.

24. See, for example, "Stalins Position . . . ," *FdK*, October 19, 1928; Stalin, "O pravom uklone v VKP(b): Rech' na plenume TsK i TsKK VKP(b) v aprele 1929 g.," in *Soch.*, vol. 12, pp. 1–107; and cf. Cohen, *Bukharin*, pp. 291–295.

25. For more details see, for example, O. K. Flechtheim, *Die KPD in der Weimarer Republik*, with an introduction by H. Weber, 2d ed. (Frankfurt am Main, 1976), pp. 48–49, 249–256.

26. "Pis'mo M. iz Moskvy ot 12.10.1928 g.," *Sots. vestnik*, no. 20 (186), October 28, 1928; for details, see Carr and Davies, vol. 2, pp. 61–63.

27. L. Trotsky, "Zur Lage in Russland, Alma-Ata, 21.10.1928," *FdK*, January 4, 1929; information of December 13, 1928, in PA, IV Ru, 2–I, 6; also other materials of this archive.

28. N. A. Uglanov, "O blizhaishikh zadachakh moskovskoi organizatsii: Doklad na ob"edinennom plenume MK i MKK 11.9.1928 g.," *Pravda*, September 21, 1928.

29. Vaganov, *Pravyi uklon*, pp. 160–167; also Daniels, *Conscience of the Revolution*, pp. 337–344.

30. Ibid.

31. Stalin, "O pravoi opasnosti v VKP(b), 19.10.1928 g.," *Soch.*, vol. 11, pp. 222–238; V. Tsifrinovich, "Pod znakom bor"by za resheniia XV s"ezda: Nekotorye itogi obsuzhdeniia reshenii plenuma MK," *Pravda*, November 14, 1928.

32. "Ko vsem chlenam moskovskoi organizatsii VSP(b). Ot TsK VKP(b), 18.10.1928 g.," *Pravda*, October 19, 1928.

33. Stalin, "O pravoi opasnosti v VKP(b)," *Soch.*, vol. 11, pp. 222–238.

34. Vaganov, *Pravyi uklon*, pp. 168–171; also Daniels, *Conscience of the Revolution*, p. 340–341.

35. Vaganov, *Pravyi uklon*, pp. 172–173; also *Pravda* for the second half of October 1928.

36. F. Dan, "Osnovnoi vopros," *Sots. vestnik*, nos. 22–23 (188–189), December 5, 1928 (citing data from Ryazan).

37. Information obtained from a Soviet courier in Berlin (information of November 5, 1928), in PA, IV Ru, 2–I, 6; also other documents of this archive.

38. Letters of October 22 and November 12, 1928, by the head of the Political Directorate of the Red Army (information of November 9 and November 23, 1928), in ibid; also, information of December 13, 1928, in ibid.

39. The first report of arrests of "right-wing Communists" dates from the second half of October (information of October 30, 1928), in ibid.; subsequently, the number of such reports increased.

40. See the resolution of the Presidium of the VTsSPS dated November 27, 1928, in *Trud*, November 30, 1928; also see *Pravda*, November 30, 1928.

41. Information of December 13, 1928, in PA, IV Ru, 2–I, 6; "Pis'mo A.: Vokrug plenuma TsK VKP(b)," *Sots. vestnik*, no. 22–23 (188–189), December 5, 1928.

42. Information of November 23 and December 13, 1928, in PA, IV Ru, 2–I, 6.

43. Ibid.; see also "Pis'mo A.: Vokrug plenuma TsK VKP(b)," *Sots. vestnik*, No. 22–23 (188–189), December 5, 1928.

44. Dirksen's telegram from Moscow, dated March 22, 1929, speaks in a very definite tone of the existence of a "group of five" *(pyaterka)* in the Politburo, as confirmed by two sources. The group had reportedly fallen apart again in January 1929 (PA, IV Ru, 5, Bd. 3–4).

45. Vaganov, *Pravyi uklon*, p. 176.

46. Information of December 13, 1928, in PA, IV Ru, 2–I, 6.

47. "Za kulisami VKP," *Sots. vestnik*, no. 9 (199), May 4, 1929.

48. Ibid.; also Vaganov, *Pravyi uklon*, p. 177 (based on the Central Party Archives).

49. Ibid.

50. Stalin, "Ob industrializatsii strany i o pravom uklone v VKP(b)," *Soch.*, vol. 11, pp. 245–290; A. I. Rykov, "Itogi noiabr'skogo plenuma TsK," *Pravda*, December 4, 1928.

51. "Pis'mo X. iz Moskvy, 3.12.1928," *Sots. vestnik*, no. 24 (190), December 19, 1928.

52. Vaganov, *Pravyi uklon*, p. 184 (based on the Central Party Archives); also "Za kulisami VKP," *Sots. vestnik*, no. 9 (199), May 4, 1929.

53. Vaganov, *Pravyi uklon*, pp. 178–183; A. I. Rykov, "Itogi noiabr'skogo plenuma TsK," *Pravda*, December 4, 1928.

54. "Pis'mo I. iz Moskvy ot 23.11.1928 g.," *Sots. vestnik*, no. 25 (191), January 9, 1929.

55. Stalin, "Ob industrializatsii strany i o pravom uklone v VKP(b), 19.11.1928 g.," *Soch.*, vol. 11, pp. 245–290.

56. *KPSS v rezoliutsiiakh*, vol. 4, pp. 142–149 (the Central Committee plenum of November 16–24, 1928).

57. "Za kulisami VKP," *Sots. vestnik*, no. 9 (199), May 4, 1929.

58. Deutscher, *Prophet Unarmed*, pp. 401–402. This is confirmed in memoirs by contemporaries and by other sources.

59. "Kievskaia demonstratsiia," *Sots. vestnik*, no. 22–23 (188–189), December 5, 1928; "Pis'mo I. iz Moskvy, 23.11.1928 g.," *Sots. vestnik*, no. 25 (191), January 9, 1929; Menzhinsky's letter of November 30, 1928, with a warning that party

organizations in the factories were not fighting the opposition, in PA, IV Ru, 2–I, 7.

60. "Pis'mo I. iz Moskvy, 23.11.1928 g.," *Sots. vestnik*, no. 25 (191), January 9, 1929.

61. Stalin, "Dokatilis'," in *Soch.*, Vol. 11, pp. 313–317. (The quotation is from p. 314.)

62. Cf., for example, I. Miroshnikov, "Pervye itogi pervogo polugodiia piatiletki," *Pravda*, May 26, 1929. Similar data appear in all the official documents of the time.

63. N. I. Bukharin, "Politicheskoe zaveshchanie Lenina: Doklad na traurnom zasedanii, posviashchennom piatiletiiu so dnia smerti Lenina," *Pravda*, January 24, 1929. These assertions are confirmed by the statistical material published in the press.

64. Vaganov, *Pravyi uklon*, p. 192; this is confirmed by the content of later resolutions (see no. 65).

65. "Vnutri pravo-tsentristskogo bloka (Pis'mo M. iz Moskvy ot 20.3.1929 g.)," *Biulleten' oppozitsii*, no. 1–2, July 1929; "Za kulisami VKP," *Sots. vestnik*, no. 9 (199), May 4, 1929.

66. Vaganov, *Pravyi uklon*, p. 193.

67. Ibid., pp. 194–195.

68. Kalinin's letter of November 14, 1928 (information of November 23, 1928), in PA, IV Ru, 2–I, 7.

69. "Rezoliutsiia ob"edinennogo zasedaniia Politbiuro TsK i Prezidiuma TsKK po vnutripartiinym delam ot 9.2.1929 g.," *KPSS v. rezoliutsiiakh*, vol. 4, pp. 187–199.

70. *Pravda*, January 24, 1929.

71. "Kak Politbiuro razreshilo vopros o vysylke tov. Trotskogo v Turtsiiu (Soobshchenie iz Moskvy), 22.3.1929 g., *Biulleten' oppozitsii*, no. 1–2, July 1929. For further detail, see Carr and Davies, vol. 2, pp. 82–84; also, L. Trotsky, *Chto i kak proizoshlo* (Parish, 1929), and *My Life*, pp. 558–566.

72. "Kak Politbiuro razreshilo vopros o vysylke tov. Trotskogo v Turtsiiu (Soobshchenie iz Moskvy), 22.3.1929 g.," *Biulleten' oppozitsii*, no. 1–2, July 1929.

73. "Za kulisami VKP," *Sots. vestnik*, no. 9 (199), May 4, 1929.

74. Kalinin's letter of January 24, 1929, in PA, IV Ru, 2–I, 7.

75. "Postanovlenie SNK i TsIK ob izmeneniiakh sel'skokhoziaistvennogo naloga," *Pravda*, February 8, 1929.

76. See the editorial "Revoliutsionnaia zakonnost'—orudie klassovoi bor'by," in *Pravda*, February 2, 1929.

77. Rudzutak's circular letter (of late January or early February 1929), in PA, IV Ru, 2–I, 7.

78. "Vnutri pravo-tentristskogo bloka," *Biulleten' oppozitsii*, no. 1–2, July 1929.

79. "Za kulisami VKP," *Sots. vestnik*, no. 9 (199), May 4, 1929.

80. "Vnutri pravo-tsentristskogo bloka," *Biulleten' oppozitsii*, no. 1–2, July 1929.

81. "Za kulisami VKP," *Sots. vestnik*, no. 9 (199), May 4, 1929.

82. "Dokatilis' ", *Pravda*, January 24, 1929; Kalinin's letter to the chairmen of the Central Executive Committees of the union republics (apparently dating from the end of January 1929), in PA, IV Ru, 2–I, 7.

83. For the discussion in the Politburo, see Vaganov, *Pravyi uklon*, pp. 199–208; Stalin, "Gruppa Bukharina i pravyi uklon v nashei partii," *Soch.*, vol. 11, pp. 318–325; "Rezoliutsiia ob"edinennogo zasedaniia Politbiuro TsK i Prezidiuma TsKK VKP(b) po vnutripartiinym delam ot 9.2.1929 g.," in *KPSS v rezoliutsiiakh*, vol. 4, pp. 187–199.

8. THE STALINIST REGIME TAKES SHAPE

1. V. V. Kuibyshev, "Piatiletnii plan razvitiia promyshlennosti: Doklad na

VIII s"ezde profsoiuzov," *Pravda,* December 25, 1982.

2. Ibid.; on problems of the plan, see, for example, Nove, *An Economic History,* pp. 142–148.

3. "Rezoliutsiia o piatiletnem plane razvitiia narodnogo khoziaistva," in *XVI konferentsiia VKP(b),* p. 621.

4. Ibid., p. 622.

5. Ibid., pp. 624–625.

6. Ibid., p. 71 (speech by Kuibyshev).

7. Ibid., pp. 68–69 (Kuibyshev's speech). The figures given in the resolution on the five-year plan were somewhat smaller (ibid., p. 623).

8. Ibid., p. 11 (speech by Rykov).

9. Ibid., p. 10 (Rykov's speech).

10. V. M. Molotov, "Ob uspekhakh i trudnostiakh sotsialisticheskogo stroitel'stva: Doklad na XVII moskovskoi gubpartkonferentsii, 23.2.1929 g.," *Pravda,* February 26, 1928; A. I. Rykov, "Otchet pravitel'stva na IX moskovskom gub. s"ezde Sovetov i sokrashch. stenogramma zakliuchitel'nogo slova po etomu otchetu," *Pravda,* April 13 and 14, 1929; A. I. Rykov, "Otchet pravitel'stva na V s"ezde Sovetov Soiuza, 20 i 21.5.1929 g.," *Pravda,* May 23, 1929.

11. See, for example, "Zaiavlenie Predsedatelia pravitel'stvennoi komissii t. Piatkova na sobesedovanii s delegatsiei angliiskikh promyshlennikov, 5.4.1929 g.," *Pravda,* April 6, 1929.

12. *Hamburger Correspondent,* June 23, 1929; *XVI konferentsiia VKP(b),* pp. 17–22 (Rykov's speech); also, tangentially, G. Krumin, "V zashchitu khoziaistvennogo plana," *Pravda,* March 31, 1929.

13. *XVI konferentsiia VKP(b),* pp. 9 and 770 (Rykov's speech and the editors' note on it).

14. Ibid., pp. 9–10 (Rykov's speech). This situation was also ratified by the Sixteenth Conference resolution on the five-year plan.

15. See in particular: "Sovnarkom i STO odobrili ustanovki piatiletnego plana (Vystuplenie Rykova)," *Pravda,* April 6, 1929; A. I. Rykov, "Otchet pravitel'stva na IX moskovskom gub. s"ezde Sovetov," *Pravda,* April 13, 1929; A. I. Rykov, "Doklad o piatiletnem plane," *XVI konferentsiia VKP(b),* pp. 5–24.

16. These phrases are taken from *Kontrol'nye tsifry narodnogo khoziaistvo na 1929–30 g.,* p. x. Certainly they were not used without instructions from on high, and in any case they expressed the spirit of the times.

17. "Vnutri pravo-tsentristskogo bloka," *Biulleten' oppozitsii,* nos. 1–2, July 1929.

18. V. M. Molotov, "Ob uspekhakh i trudnostiakh sotsialisticheskogo stroitel'-stva: Doklad na XVII moskov. gubpartkonferentsii, 23.2.1929 g.," *Pravda,* February 26, 1929.

19. For an account of this development in the relatively narrow sphere of the "ideological front," see "The Philosophical Controversy," in Daniels, *Conscience of the Revolution,* pp. 360–362; also Avtorkhanov, *Tekhnologiia vlasti.*

20. Some of the relevant documents have been cited above. They are widely represented in the first half of 1929 (in a series of letters by Rykov, Kalinin, and other party and government leaders, as well as various informational reports from Moscow, in PA, IV Ru, 2–I, 7).

21. Em. Iaroslavskii, "Rabota Tsentral'noi kontrol'noi komissii VKP(b): Doklad na XVII moskov. gubpartikonferentsii VKP(b), 26.2.1929 g.," *Pravda,* March 2, 1929.

22. Information of February 21 and 26, 1929, in PA, IV Ru, 2–I, 7.

23. *XVI konferentsiia VKP(b),* p. 19 (Rykov's speech).

24. M. I. Kalinin, "Doklad na Uchreditel'nom s"ezde Sovetov Ivanovskoi promyshlennoi oblasti," *Pravda,* July 19, 1929.

25. *Pravda*, February 20, 1929. The "zabornye knizhki" (ration books) were instituted in Moscow on March 15, 1929; in many cities they had existed well before that.

26. Even the official *Kontrol'nye tsifry narodnogo khoziaistva na 1929–30 g.* (p. 4); noted substantial losses in livestock.

27. *Industrie und Handelszeitung*, March 10, 1929; *Frankfurter Zeitung*, April 17, 1929. O. Auhagen, a specialist at the German embassy in Moscow, denied in his reports for 1929 that German colonists in Russia had died of starvation in the spring of 1929. On the other hand, he confirmed the fact that conditions were becoming more and more disastrous over the course of the year and that by the autumn they were unendurable. See O. Auhagen, *Die Schicksaalswendungen des russlanddeutschen Bauerntums in den Jahren 1927–1930* (Leipzig, 1940).

28. *XVI konferentsiia VKP(b)*, p. 20 (Rykov's speech).

29. See M. A. Tolstopiatov, "Bol'she vnimaniia trudovoi distsipline," *Pravda*, January 11, 1929; the editorial "Povysim trudovuiu distsiplinu," *Pravda*, January 31, 1929; and other material from the press campaign.

30. Rykov's letter of October 30, 1929, in PA, IV Ru, 2–I, 7.

31. A. Iugov, "Front protiv 'lodyria,'" *Sots vestnik*, no. 7–8 (197–198), April 12, 1929, with quotations from relevant Soviet materials.

32. *Kontrol'nye tsifry narodnogo khoziaistva na 1929–30 g.*, p. 6; *Hamburger Correspondent*, June 23, 1929.

33. *XVI konferentsiia VKP(b)*, p. 20 (Rykov's speech).

34. Rudzutak's circular letter, in PA, IV Ru, 2–I, 7; information apparently of February 21, 1929, in ibid; *Deutsche Tageszeitung*, January 17, 1929.

35. *Industrie und Handelszeitung*, March 10, 1929.

36. Lewin, *Russian Peasants*, pp. 267–268.

37. K. Ia. Bauman, "Otchet MK VKP(b): Iz doklada na XVII moskov. gub-partkonferentsii," *Pravda*, March 7, 1929; A. I. Rykov, "Otchet pravitel'stva na IX mosk. gub. s"ezde Sovetov," *Pravda*, April 13, 1929; and elsewhere.

38. *Kontrol'nye tsifry narodnogo khoziaistva na 1929–30 g.*, p. ix.

39. "Pis'mo M. iz Moskvy ot 5.5.1929 g.," *Sots. vestnik*, no. 10–11 (200–201), May 25, 1929.

40. Ibid.; also "Pis'mo B. iz Moskvy ot 23.2.1929 g.," *Sots. vestnik*, no. 6 (196), March 22, 1929.

41. See, for example, K. V. Ukhanov, "Doklad na plenume Mossoveta, 1.2.1929 g.," *Pravda*, February 7, 1929; "Pis'mo X. iz Moskvy ot 26.3.1929 g.," *Sots. vestnik*, no. 10–11 (200–201), May 25, 1929.

42. From the fall of 1928 on, there were an increasing number of arrests in the Ukraine. This was connected with the growth of nationalist attitudes directly inside the Communist Party (Bolshevik) of the Ukraine, going so far as consideration of the possibility of cooperation with bourgeois parties on the national question. See, for example, the informational reports on December 10, 14, and 19, 1928 (the report of December 19 contains a letter by a Ukrainian Communist dealing with these questions), in PA, IV Ru, 2–I, 6.

43. See K. Ia. Bauman, "Otchet MK," *Pravda*, March 7, 1929; *Rhein-West. Zeitung*, February 12, 1929. Most typical was *Pravda's* publication on June 2, 1929, of a series of materials under a heading in large type, "Not Terror, Not Dekulakization, but a Socialist Offensive on the Rails of NEP."

44. V. M. Molotov, "Ob uspekhakh i trudnostiakh sotsialisticheskogo stroitel'stva, 23.2.1929 g.," *Pravda*, February 26, 1929.

45. *Kontrol'nye tsifry narodnogo khoziaistva na 1929–30 g.*, p. 6.

46. Ibid., p. x.

47. Bukharin was removed from the Politburo by a Central Committee resolution "On the Bukharin Group" at the plenum of November 10–17, 1929;

Tomsky was not reelected to the Politburo after the Sixteenth Party Congress in June–July 1930; Syrtsov replaced Rykov as chairman of the RSFSR Council of People's Commissars in May 1929 (see *Pravda*, May 19, 1929); both Rykov and Syrtsov were finally dropped as members of the party leadership in December 1930; see Michal Reiman and Tamara Reimanova, "Prehled nejvyssich organu KSSS," *Revue dejin socialismu* (Prague), 1968, no. 3

48. Note for Trautmann, October 25, 1929 in PA, IV Ru, Allg. I, Russland, 95.

APPENDIX I

DOCUMENT NO. 1

1. The celebrations of the tenth anniversary of the October revolution, November 7, 1927.

2. the Fifteenth Party Congress, held December 2–19, 1927. During the commemoration of the anniversary of the revolution in 1931, Stalin made an attempt to revive publicly the charge that the opposition had planned an insurrection in 1927. This was immediately and decisively refuted by Trotsky in the *Biulleten' oppozitsii*, no. 27, March 1932, pp. 15–16 (for an English translation, see *Writings of Leon Trotsky [1932]*, New York, 1973, pp. 15–17).

3. The term "combat organization" *(boevaya organizatsia)* is used by Menzhinsky for the obvious purpose of making an association with the Combat Organization of the Socialist Revolutionary (SR) Party, which, before the revolution, had organized the general combat activities of the SRs, as well as specific terrorist acts against representatives of the power structure. The existence of a "combat organization" of the opposition has to be ascribed entirely to the imagination of the GPU and its agents. It is significant that such an organization was never mentioned in any officially published document of the Soviet Communist Party.

4. Surviving accounts of the events in Leningrad on November 7, 1927, do not mention any open expressions of pro-opposition sentiment in the army.

DOCUMENT NO. 2

1. Apparently this refers to an incident in the Urals region in which Beloborodov, the people's commissar of internal affairs of the RSFSR, "enlightened" a Red Army sentry as to "whose cause he should serve." This was regarded as an offense equivalent to high treason.

DOCUMENT NO. 3

1. The Political Archives of the German Foreign Ministry contain the undated text of a memorandum by Chicherin on these questions. However, the quotations in Stalin's letter do not correspond to that text. Later in this letter Stalin refers to another text by Chicherin (of October 27, 1927), which deals with the same questions.

2. For more on this matter, see above, ch. 4.

3. Aleksandr Serebrovsky: member of the Presidium of the Supreme Council of the National Economy (Vesenkha). N. P. Bryukhanov: people's commissar of finance.

4. N. P. Bryukhanov.

5. The treaties with Latvia and Persia, concluded respectively on June 2 and October 1, 1927, contained paragraphs that represented some modifications in the usual implementation of the foreign trade monopoly. These were intended to arouse interest in the industrialized countries. (For the full texts of the treaties, see *DVP*, vol. 10, pp. 67–70 and 396–434.)

6. N. N. Krestinsky: authorized representative (ambassador) of the USSR in Berlin.

7. A. P. Rozengolts: authorized representative of the USSR in London. His "departure" refers to his leaving London after the break in Anglo-Soviet relations in May 1927.

8. L. B. Krasin: a leading Soviet diplomat, who carried out numerous missions for the Soviet government in other countries. In the last period of his life (he died in 1925) he was the authorized representative of the USSR in London.

9. This refers to the Franco-Soviet economic negotiations on the prerevolutionary Russian debts and the question of French credits to be granted to the USSR. The French delegation at these talks was led by de Monzie; the Soviet delegation, by Rakovsky, the authorized representative of the USSR in Paris.

10. See note 1.

11. This apparently refers to opposition statements against any relaxation of the foreign trade monopoly, one of the main themes in opposition attacks on the party leadership.

12. I am unable to determine what measures were proposed in these particular paragraphs.

DOCUMENT NO. 4

1. The main point on the agenda of this meeting was a report by Voroshilov on calling up officers of the old army for reserve duty in the Red Army.

2. It was under Article 58—whose wording allowed very broad possibilities for interpretation—that cases of counterrevolutionary activity, that is, political offenses, were tried.

3. The German "law for the protection of the republic" was ratified on July 1, 1922, as a result of the assassination of Foreign Minister Walter Rathenau. It went into effect for a five-year period with the possibility of prolongation after that. Crimes against the constitution and the state order were punishable under this law. At the same time, a supreme court for the protection of the republic (Staatgerichtshof zum Schutz der Republik) was established in Leipzig, to hear cases involving offenses of this kind.

4. The party leadership approved these measures against oppositionists in late 1927 and early 1928.

5. The above-mentioned German law for the protection of the republic is an example of what is meant here.

6. This refers to the GPU's cooperation with the party's Central Control Commission, which was headed by Ordzhonikidze.

7. Compare document no. 2.

8. Two paragraphs, in which Menzhinsky expresses his approval of Voroshilov's proposals, are omitted at this point.

9. This refers to the several existing left opposition groups, among which the German group headed by Ruth Fischer, Arkady Maslow, and Hugo Urbahns was considered the most important. The prevailing view in the Comintern at the time was that these groups could prove to be dangerous competitors of the official Communist parties in the elections to be held in Germany and France in 1928; in reality the left groups won only a tiny percentage of the votes.

10. The GPU and its agencies in foreign countries, especially its agents in Berlin, spread rumors according to which the "lefts" were financed by the Social Democratic party. Actually, their obvious lack of financial strength was one of the main reasons for the failure of the left groups in the elections.

11. This supposition was apparently based on the fact that Zinoviev had previously been the head of the Comintern.

12. The meeting took place on February 26, 1928, and issued the resolution which is reproduced below as document no. 7.

13. I have omitted the opening part of Kuibyshev's speech, two-and-a-half typed pages long, which does not deal directly with the economic situation.

14. This refers to Chicherin's proposals for a relaxation of the foreign trade monopoly.

15. For more on the question of grain procurements during fiscal year 1927–1928, see ch. 4.

16. A request by Kalinin that people stick to the agenda point under discussion is omitted at this point.

17. This refers to the critical situation in 1921, the end of the period of "war communism," which was resolved by the transition to the New Economic Policy.

18. Four lines containing general remarks only are omitted here.

19. Six lines with general remarks only are omitted here.

20. Two sentences with general remarks only are omitted here.

21. One sentence containing general remarks only is omitted here.

DOCUMENT NO. 5

1. Litvinov was informed about the Sovnarkom meeting of February 8, 1928, in a long talk with Rykov. It may be assumed that in the present document Litvinov accurately reflects the substance of that conversation and, consequently, the assessment of the situation made at the Sovnarkom meeting. The main point on the agenda of that meeting was a discussion of the possibilities of obtaining foreign aid and, in that connection, of further relaxing the foreign trade monopoly.

2. This notion of Britain's role (often greatly exaggerated) had existed since the break in Anglo-Soviet relations.

3. A. I. Rykov.

4. The meeting most probably took place on February 6, 1928, with follow-up decisions being adopted by the Sovnarkom on March 2, 1928 (see documents no. 6 and 7).

5. This development was prevented by the decisions of the Politburo at its meeting of February 26, 1928 (see ch. 4).

6. N. P. Bryukhanov.

7. A reference to the Fifteenth Party Congress.

8. This apparently refers to reports and analyses presented by Chicherin in support of his proposal for a relaxation of the foreign trade monopoly (cf. document no. 3 and the notes to it).

9. The reports and evaluations sent in by Soviet diplomats in response to this request turned out to be quite pessimistic.

10. At this point, I have omitted a passage in the text, one typewritten manuscript page in length, which discusses certain international events of the time.

DOCUMENT NO. 6

1. N. A. Kubyak.

2. V. R. Menzhinsky.

3. This refers to party, state, and other functionaries.

4. A reference to the effect of the poor economic situation on negotiations with other countries. The role of opposition propaganda is grossly exaggerated, and its aims are presented in such a way as to take blame away from the party leadership for its own miscalculations.

Document No. 7

1. At this time Kharkov was the capital of the Ukraine and consequently also the headquarters of the Ukrainian GPU.

2. Goldstein and Wagner, who were working in the USSR for the German firm Allgemeine Elekrizitäts-Gesellschaft, were arrested during the night of March 5–6. After strong protests by the German government, they were released for lack of evidence ten days later.

3. Although the mining town of Shakhty belonged to the region of the Northern Caucasus, most of the industrial area called the Donbass was on Ukrainian territory. Arrests in the Shakhty case were made by the Ukrainian GPU, the head of which was Balitsky. This letter confirms the major role played by the Ukrainian GPU in fabricating the case.

4. For details on the resolution of February 26, 1928, see ch. 4. Both inside the USSR and abroad, the resolution was seen as a departure from the policy of international cooperation.

5. For Chicherin's point of view, see document no. 8.

6. Presumably, this refers to a Central Committee decision that resulted in the release of two German and four Soviet specialists as well as the dispatch of A. S. Bubnov (and others too, later on) to the Donbass to investigate the case.

Document No. 8

1. Authorized representative of the USSR in Berlin.

2. A Soviet-German agreement precisely specified the time limits within which the Soviet government was obliged to inform the German government about the nature of the charges if a German citizen were arrested. Chicherin informed the German ambassador about the arrests on March 6, but information about the charges was not provided in a satisfactory manner, causing great indignation in Germany.

3. This refers to Germany's retreat from a policy of cooperation with the USSR and the beginning of a decline in Soviet-German relations.

4. Nothing is known about the exact nature of the decisions of March 11. For the general circumstances, see ch. 5.

5. At about this time, France filed a suit asking that Soviet gold deposits in the United States be seized as compensation for French gold that had been deposited in the Russian state bank before the revolution and had not been returned to France after the revolution. (see ch. 5.)

6. The negotiations were indeed broken off on March 15 by the decision of the German government.

7. K. Ulrich, Count of Brockdorf-Rantzau.

Index

Accidents, industrial, 54, 58, 59–60
Administrators, 56, 82
Agricultural policies, 42, 69, 74, 79, 89
Agricultural production, 38, 111–12, 116–17; under five-year plan, 102, 103; under NEP, 4, 6, 8, 155 n.1. *See also* Grain procurement; Grain production; Grain supplies
Agriculture, Commissariat of, 80
All-Union Central Trade Union Council (VTsSPS), 98
Andreyev, Andrey, 70
Anglo-Russian Trade Union Committee, 23
Anti-Semitism, 56–57, 112–13
Antonov-Ovseyenko, Vladimir, 24, 68 n
Antonov-Saratovsky, V. P., 63
Armed forces, 5, 24, 33, 53, 94; opposition influence in, 20, 28, 125; provision of food for, 109; and war scare, 13
Arrests, 112, 177 n.42; in Shakhty affair, 59, 60
Astrov, V., 72, 92
Austria: opposition movement in, 134

Balance of trade. *See* Foreign trade balance
Balitsky, Vsevolod, 33, 59, 146, 181 n.3
Bashkiria: grain procurement from, 42
Belgium, 21
Beloborodov, 32, 127, 178 n.1
Briand, Aristide, 15
Bryukhanov, N. P., 16, 129, 178 n.3
Bubnov, Andrei, 60
Bukharin, Nikolai, 8, 17, 40, 47, 48, 73–74, 95; China policy, 11; conflict with opposition, 23; conflict with Stalin, 70–71, 99, 100–101; Menzhinsky on, 134; 1929 campaign against, 107; removal from Central Committee and Politburo, 113, 177 n.47; on repression, 46, 52; and Shakhty case, 65 n; speech on anniversary of Lenin's death, 98, 100; on Stalin, 67, 70, 90–92; support for in ECCI, 21
Byelorussia, 16; anti-Semitism in, 56; Polish claims to, 13

Capital investment, 37, 88 n, 90–91, 102–103
Capitalism, 40, 55, 69

Cattle, slaughtering of, 53
Central Committee, 20, 71, 87, 88 n, 107–108; joint plenums with CCC, 31–32, 113; plenum of February 1927, 9, 37; plenum of April 1927, 20; plenum of July 1927, 24–26; plenum of July 1928, 72–74; plenum of November 1928, 95–96; role in conflict between opposition and Stalinists, 23, 24–26, 34; and the Shakhty case, 62
Central Control Commission (CCCO), 22–23, 24–26, 34, 49, 108; joint plenums with Central Committee, 31–32, 113; and Shakhty case, 62
Central Council of Trade Unions, 54, 110
Central Executive Committee (CEC), 38 n, 52, 54, 79–80
Centrists: Stalinists as, 30
Chamberlain, Neville: Litvinov's meeting with, 39 n
Chicherin, Georgy, 24, 46, 134; on foreign relations, 9, 15–16, 17, 39, 76, 156 n.15; on foreign trade, 128–30, 132–33; on GPU, 148–49; and Shakhty affair, 59, 60, 61
China, 9, 20; Soviet foreign policy on, 11, 16, 23, 25, 158 n.25
Chubar, Vlas, 30
Cities, 5, 53–55, 56, 109
Civil war: social consequences of, 1–2
Class struggle, 73, 113
Coal industry: and the Shakhty affair, 57–65
Collective contracts, 54
Collective farms, 78, 79, 112; Bukharin on, 90; Rykov on, 96; Stalin on, 52, 69, 73
Collectivization, 45, 70
Combat Organization of the Socialist Revolutionary (SR) Party, 178 n.3
Combat organizations, 33–34, 125, 178 n.3
Comintern, 46, 47, 48–49, 165 n.44; foreign policy of, 9, 16; and the opposition, 23, 25, 179 n.9; 6th Congress of, 20, 92
Communist Party, Soviet, 15, 28, 30, 35, 119; arrests of members, 108; and the Comintern, 47; 10th Party Congress, 2; 14th Party Congress, 3; 15th Party Conference, 9; 15th Party Congress, 20, 24,

35, 71; 16th Party Conference, 106, 113; Stalin's responsibility for political line, 107

Communist Party of Czechoslovakia, 21, 92 n

Communist Party of Germany (KPD), 21, 25, 47, 91

Communist Party of the Ukraine, 14, 57

Concentration camps, 47

Conservative party, British (Tories): and relations with Soviet Union, 11

Construction, 4, 55

Cottage industries: effects of taxation on, 78

Council of People's Commissars. See Sovnarkom

Counterrevolutionary movement: among the kulaks, 81; and the Shakhty affair, 59

Countryside. See Peasants; Rural areas

Coup d'etat: plans for, 33–34, 124, 125

Crimea: grain procurement from, 42

Czechoslovakia, 12; Communist Party of, 21, 92 n

Death penalty, 2, 80; for Shakhty case defendants, 65. See also Executions

Declaration of the Eighty-Four, 21, 23

Defense spending, 5, 37, 75

Democratic Centralists, 19, 25

Demonstrations: in fall of 1927, 32–33

De Monzie, 130, 179 n.9

Dictatorship of the proletariat, 49, 131–32

Diplomatic corps, Soviet, 24, 26

Dirksen, Herbert von, 99 n

Disarmament conference (Geneva, Dec. 1927), 39

Disease rates, 55

Donbass (Donetsk Basin) coal industry: and the Shakhty affair, 59–62

Eastman, Max: The Real Situation in Russia, 99 n

Economic management: under five-year plan, 105–106

Economy (economic conditions), 30, 37–50, 51; in 1928, 67–70, 85–86; Kuibyshev on, 135–37; Litvinov on, 138–42; Opposition Platform on, 29

Engineers, 56; and the Shakhty case, 57, 65, 82

England. See Great Britain

Executions: by the GPU, 15, 16, 158 n.19; of peasant terrorists, 112; of transport specialists, 113 n. See also Death penalty

Executive Committee of the Communist International (ECCI), 20–21, 31–32

Existing socialism, 121–22

Extraordinary measures, 44–46, 51–53, 68–70, 74; reinstitution of, 79–80, 83; Stalin on use of, 72–73

Factories: conditions of workers in, 110; unrest in, 56

Famine, 81, 98, 109, 111

Fifteenth Party Conference, 9

Fifteenth Party Congress, 20, 24, 35, 40–41, 71

Finance, Commissariat of, 80, 88 n, 89

Fischer, Ruth, 21, 25, 179 n.9

Five-year plan, 38, 67, 102–106, 112, 113–14

Fon-Meck, M. K., 113 n

Food supplies, 38, 42, 53–54; Litvinov on, 138, 140, 141; 1928 shortages, 52–54, 70, 81; 1929 shortages, 108–10, 113; rationing of, 44, 109

Foreign Affairs, Commissariat of (Narkomindel), 24, 47, 61

Foreign currency reserves, 43, 48, 109

Foreign relations, 11–18, 26–27, 38–39, 75–77, 103; opposition on, 20, 30

Foreign trade, 26–27, 38–39, 87; and grain exports, 42, 43; Kuibyshev on, 136–37; under NEP, 4, 6–7, 9, 155 n.2

Foreign trade balance (balance of trade), 43, 74, 109 n, 136

Foreign trade monopoly, 7, 46, 49; Chicherin on, 39, 162 n.8; Litvinov on, 139–40; Stalin on, 39, 76, 128–33

Fourteenth Party Congress, 3

France, 21, 47, 133; opposition in, 134, 179 n.9; Soviet relations with, 12, 26–27, 27 n, 30, 39, 60, 103, 130, 139, 179 n.9

French revolution, 28

Frumkin, Mikhail, 71, 95, 96

Georgia: nationalism in, 14, 16, 57

Georgian Republic, 14

German colonists (in USSR): food supplies for, 109, 177 n.27

Germany, 47, 63, 99 n; Communist Party in, 21, 25, 47, 91; economic relations with USSR, 7, 39–40, 77; law on treason, 133, 179 n.3; opposition movement, 25, 134, 179 nn.9, 10; Soviet relations with, 11, 12, 27, 60–61, 64, 103

Goldstein, 146, 181 n.2

Goods famine, 5, 44, 82

Gosplan (State Planning Commission), 87, 104

Gottwald, Klement, 92 n

GPU (OGPU), 3, 28, 51, 53, 65, 94; anti-Semitism in, 56; Chicherin on, 16, 148–49; executions by, 15, 16, 17; and Leningrad explosions, 158 n.16; powers, 35–36, 46–47, 49–50; role in grain procurement, 45, 52, 80; Rykov on, 142–47; and Shakhty affair, 58–60, 61–62, 65; and specialists, 82, 83, 113 n; Stalin on, 127–28; support for moderates in, 70; use in party purges, 107–108; use in re-

pression of opposition, 22, 30–31, 33–34, 35, 97
Grain procurement, 41–43, 44–45, 51–53, 77–78, 78–81, 108; Kubyak on, 149–50; Kuibyshev on, 135–36; Litvinov on, 138
Grain production, 4, 6, 41, 78
Grain supplies, 41–42, 69, 108–109
Great Britain, 21–22, 23, 129–30, 133; Soviet relations with, 7, 11–13, 15–17, 39, 103, 139
Group of five, 70, 98

Herbette, J., 30
Hours (for workers), 54–55, 111

Industrial goods, supply of, 37–38, 41–42, 43
Industrialization, 37, 51, 87–89, 90, 120; under five-year plan, 104–105; under NEP, 3–6; policy of accelerated, 77, 83; Stalin's policies on, 72, 85–86; and war scare, 13
Industrial production, 37, 43, 82–83, 87–89, 116–17; under five-year plan, 102; Kuibyshev on, 135–36; under NEP, 4, 8, 155 n.1; Shakhty affair effects, 82–83
Industrial workers. See Workers
Inflation, 5, 37
Interrogation methods: used in Shakhty case, 64
Italy, 21, 26
Ivanovo-Voznesensk, 22

Japan: Soviet relations with, 26
Justice, People's Commissariat of, 110

Kaganovich, Lazar, 17, 93, 98
Kalinin, Mikhail, 15, 16–17, 70, 72, 98; on extraordinary measures, 79–80; on grain procurement, 81 n; and the opposition, 30, 46; opposition to Stalin, 94–95; on propaganda and sabotage, 151–52; and Shakhty affair, 59, 62, 64
Kamenev, Lev, 7, 24, 73–74, 100–101; role in revival of opposition, 19–20; and Shakhty case, 65 n
Kazakhstan: grain procurement from, 42–43, 80, 108
Kellogg, F. B., 75
Kellogg-Briand pact, 76
Kharkov, 5, 146, 180 n.1
Kiev, 5
Kirov, Sergei: murder of, 80
Komsomol: arrests of members, 108
Kork, A. I., 33
Kossior, Stanislas, 88
Kotov, Vasily, 94
Koverda, 14
Krasin, L. B., 130, 179 n.8
Krestinsky, Nikolai, 24, 130, 179 n.6

Kronstadt: rebellion of sailors in, 2
Krumin, Garald, 92
Krylenko, Nikolai: role in Shakhty trial, 63, 64–65
Krzhizhanovsky, Gleb, 40
Kubyak, Nikolai, 49, 111, 149–50
Kuibyshev, Valerian, 16, 48, 58, 70, 102; on economic conditions, 47–48, 135–37; as head of VSNKh, 87, 88 nn; and Shakhty affair, 59
Kulaks, 40–41, 45, 81, 112; Stalin on, 45, 68, 69
Kuomintang, 11, 20

Labor. See Workers
Labor and Defense, Council for, 83
Latvia: treaties with, 129–30, 178 n.5
Left opposition, 19–36, 46–47, 49, 97, 99, 119; collaboration with Stalinists, 73–74; on economy, 7, 9; in foreign countries, 134, 179 nn.9, 10; on foreign trade monopoly, 39; France's opposition to, 26–27, 27 n; influence on Stalin's political line, 68; on kulaks, 40–41; Litvinov on, 138–39, 140; Menzhinsky on, 124–26, 131, 133–35; Stalin on, 124, 126–28, 179 n.11; working population sympathy for, 55. See also Trotskyists; Zinovievists; members by name
Lenin, 2, 3, 130–32, 137
Leningrad, 2, 19, 22, 27–28, 32; explosions in, 14, 158 n.16
Leningrad Pravda: support for moderates, 70
Let History Judge (Medvedev), 119
Lithuania, 13
Litvinov, Maxim, 39, 138–42
Living conditions, 29, 51, 54–55, 104
Lunacharsky, Anatoly, 39

Machinery and tractor stations (MTSs), 112
Management, 56, 110
Maretsky, D., 72, 92
Maslow, Arkady, 21, 25, 179 n.9
Medvedev, Roy: Let History Judge, 119
Menzhinsky, Vyacheslav, 15, 36, 46, 48, 82–83; on opposition, 33–34, 46–47, 124–26, 133–35; Rykov on, 142–43, 145; and Shakhty affair, 56, 59–60, 61; on use of extraordinary measures, 77, 80
Metallurgical industry, 43, 88, 105
Mikoyan, Anastas, 16–17, 36, 42, 49, 72
Moderates, 67–68, 70–74, 94–96, 98–101; 1928 policies, 77–78, 80, 85, 87, 89–92, 95–96; opposition criticism of, 30; role in 1927 power struggle, 15, 16–17, 19, 21–22, 24, 28; and Shakhty affair, 59–60, 61–62, 65; support of Stalin, 34, 35; on use of extraordinary measures, 68–69

Molotov, Vyacheslav, 17, 40, 92; support for Stalin, 68, 71, 86, 87, 93
Moscow, 5, 15, 27, 92–94; opposition influence in, 20, 22
Moscow Committee, 92–93
Moscow Control Commission, 92, 93
Mrachkovsky, 31, 31 n
Murders: in countryside, 79, 80, 81

Narkomindel (Foreign Affairs, Commissariat of), 24, 47, 61
Nationalism: in national republics, 14, 16, 57; repression of, 112, 177 n.42
National regions: Opposition Platform on, 29–30
New Economic Policy (NEP), 2–10, 67, 68, 71, 72, 117; Bukharin on, 40; Opposition Platform on, 29; Stalin on, 69; as transition to state socialism, 131–32
Nin, Andres, 46
Northern Caucasus, 78, 79; grain procurement from, 42–43, 52
"Notes of an Economist: At the Start of the New Fiscal Year" (Bukharin), 90–91

October revolution, 116, 117, 121–22
OGPU. See GPU
Opposition, political, 3. See also Left opposition; Right opposition
Ordzhonikidze, Sergo, 17, 23, 25, 33, 70, 100; on industrial sabotage, 150–51; on repression of opposition, 46; and Shakhty affair, 62
Orenburg province: grain procurement from, 42

Palchinsky, P. A., 113 n
Paper currency: issuing of, 6, 37, 43, 89
Paris Conference (August 1928), 75, 76
Peasants, 38 n, 41–42, 71, 78–81, 111–12, 113; antagonism toward cities, 56; and food provisioning system, 109, 111; Kuibyshev on, 135; land ownership under NEP, 3; Opposition Platform on, 29; rebellions, 2, 53; social repression of, 51–53; as source of government revenue, 5–6, 74; Stalin on, 68, 72–73; and surpluses, 8, 12. See also Kulaks
People's Commissars, Council of. See Sovnarkom
Persia, treaties with, 129–30, 178 n.5
Petrovsky, Grigory, 30, 70
Pilsudski, Jozef, 13
Platform of the United Opposition, 28–30
Poland, 13, 16, 17, 22, 57, 61
Polish-Lithuanian-Ukrainian federation, 13
Politburo, 23–24, 70–71, 83, 87, 93, 94–95; and deportation of Trotsky, 99; and economic conditions, 38–40, 49; on foreign

relations, 9, 15–16, 17; and the opposition, 21–22, 23, 30, 33; role in Shakhty affair, 59–60, 61
Political opposition, 3. See also Left opposition; Right opposition
Political repression, 2, 93–94, 118. See also Repression
Political terror, 15, 96, 118
Pravda: on lifting of extraordinary measures, 74; publishing of opposition's "Counter-Theses," 34; on Shakhty affair, 60; Stalin's control of editorial board, 92; support for moderates, 70, 72
Preobrazhensky, Yevgeny, 7, 24, 31
Prices, 5, 54, 81–82, 109–10; for grain, 41, 42, 44, 74
Procuracy (Public Prosecutor's Office): and Shakhty affair, 60
Production quotas, 54
Propaganda, 52, 113; on Shakhty affair, 61; use by opposition, 23, 27, 125
Public show trial, 66
Pyatakov, Georgy, 24

Radek, Kark, 7, 97 n
Rakovsky, Christian, 7, 26–27, 32, 97 n; negotiations with France, 130, 179 n.9
Rationing, 44, 54, 109
Real Situation in Russia, The (Eastman), 99 n
Red Army. See Armed forces
Repression, political and social, 2, 15, 93–94, 96, 118; Stalin's justification of, 73; use in labor discipline, 110–11
Revolutionary movements (foreign): Soviet support for, 6, 156 n.11
Right opposition, 21, 101, 106–108
Rozengolt, A. P., 130, 179 n.7
Rudzutak, Jan, 58, 70, 83
Rural areas (countryside), 5–6, 29; effects of grain shortages on, 53; 1929 famine in, 109; social repression in, 51. See also Peasants
Russification: Ukrainian resistance to, 14
Rykov, Aleksei, 9, 15–17, 94–96, 99, 100–101; and economic policy, 8, 37, 42, 45, 46, 48–49, 85, 91; on five-year plan, 40, 104–106; on GPU, 142–47; and the opposition, 30, 46; on propaganda and sabotage, 151–52; and Stalin, 68, 70–71, 72; removal as chairman of Sovnarkom, 113–14, 178 n.47; and Shakhty affair, 59–60, 62, 65 n; support for specialists, 58

Sapronov, Timofei, 19
Self-criticism, 66, 93, 108
Self-taxation, 45, 52
Serebrovsky, Aleksandr, 129, 178 n.3
Serebryakov, Leonid, 31

Seven-hour day decree, 54–55
Shakhty case, 57–66, 75, 82–83, 181 n.3
Sharov, Y., 31
Siberia, 27, 137; grain procurement from, 43, 44–45, 52, 80, 108
Sixteenth Party Conference, 106, 113
Sixth Congress of the Comintern, 20, 92
Slave labor, 108
Smeral, B., 21, 92
Smilga, Ivar, 7, 21, 22, 97 n
Social conditions, 29, 51, 54–55
Socialism, 1–2, 73, 86, 121–22
Social repression, 73, 110–11. *See also* Repression
Social terror, 15, 118
Sokolnikov, Grigory, 65
Solts, Aron, 22–23
Solzhenitsyn, Alexander, 118
Sosnovsky, Lev, 68
Soviet historiography: on Stalin and Stalinism, 119
Sovnarkom (Council of People's Commissars), 15–16, 17, 48, 49, 81, 83; and foreign policy, 75–76
Specialists, 113; and the Shakhty case, 57–65, 82, 83
Stalin, Joseph, 5, 16–17, 28, 85–87, 89, 102, 119–20; and anti-Semitism, 56 n, 57; attack on Tomsky, 73; campaign against the right, 93–94; on collective farms, 52, 69, 73; on collectivization, 45; on deporting Trotsky, 99; economic policies, 8, 40, 44–46; and five-year plan, 104–105, 106–107; foreign policy, 11, 15, 48, 76; on foreign trade, 9, 39, 128–33, 156 n.16; and the moderates, 67–74, 95–96, 113–14; and Moscow Committee, 92–93; 1934 decree on dealing with terrorists, 80; and the opposition, 19, 23–24, 30, 32, 33–34, 35–36, 124, 126–28, 131, 179 n.11; power gains in 1928, 91–101; power gains in 1929, 106–107, 108; rumors of mental illness, 114; and Shakhty affair, 56, 59–60, 63, 65; and 6th Congress of the Comintern, 91; social policies, 82–84; support for in the ECCI, 21
Standard of living, 2–3, 29, 51, 54–55, 104, 110; in prerevolutionary Russia, 4
State farms: moderates on, 90, 96; Stalin's policy on, 69, 73
State industry, 5, 7, 155 n.6
State Planning Commission (Gosplan), 87, 104
Stern, V., 21
Stresemann, Gustav, 12
Strike committees, 22
Strikes, 54, 58
Supreme Court of the RSFSR: Shakhty trial, 63

Supreme Economic Council (VSNKh), 54, 87, 88 n
Surplus agricultural products, 6, 12, 156 n.10
Surveillance cells, 133
Syrtsov, S. I., 113, 178 n.47

Tataria: grain procurement from, 42
Taxation, 5–6, 43, 77–78, 98–99; agricultural, 45, 52, 74, 78, 80
Technicians, 56; and the Shakhty case, 57, 65, 82
Tenth Party Congress, 2
Terror, political and social, 15, 96, 118
Textile mills: 3-shift workday at, 54
Thaelmann, Ernst, 21
Thermidorian degeneration, 23, 25
Tomsky, Mikhail, 15, 16–17, 28, 95, 98, 100–101; conflict with Stalin, 70–71, 73, 75; opposition criticism of, 30; removal from Central Committee and Politburo, 113, 178 n.47; and Shakhty affair, 62, 65 n
Totalitarianism: Stalinism as, 120
Trade unions, 23, 58, 110
Trade Unions, Eighth Congress of, 98
Transcaucasia, 19–20, 27; nationalism in, 14, 16, 57
Treason, 133, 179 n.3
Treint, Albert, 46
Trials: in the Shakhty case, 63–66; use of public show trial, 66
Trilisser, Mikhail, 70
Trotsky, Leon, 7, 19–23, 24 n, 25–26, 31–32, 97 n; arrest and internal deportation, 34–35, 97; deportation of, 99, 99 n, 100; opposition to coup attempt, 33, 125; and Stalin, 56 n, 73, 90
Trotskyists, 19, 35, 47, 68 n, 97, 100. *See also* Left opposition

Uglanov, Nikolai, 70, 74, 92, 94
Ukraine, 78, 79, 81, 137; anti-Semitism in, 56; grain procurement from, 42, 52; nationalism in, 14, 16, 57, 112, 177 n.42; opposition activity in, 19, 27–28
Ukrainian Communist Party, 14, 57
Ukrainian GPU, 59–60
Ulrich, K. (German ambassador), 148–49, 181 n.7
Underground movements, 14, 22, 57, 97, 100
Unemployment, 5, 55, 155 n.6
Union republics: Opposition Platform on, 29–30
Unions. *See* Trade unions
United States: Soviet relations with, 7, 16, 26, 39, 103, 129–30

Urals, the, 137; grain procurement from, 43, 80, 108; opposition activity in, 20, 27
Urals-Siberian method of procurement, 80
Urbahns, Hugo, 21, 25, 179 n.9
Urquhart, Leslie, 137

Vasilyev-Yuzhin, M. I., 63
Velichko, A. F., 113 n
Village soviets, 111
Voikov, P. L., 14
Volga region: grain procurement from, 42–43, 80
Voroshilov, Kliment, 17, 33, 36, 94, 124, 125; and the moderates, 70, 72; on repression of opposition, 46
VSNKh (Supreme Economic Council), 54, 87, 88 n
Vujovic, V., 21, 31–32
Vyshinsky, Andrei, 63

Wages, 38, 54, 82, 113
Wagner, 146, 181 n.2
War communism, 1–2, 15, 16, 39, 51; Stalin on, 69, 130–31
War industry: 1928 program for, 75
War scare (in USSR), 12–13
Wildcat strikes: in Donbass coal industry, 58

Wilno, 13
Workers, 56, 113; living and working conditions, 29, 38 n, 54–55; lack of discipline among, 82–83, 110–11; and the opposition, 21–22, 29, 55; and Shakhty affair, 58, 65
Workers' and Peasants' Army, 125–26, 127, 144
Workers' and Peasants' Inspection, 80, 107–108, 150, 151
Working conditions, 29, 51, 54–55, 104, 111
Work shifts, 111

Yagoda, Genrikh, 70
Yakir, Iona, 33
Yaroslavsky, Yemelyan, 62, 108
Yevdokimov, Grigory, 21
Yevdokimov, Yefim, 59
Yugoslavia: relations with USSR, 12

Zinoviev, Grigory, 7, 19–20, 23, 25–26, 32; arrest and internal deportation, 34–35; influence on Opposition Platform, 30; and Stalin, 74
Zinovievists, 19, 35, 47, 68 n. See also Left opposition